PERSPECTIVES ON POWER: INDIA AND CHINA

PERSPECTIVES ON POWER: INDIA AND CHINA

An Analysis of Attitudes Towards Political Power in the Two Countries Between c. Seventh and Second Centuries B.C.

P.V. PILLAI

MANOHAR
2025

First published 1977
Reprinted 2023, 2024, 2025

ISBN 978-93-91928-87-2

Published by
Ajay Kumar Jain *for*
Manohar Publishers & Distributors
4753/23 Ansari Road, Daryaganj
New Delhi 110 002

Printed at
Replika Press Pvt. Ltd.

TO MY PARENTS

FOREWORD

It has frequently been remarked that China and India underwent political experiences of considerable similarity between the seventh and second centuries B.C. The states of Ch'in in China and Magadha in India both emerged to positions of undisputed sway in their respective countries through the assimilation and conquest of states which had been their equals. And the centralization implicit in this replacement of a welter of states by a single power was of the greatest importance. In both cases, the powers that were to become paramount were outsiders to the traditional centres of culture, and in this sense representative of the changing and radical nature of the epoch in which Chou feudalism finally died in China and India saw the rise of major heterodox religious movements such as Buddhism. It is also noteworthy that it is in this period of savage inter-state conflict and fluctuating political fortunes—preceding unification—that both China and India saw the development of a literature of Realpolitik which aimed frankly at the aggrandizement of political might—a concern which links the Legalists of China with the Arthaśāstra authors of the subcontinent.

These affinities are striking, and it is the purpose of this study to determine the precise nature of these similarities; whether or not they spring from shared perspectives towards political power. The question is one of some importance as the answer may provide a clue to the further question as to why, after this period of comparable experiences, China became in spirit and intent—if not always in fact—a bureaucratic and centralized state while India did not. If the similarity between India and China in this period does imply similar political attitudes then this is difficult to explain; if it does not, the ways in which the two differ are still worth clarifying. We have sought to answer this question on the basis of the analyses of a number of contemporary texts in the hope that this theoretical literature will reveal crucial distinctions disguised by the affinity of historical patterns.

We shall now deal with the specific issues concerning the dating of these sources, and for the present will limit ourselves to some general observations regarding their nature. On the Indian side, after a brief discussion of the nature of temporal authority in the *Brāhmaṇas*, we commence our analysis with the Dharmasūtras which are essentially religious works devoted to sacrificial ritual and the duties of those in each of the four classes—*varṇas*—and stages of life. The importance of these works for our purpose is that they provide a graphic picture of the position allotted to the king in religious literature and thus offer a standard of comparison in relation to which we can study other genres in order to determine whether there is a change of viewpoint. Government organization as reflected in the Dharmasūtras is of a relatively simple nature, and the society it portrays is one of scattered rural communities functioning largely on the basis of custom and caste usage. The role of the king is seen as being one of supporting the *varṇāśramadharma*—the sacrally ordained distinctions of class and stages of life. In the next text studied, the *Arthaśāstra* of Kauṭilya—a work belonging to the category of treatises devoted to the science of acquiring wealth (Artha) which, along with Dharma (the transcendental religious law), and Kāma (sensual pleasure), are traditionally regarded as the three aims of life and thus not seen as being mutually opposed—we see an entirely different situation. The state has now attained a highly complex stage with a centralized administration having responsibilities in almost every activity. The infra-structure presumed or mentioned in Kauṭilya's work, whether it relates to the trained officials who staff the various departments or the functional subdivisions of the army, are unthinkable in the rustic context of the Dharmasūtras. It comes as a considerable surprise, therefore, to discover that in the final analysis its conception of the royal duty remains the same as in the Dharmasūtras, that is, subordinate and supportive of the *varṇāśramadharma*. The edicts of Aśoka reveal a world which obviously has experience of the sophisticated administration of which the *Arthaśāstra* of Kauṭilya gives us a glimpse. At the same time, we are witness to the attitudes towards kingship of those outside the framework of Brāhmanical orthodoxy. For the first time kingship becomes autonomous and defines its own systems, an autonomy which is again lost with the recrudescence of Brāhmanical forms as represented by Manu. Although the *Manusmṛti*, having absorbed the lessons of Arthaśāstra, is much more emphatic on matters of temporal import than the Dharmasūtras, it does not move from the position taken by the latter regarding the subordinate nature of the royal function.

Our sources on the Chinese side are far more uniform and need not be described in terms of varying concerns as they are unified by one overriding preoccupation—that of the establishment of political order. From Confucius to Li Ssu, they all reflect the loss of a traditional order and the attempt at finding or forging a new one to replace it. Thus while the Indian texts largely deal with the question of regnal authority and function only in a peripheral manner, the Chinese ones address themselves specifically to these issues, and this can be said to constitute the main difference between them.

As regards the chronology of the sources, we have followed, on the Indian side, the dating of Bühler and Kane for the Dharmasūtras and the Manusmṛti. Despite certain differences of detail, the two scholars are agreed on accepting the Dharmasūtra of Gautama as being the oldest followed by those of Baudhāyana and Āpastamba respectively.[1] Bühler refrains from suggesting any date for Vasiṣṭha, but Kane proposes some time between 300 and 100 B.C. and sees him as being the latest of the four.[2] Bühler refuses to commit himself to any definite datings for the specific authors save for the very wide

[1]*The Sacred Laws of The Aryas, Part I, Āpastamba and Gautama*, trans. by Georg Būlher in *The Sacred Books of the East*, ed. by Max Mueller, Vol. II (Delhi: Reprint by Motilal Banarsidass, 1965), p. xlix.

[2]P.V. Kane, *History of Dharmaśāstra*, Vol. I, Part 1 (Poona: Bhandarkar Oriental Research Institute, 1968).

estimate—between the fifth and first centuries B.C.—that he tentatively puts forward for Āpastamba.[3] Kane, though equally aware of the perils of advancing a definitive chronology,[4] provisionally accords the following dates to the authors: Gautama, 600-400 B C.;[5] Baudhāyana, 500-200 B.C.;[6] Āpastamba, 450-350 B.C.;[7] Vasiṣṭha, 300-100 B.C.[8]

These are very catholic estimates, so undogmatic as to be distressing, but dates of greater certainty and precision are yet to be justifiably asserted. The date of the *Arthaśāstra* of Kauṭilya has been the subject of relentless controversy, and estimates range from the third century B.C. (Jacobi)[9] to the third century A.D. (Winternitz and Jolly).[10] Kane simply notes that the the work cannot be later than the second century A.D.[11] Recent scholarship tends in the same direction, and Trautmann, who holds the work to be of composite authorship, is inclined to accept the second century A.D. as the date to which the evidence—taken altogether—converges.[12] He also notes, however, that certain parts of the work, Books Three and Four and, possibly, Seven, may enjoy a higher antiquity.[13] As has been mentioned in the text, the *genre* of Arthaśāstra literature almost certainly pre-dates the *Manusmṛti*—the earliest of the smṛtis—which both Bühler and Kane see as having achieved its present form between the second century B.C. and the second century A.D. Thus the work attributed to Kauṭilya is by no means the earliest of its kind.[14] In conclusion, despite the variance in chronological estimates, it seems to be a matter of common acceptance that the administrative complexity evident in the *Kauṭilīyan Arthaśāstra* does reflect in general

[3]Bühler, *Āpastamba*, p. xviii.
[4]Kane, History, p. 105.
[5]*Ibid.*, p. 36.
[6]*Ibid.*, p. 51.
[7]*Ibid.*, p. 70.
[8]*Ibid.*, p. 105.
[9]*Ibid.*, p. 191.
[10]*Ibid.*, p. 170.
[11]*Ibid.*, p. 209.
[12]Thomas R. Trautmann, *Kauṭilya and the Arthaśāstra*, (Leiden: E.J. Brill, 1971), p. 183.
[13]*Ibid.*, pp. 184-185.
[14]*Ibid.*, p. 185.

and abstract terms the practices of the Mauryan court, and this fact, along with the point that the work is the earliest extent representative of a tradition which certainly goes further back than the second century B.C., justifies its inclusion among our sources.

On the Chinese side, the issues concerning the dating of the *Lao-tzu*, the *Chuang-tzu*, the *Shang-chün Shu*, the *Han Fei Tzu* and the *Kuan-tzu* have been touched upon in the text and notes and will not be repeated here. The *Analects of Confucius* is generally conceded to be authentic although Creel, following Ts'ui Shu, is convinced that Chapters 16-20 are later additions.[15] But he goes on to emphasize that this does not mean that their contents were not of an early date,[16] and it would perhaps be in accord with the bulk of scholarly opinion if the work is dated to around a generation after the death of the Master. Ts'ui Shu and modern scholars generally believe that the first ten chapters of the *Analects* are more authentic than the last ten which include later additions. The more dubious sections have been pointed out by Creel,[17] but it is likely that even these are of a period preceding the Han. Like the *Analects*, the *Mencius* too is probably the work of disciples, and it enjoys a similar reputation for reliability—constituting an important source for the Chan Kuo period as also for the tradition regarding Confucius.[18] According to Liang Ch'i-chao, the *Hsün-tzu* can be considered reliable on the whole despite the fact that certain chapters may date as late as the Han.[19] Hsu Cho-yun holds that although the work may be a composite creation of Hsün-tzu and his disciples, it does seem to be composed of pre-Ch'in materials[20] and is thus suitable for our period. The *Mo Tzu*, like the *Analects* and *Mencius*, is a work composed by the disciples of the putative author and its composite nature is

[15]H. G. Creel, *Confucius, The Man and the Myth* (New York: The John Day Co., 1949), p. 291.

[16]*Ibid.*, p. 292.

[17]*Ibid.*, p. 293-294.

[18]Hsu Cho-yun, *Ancient China in Transition*, (Stanford: Stanford University Press, 1965), p. 188. Creel, *Confucius...*, p. 10.

[19]Chang Hsing-cheng, *Wei-shu T'ung-kao* (Shanghai 1939; reprint, 1954), p. 620.

[20]Hsu, *Ancient China in Transition*, p. 189.

generally conceded.[21] Hsu Cho-yun, following Hu Shih, divides it into five sections of which the second and fourth respectively are reckoned to be reliable and dateable to about a generation after Mo Ti's death[22]—sometime towards the later part of the last quarter of the fourth century B.C. These are the divisions dealing with the primary tenets of the Mohist school[23]—Agreement with the Superior, the doctrine of Universal Love and so on, which are our main concern.

All the texts referred to above have generally been utilized through the translations detailed in the bibliography; reference to the originals being limited to cases where the translation is dubious or a matter of disputed interpretation.

There remains the pleasurable task of thanking the institutions and individuals whose help and support were vital to this work. Of the former, my gratitude is due to the Centers of Chinese and South and Southeast Asian Studies, the Department of History and the Rackham School of Graduate Studies, all of The University of Michigan, whose generous aid over five years was invaluable. My debt to the many people whose kindness, tolerance and fertility of mind did much to make my stay at the University the very pleasant experience that it was is less easily expressed, but I should like in particular to make what paltry acknowledgment I can to Professors Chun-shu Chang and Thomas R. Trautmann for all that they have done to bear me along what often seemed to be a trackless infinity. They have proved accessible and helpful to a degree beyond any possible call of duty, and if I have benefited greatly from their erudition and critical acumen, they have always gracefully refrained from overwhelming my fledging efforts with these attributes. Dr. Chou Min-chih, my friend and colleague, has placed me further in his debt by contributing the Chinese characters in the glossary, and I trust this touch of elegance will

[21]Chang, *Wei-shu. . .*, pp. 753-762.

[22]Hsu, *Ancient China in Transition*, p. 187.

[23]*Ibid.* See also Fung Yu-Lan, *History of Chinese Philosophy*, Vol. I, trans. by Derk Bodde (Princeton University Press, 1952), p. 81, where, by implication, he accepts the authenticity of the *Mo-Tzu* except for the chapters on dialectical and semantic subjects—the third section of Hu Shih.

do something to mitigate the many pedestrian deficiencies of this work. In closing, I would like to express my deep appreciation of the skill and patience with which Mrs. Norma Feldkamp has undertaken the typing of this manuscript.

Ann Arbor
Michigan
Oct 1975

Padmanabh Vijai Pillai

CONTENTS

CHAPTER I

The Regnum Delimited

CHAPTER 1

Section 1. The Archetypal Syzygy

Ananda Coomaraswamy commences his work on spiritual authority and temporal power in India with the observation that the Indian concept of kingship can be summarized in the words of the marriage ceremony;[1] "I am He, thou art She; I am the Harmony, thou the Words; I am Sky, thou art Earth. Let us twain here become one; let us bring forth off-spring."[2] This is perhaps an apposite point for a background discussion on the mystique of kingship as it exists in the Brāhmaṇas and some of the older Vedic works.[3] We shall have occasion to note later whether the ethos remains the same in the Dharma-sūtras, the *Kauṭilyan Arthaśāstra*, the Aśokan edicts, and, finally, the *Manusmṛti*.

Central to the whole scheme is the concept of syzygies or procreative pairs whose productive union is responsible for the creation of the cosmos and all within. The archetypal example of such a relationship is that of the Sky and the Earth, which finds a place in the marriage formula quoted above. It is also the Sun which takes the forms of Agni, Vāyu and Āditya in relation to the Three Worlds of Earth, Air and Sky[4]—a sequence of correspondences which are also spoken of in terms of the "Three Skies" and "Three Earths"[5] on the pattern of the primary paradigm. This relationship, constituting as it does the vital logic of procreation, is sustained all the way down the hierarchy from the Sun and the Sky to the Husband and Wife. Thus the union of Mitra and Varuṇa, like that of Indra and Agni or Indra and Bṛhaspati, where Mitra, Agni and Bṛhaspati are divine archetypes of the Sacerdotium of Spiritual Authority (Brāhma), and Varuṇa and Indra those of the Regnum or Executive Power (Kṣatra), are merely particular instances of a cosmic and eternal principle. In this union, however, complementary though it is, it is a complementarity involving unequal partners, for the Sacerdotium is always given preeminence. In the *Śatapatha Brāhmaṇa*, for instance, we are shown a time when the two, Mitra and Varuṇa, were distinct, and when, though Mitra could do without Varuṇa, the latter could not as he needed Mitra to "quicken" (*aprasutam*) his actions and thus bring them successfully to fruition. He therefore said to Mitra, "Turn thou unto me that we may unite; I assign to you the precedence; quickened by thee I shall do deeds."[6] It is with this act of being quickened, of ceding the precedence unto the Sacerdotium, that the essential rite of *abhiṣeka* in the *Rājaśūya*, or anointment ceremony, is concerned. The initiatory 're-birth' of the king takes place under the aegis of the officiating priests who thereby attain to a paternal status, while a fresh purity is bestowed upon the king.[7] It is in this context that the *purohita* earns his name—the "one put in front"—and it is as a consequence of the beneficial results flowing from this act of subordination that it is said—"To him the people of themselves pay homage, in whose realm the Brāhma goeth first."[8]

The alliance between the *purohita* and the king is cemented in a formula very similar to the marriage one, and is uttered by the *purohita* who has been chosen as the pastor of the realm (Rāṣṭragopa)· "I am That; thou art This; thou art This, I am That. I am Sky, thou art Earth. I am the Harmony, thou the Words. Let us twain here unite our houses. Thou art the body, protect thou my body from this Great Dread." This formula, as Coomaraswamy goes on to say, is clearly apotropaic of death by way of drought—"this Great Dread."[9] The result of the congress of Mitra and Varuṇa is a metamorphosis in the nature of the latter, a kind of 're-birth' in the course of which he sheds his "wrath"—hitherto primarily expressed in the form of drought. Thus, if the independent Varuṇa is a god of drought and privation, the joint Mitrāvaruṇāu are gods of rain.[10] And similarly all syzygies are principles of fecundity as their individual components are of aridity, and thus, like Sky and Earth, the priest and king too are jointly rain-givers, and the physical well-being of the land depends, quite literally, upon the king being duly cognizant of the spiritual element, just as "When Sky and Earth consent (or 'know' one another) then indeed it rains."[11]

The Regnum is thus not its own principle but is controlled by another, that of Dharma or Satyam, which is the Kṣatrasya Kṣatram or the ruler of the Kṣatra.[12] This supreme principle overrides both king and sage, but between these two, the king is food for the Brāhman[13] just as the people are food for the king.[14] There are no absolute identities in such a hierarchy, and each link is defined relationally rather than absolutely. As the Brāhman is male in relation to the king, so the king is male in relation to the people. In the delegation of the sceptre (*vajra*) by the priest to the king, for instance, the king is strengthened in relation to the Sacerdotium, just as when the king himself delegates authority to others they become his vassals.[15] The relationship therefore involves a certain opposition which is overtly recognized by the *Śatapatha Brāhmaṇa* when it says, "that which is of Mitra is not of Varuṇa,"[16] and this bipolarity is an essential feature of the entire chain of syzygies, for, in fact, the very fecundity of the union of the progenitive pairs is conditional upon the bringing together of opposed poles. And this is why *Anṛta*—disorder—is the consequence of rule by the Regnum untempered by the Sacerdotium.

Summing up by way of a brief critique, the following would seem to be the pertinent points: kingship is not an autonomous principle, its exercise is contingent upon being penetrated by the opposed principle of the moral order or Sacerdotium. This symbiotic union, in turn, is but one particular instance of a given cosmological scheme. Just as the union of Sky and Earth gives birth to the world of nature, so the union of priest and king gives birth to that of political and social norms. But it is a union between unequal partners, for the Sacerdotium also represents the fundamental principle of the union of opposites, while the Regnum is constantly tempted in the direction of a unilateral declaration of independence which, if successful, would impede its primary function of being the patron (*yajamāna*) of the sacrifice by which it is ensured that the ceaseless downward flow of food as rain is returned in the smoke of the sacrificial offering.[17] In this, of course, the Regnum is dependent upon the Sacerdotium, but the latter needs the former only in order to re-create, mimetically, the archetypal syzygy. What follows from this is that the Sacerdotium is indifferent to all specific acts of the Regnum—political acts—unless they simultaneously violate and threaten the very system of creation engendered by the syzygy principle, such as, for example, those which tend to the interruption or termination of sacrifices. Or, to put it the other way about, the Regnum is of significance only to the extent that it subserves the spiritual principle of which, in social terms, the *varṇāśramadharma*—the four stages of life and the fourfold order of caste—is the embodiment.

The Sacerdotium does not, in fact, penetrate the Regnum—the Regnum in itself is not spiritualized—but is satisfied with utilizing it to fulfill the formal requirements of a congress with its opposite. With all that pertains to the Regnum outside this context, the Sacerdotium remains ambivalent if not uninvolved, and in this it is possible to discern why the temporal power in ancient India seems to be both merely supportive (the sacrificial role of re-creation and the social and political one of protection) and, in the absence of spiritual support in its specifically political aspect, amoral (Arthaśāstra doctrines). What concerns us in the rest of this work is to determine whether the concept of kingship outlined above persists through the Dharmasūtras, the *Kauṭilyan Arthaśāstra*, the Aśokan edicts and Manu, or whether the king, and political power, attain to a more assertive status. The first step will be, by way of defining temporal power through its manifestation in positive law, an analysis of the injunctions, penances and sanctions in the Dharmasūtras. And to this we now turn.

CHAPTER I

Section 2. The King in the Dharmasūtras

The Dharmasūtras are essentially concerned with codifying, in a very terse fashion, the rules of behaviour to be found in the Vedas and hence believed to be based on *śruti*—what is heard. The rules are specifically assembled in order to clarify the role of each class (*varṇa*) and the duties of those at each of the four stages of life. Its concern is thus the *varṇāśrama-dharma*. Together with the Śrauta, Gṛhya and Sulva Sūtras they form a part of the Kalpasūtras,[18] a body of aphoristic works dealing with sacrificial ritual and the duties of the twice-born. The Dharmasūtras derive part of their content from the Gṛhyasutras—which deal with domestic ceremonies such as the obligatory daily rites and the "rites of passage" (samṣkāras)—and consequentially partially overlap with them.[19] In addition, they deal with civil and criminal law and the functions of the king, although, of course, their main orientation is religious and soteriological—the attainment of heaven by scrupulous adherence to the prescribed rites. As we are concerned with the question of political authority, attention will be focused on the legal aspects and the position of the king.

A beginning may be made with a review of their formal statements regarding the status allotted to the king. Gautama commences his section on the duties of a king with the observation that the "king is master of all, with the exception of the Brāhmaṇas."[20] With the further assertion that "Kṣatriyas, who are assisted by Brāhmaṇas, prosper and do not fall into distress,"[21] we are clearly still within the general idea of kingship outlined above in relation to the Brāhmaṇas. In more concrete terms, however, his duties are to protect the castes[22] and to lead back those who stray from the paths prescribed for them.[23] His administration of justice is to be regulated by the Vedas, the Dharmasūtras, the Aṅgas and the Purāṇas.[24] The laws of countries, castes and families are to be respected unless in flagrant opposition to the sacred texts, and cultivators, traders, herdsmen, money-lenders and artisans are entitled to legislate for themselves.[25] Thus far, therefore, the function of the king is patently supportive: he is eulogized for being the protector of a scheme which owes its genesis to a force quite independent of him, and similarly his power as a legislator is curtailed both by the fact that he is the enforcer of pre-existent rules and that, even in those instances where he may be expected to innovate, he is to uphold the norms of localities or those of professions. So much for the formal evaluation of the king's power; it still remains to be seen whether one can discern, in the circumstances described or implicit in the Dharmasūtras, situations which cannot be tackled by the scriptural codes and which therefore demand a power separate from what we may call the sacro-social nexus of priestly injunctions and social sanctions. To this end, an analysis of the proscriptions in the Sūtra literature will be undertaken in which the main questions will be: the nature of the proscription, the penalties imposed, and finally, the agent of the punishment. J.D.M. Derrett has pointed out[26] that much of what exists in the Sūtras and Śāstras are in the form of exhortations and moral advice, and that, even in the case of practical (*vyavahāra*) law, we are not really dealing with law properly so-called in that no distinction is drawn between the obligatory and the morally imperative. Further, many of the rules are unenforceable and hence non-legal, while many of the penalties imposed, being of a *karmic* nature, have to be seen in the same light. But, as he goes on to say,[27] the Sūtras constitute an organic whole in which there is no distinction between law and morality, in which the individual conscience plays an important part, and in which therefore, one can further argue, the sense of guilt and sacrilege attain to the strength of legal sanctions. It will be with this view of sanctions in mind that the analysis will be undertaken.

Five main types of proscriptions appear in the Ḍharmasūtras. There are, to begin with, the ritual proscriptions specifying conditions and circumstances which are unfavourable to sacrifice or Veda study or, in general, to the formal duties of the twice-born. Examples of these are, "At night (he shall not study) in a wood where there is no fire nor gold."[28] "He shall not sip rain-drops."[29] He (shall) not choose (for the performance of a Śrauta-sacrifice) a priest who is unlearned in the Veda, nor one who haggles about his fee."[30] In each of these cases the fundamental concern is for the purity essential to the undertaking which will be violated if these precepts are not followed. The sanction therefore inheres in the failure and frustration which such non-compliance will inevitably entail, and thus stands in no need of an external executor. The second type of proscriptions are to be found in the sections dealing with permissible modes of livelihood. Such for instance are injunctions like "Trade is not lawful for a Brāhmaṇa,"[31] and then, having permitted it in times of distress, "Among the various kinds of grain he shall specially not sell sesamum or rice (except he shall have grown them himself)."[32] Penalties for the infraction of such rules are left unspecified, and one can infer either social opprobrium, or an appeal to caste purity, or both.

The next category involves the various acts of omission and commission for which reparation can be made through penances. Foremost amongst these are the heinous crimes of murdering a Brāhman and violating a guru's bed[33]—the penances for which are tantamount to a death sentence. "He (the violator of a guru's bed) shall perform to his last breath (the penance) prescribed by that rule (sūtra 11). He cannot be purified in this world. But (after death) his sin is taken away."[34] Penances are, however, backed by something more than religious imperatives. Āpastamba[35] says that the spiritual guide is to prescribe penances proportionate to the sins committed in accordance with the precepts of the Smṛtis. If the teacher's orders are ignored, he shall take the transgressor before the king, who, in turn, will enforce the penance—corporally if necessary—*via* his domestic priest. The king is seen to be, once more, the executive wing of theologically ordained law.

The fourth category pertains to that relatively small number of instances where the king is delegated, not an autonomous, but a direct and practical role in justice. "A thief shall go to the king with flying hair carrying a club on his shoulder, and tell him his deed. He (the king) shall give him a blow with that club. If the thief dies his sin is expiated."[36] And this is followed by "If he is forgiven by the king, the guilt falls upon him who forgives him,"[37] thereby effectually curbing the king's freedom of choice. A similar instance is afforded by the case of the proven adultress who has also violated caste laws: "A woman who commits adultery with a man of lower caste the king shall cause to be devoured by dogs in a public place."[38]

The fifth and most significant category, however—significant for what it implies regarding the possibility of growth in the king's role—is to be found in those exhortations of practical import which are not backed by the usual penitential or eschatological sanctions and utilize either no sanctions at all, or purely secular ones which imply the need for an executor—without anyone, however, being thus designated. It may be useful to give a relatively wide range of examples. "If a person who has taken a lease of land (for cultivation) does not exert himself, and hence (the land) bears no crop, he shall, if he is rich, be made to pay (to the owner of the land the value of the crop) that ought to have grown."[39] Regarding damage done by cattle, "If all is destroyed, (the value of) the whole crop (must be paid and a fine in addition)."[40] "The heirs shall pay the debts (of a deceased person)."[41] When matters of commercial import, such as interest, are dealt with, conflicting positions would seem to demand the king's final arbitration. "The legal interest for money lent (is at the rate of) five Māshas a month for twenty (Karshāpaṇas)."[42] "Some (declare that this rate should not be paid) longer than a year."[43] "A loan secured by a pledge that is used (by the creditor) bears no interest."[44] "Nor money tendered, nor (a debt due by the debtor) who is forcibly prevented (from paying)."[45] It is pertinent to note that the attitude towards interest itself is ambivalent. Whereas Gautama above accept and seeks to systematize it, Āpastamba regards it as a fairly serious crime. "He who co-habits with a non-Aryan woman, he who lends money at interest, he who drinks (other) spirituous liquors (than Sūra), he who praises everybody in a manner unworthy of a Brāhmaṇa, shall sit on grass, allowing his back to be scorched (by the sun)."[46]

The very amorphousness of these stipulations, their lack of definition, would seem to indicate that the code to cover these various contingencies developed organically rather than through royal fiat, but the king's role would nevertheless emerge in the need for implementation, and in cases of conflicting customary law—whether, for instance, the rate of five Māshas a month for a loan of twenty karshāpaṇas could be maintained only for a year—he could exercise his power through a final decision. The Dharmasūtras reveal a situation in which the emergence of positive law is implicit in the need to adjust conflicting sets of customary law. They further reveal the need for an external agent to stand behind those laws which have arisen through usage and inter-action. In the course of their gradual migration eastwards across India, the Aryans were often confronted by practices and customs quite different from, if not altogether opposed to, their own, but the answer lay in a slow, natural accommodation, and not in a diktat issued from above which assimilated everything into a new scheme which entirely transcended the old. This was, moreover, quite impossible in the nature of things. The Aryans infiltrated eastwards in small drifts, it was not a concerted drive for conquest undertaken by a powerful ruler. Gautama's dictum that the king in his administration of justice was to be guided by the Vedas, the Sūtras, and the local laws of countries, castes and professions,[47] reflects the flexibility of the process of legal adaptation. But this is not to deny an important part to the king, for, as J.D.M. Derrett has indicated,[48] although the Śāstric injunctions in themselves were beyond his pale, he could, by the fact that a decision in a dispute could center around a royal decree given in another context, modify the dictates of the Sūtras and of custom in accordance with his own determination.

The very blurring of the distinction between law and morality however, tends to make positive legislation suspect, and whenever possible the Dharmasūtras incline to prohibit an undesirable act by bringing it under the rubric of religious prohibitions rather than banning it under the aegis of kingly authority. An instance of this is noted above where the lending of money is lumped together with questions of religious impurity—drinking liquor and cohabiting with a non-Aryan woman. It may be argued that given the priestly provenance of the Sūtras this is to be expected, but it would be simplistic, perhaps, to see in this merely another attempt at priestly usurpation. The latter makes sense only in the presence of a dichotomy between the spiritual and temporal realms which is totally lacking in the Dharmasūtras. There is no distinction between what is God's and what Caesar's. Indeed, as is ceaselessly reiterated, the king exists to protect; protection is his duty par excellence, and what he protects in upholding the *varṇāsramadharma* is precisely the spiritual order which is co-extensive with the social scheme. It is natural, therefore, that the Sūtras concern themselves not only with religious obligations in the strict sense, but also with larger aspects of community life—hence the chapters on civil and criminal law. But, as the social structure is a reflection of the cosmic order and thus immutable, the Sūtras are committed to the status quo. They are by their very quiddity ill-equipped to deal with social mutations caused by changed geographical, political and economic settings. Thus, as the diffuse and occasionally contradictory strictures of the fifth category reveal, they are prone to a faltering of authority, a consistent ambiguity, in matters of practical, and, as we shall see, political, import.

It is also to be noted that in periods of change when the social fabric alters along with much that sustains it, the primary weapons in the Śāstric armoury, those of penance and exclusion from caste, necessarily lose much of their potency. Nevertheless, as a study of Manu will prove, far from retreating into exclusively ritualistic and religious concerns, the Śāstra places, as a result of current exigencies, relatively greater emphasis on matters pertaining to the elucidation, systematization and implementation of practical law, although, as we have seen, it is precisely in this realm that it lacks coercive power. And this paradoxical situation, stemming from the inability of the Sūtras to cope with change, finds a correspondence in the relation between the Sūtras and the king. In so far as the king duly supports the divinely ordered society the Sūtras are entirely behind him, but when, confronted with change, he seeks to reduce the social flux and chaos of a given historical period to order, they refuse to commit themselves firmly. To the extent that he is presumably fighting to restore social stability and the sacred order they support him, but since in such a situation orthodoxy will inevitably be compromised by immediate pressures, and the king will inexorably be driven into being far more than a protector—the thrice-blessed role—the Sūtras are uneasy. The nature and strange consequences of this ambiguity are further explored in the chapter on Manu. We shall now turn to a brief study of the historical conditions attendant upon the growth of Arthaśāstra literature with its marked emphasis on political imperium.

CHAPTER II

Realpolitik in Fact and Theory

CHAPTER II

Section 1. The Historical Context of the Arthaśāstra Literature

The course and the spirit of political developments in our period are best characterized in terms of two major motifs; the geographical movement eastwards to the mouth of the Ganges coupled with the growth of strong monarchical states, and the ideological movement glorifying the concept of the all conquering monarch. Both of these find expression in the literature of the Brāhmaṇas, and the first book of the *Śatapatha Brāhmana* traces, in semi-allegorical form, some of the steps in the eastward migration.[1] The king of Videha, Māthava, and his priest, Gotama Rahugāna, said to have followed Agni, the purificatory fire, as it went along burning the ground until making a stop at the river Sadānīra, a tributary of the Ganges flowing down from the northern mountains. This river marked, for a time, the limit of Aryan advance, the territory beyond being unfit for human habitation as it had not been "burnt over by Agni Vaiśvanāra."[2] The *Śatapatha Brāhmaṇa* goes on to say that since then the land has been highly cultivated as the Brahmins had caused Agni to taste it through sacrifices.

The *Punār-abhiṣekha* or Renewed Anointment[3] described in the *Aitareya Brāhmaṇa*[4] gives us the ideal of kingly power: "Do thou become here the over-king of kings; the great of the great people, the supreme ruler of the people." And the object of the *Aindra Mahābhiṣekha*, another ritual anointment at the Royal Inauguration, was much the same.

"May he win all victories, find all the worlds, attain the

> superiority, pre-eminence and supremacy over all kings and overlordship, paramount rule, self-rule, sovereignty, supreme authority, kingship, great kingship and suzerainty, may he be all-encompassing, possessed of all the earth, possessed of all life, from one end up to the other side of the earth bounded by the ocean, sole ruler."[5]

The attention paid to titular dignities further testifies to the concern with imperium, and the *Śatapatha Brāhmaṇa* explains the difference between Samrāṭ and Rājan in these terms, "by offering the Rājasūya he becomes king (Rājan), and by the Vājapeya he becomes Samrāj; and the office of the king is lower, and that of Samrāj the higher."[6] The very structure of Brahmanical rituals, as analyzed by Heesterman, reveals a change which is reflective of the idea of paramount power. Thus, in analyzing the ritual of the saṃjñāneṣṭiḥ (the "concord iṣṭi") he says[7] that it was "manifestly intended to be performed by rival groups in order to unite under a common leader."[8] In the Maitrāyaṇī-saṃhitā 2.2.6, the gods are divided into four groups unable to agree on the question of leadership. Bṛhaspati makes them perform the saṃjña-neṣṭi, and turning to Indra they agree on him as their leader. The classical ritual, however, does not admit this situation, but transforms the saṃjñana ceremony into a standard iṣṭi to be performed by a single yajamāna (patron) "who wishes that the others will agree on his leadership but without their participation in the ceremony."[9] In this way, a communal elevation to power is replaced by a process of self-ascription in which one can perhaps see the ritualistic and symbolic equivalent of the over-king of kings, the cakravartin. It is to be remembered, however, that this still remains a modality of the scheme of complementarity that was discussed in the previous chapter. The sacrificer or the patron of the sacrifice does not do away with the priest, the Sacerdotium, but in effect utilizes him to gain the ascendancy over his colleagues. The continuing subordination to the sacral power is attested to by the fact that in the ceremony of the *Punār-abhiṣekha* mentioned above, the king, after he is asked to become the over-king of kings, is required to descend from the throne and make obeisance to the Brahman—"verily thus the lordly power (kṣatra) falls under the influence of the holy power (Brāhma)."[10] We shall now trace the vicissitudes of political power as it develops in the context of the political tensions and forces of this period and the accompanying Arthaśāstra literature typified by Kauṭilya's work.

Towards the 7th century B.C.,[11] the old heart-land of the Aryans, the land of the Kuru-Pancālas, had faded in importance, and had become subordinate to Videha under King Janaka in the east both in status and as the breeding ground of philosophical ideas—those of the *Upaniṣads*.[12] The other important states of this period, stretching in a chain from the Northwest to the Southeast, were Gandhāra, Kekaya, Madra, Uśināra, Matsya, Kāśī and Kosala. The Videhan monarchy appears to have collapsed sometime near the beginning of the 6th century B.C., and was replaced by the confederation of the Vṛjjis in which the Licchavis and the Videhas were the predominating elements.[13] No mention is made of it in the list of sixteen peoples found in the *Aṅguttara Nikāya* which runs as follows: Kāśī, Kosala, Aṅga, Magadha, Vṛjji, Malla, Cedi, Vatsa, Kuru, Pancāla, Matsya, Śūrasena, Aśmaka, Avanti, Gandhāra and Kamboja.[14] While some of these people—for they are yet to be defined in territorial terms—were to exist into the period of the great Gangetic kingdoms, many would be subsumed into the latter. By the middle of the 6th century B.C., the political centre of gravity had shifted decisively toward the lower end of the Gangetic basin, and the main protagonists for supremacy are all to be found in this area. A few kings to the West and Northwest, Caṇḍa Pradyota Mahāsena of Avanti and Puskarasārin of Taxila, exercised considerable power, but their role in the ultimate analysis was peripheral. Of all the newly emergent powers, Magadha was to prove to be the most significant, but its early history is very obscure. It is first mentioned in the *Atharvaveda*[15] where fever is wished away upon its inhabitants by its pious authors, but this indicates nothing more than the fringe status of the Magadhis in Aryan society. The main architect of its future strength was Bimbisāra who attacked and annexed Aṅga after defeating its ruler—a victory which is elliptically attested to by the *Sonadaṇḍa Sutta* of the *Dīgha*

Nikāya in which the Brahmin Sonadaṇḍa is said to have been given a large estate in Campā by Seniya Bimbisāra.[16]

It would be reasonable to speculate with Basham[17] that part of the significance of this conquest lay in giving Magadha an outlet to the sea and the chance to participate in coastal trade, while it strengthened its hold over the lower reaches of the Ganges. In Kosala, Mahākosala was succeeded by his son Prasenajit who is said by the *Samyutta Nikāya* to have been at the head of five Rājas which probably included those of Kāśi, the Kalāmas and the Śākyas.[18] Avanti was to remain a major power to the west for sometime to come, and a measure of its aggressive policy under Canda Pradyota Mahasena is provided by the fact that Ajātaśatru, the son and successor of Bimbisāra, felt compelled to fortify the walls of Rājagṛha against him.[19]

The conflict for power intensifies with Ajātaśatru, and his wars against both Kosala and the Vṛjjian confederacy are to be seen as part of the drive towards Magadhan hegemony. The *Samyutta Nikāya* mentions a conflict between Kosala and Magadha over Kāśī in which Prasenajit, after initial set-backs, finally defeats and captures Ajātaśatru, but then releases him after confiscating his elephants, horses, chariots and infantry.[20] Despite this victory, however, the decline of Kosala as a major power after the death of Prasenajit is relatively rapid, and Sumitra—fourth in line from Viḍūḍabha, the son of Prasenajit —is said to have been the last independent sovereign of Kosala.[21] The war with the Vṛjjian confederacy again stems from a territorial dispute, and the *Mahāparinibbāna Sutta* of the *Dīgha Nikāya* tells us that a port half in Magadha and half in Vṛjji produced a scented substance highly valued in both countries.[22] When Ajātaśatru sent men to secure his share, they found that the Vṛjjians had appropriated the entire amount. Ajātaśatru then sent his chief minister, Vassakāra, to inquire of the Buddha whether it would be possible to exterminate the Vṛjjians, and received the answer that it would be impossible so long as the latter maintained their folk-moots and revered their shrines. Vassakāra thereupon pretended to have fallen out with Ajātaśatru and went to Vaiśāli as a refugee—where he was received and accepted in council. He then took advantage of his position to sow dissension amongst his hosts and so divided them that Ajātaśatru was able to overcome them with little fighting. The episode is interesting, for it also affords an illustration of one of the techniques recommended by Kauṭilya in the Eleventh Book of his work for dealing with republics. The defeat of the Vṛjjians made Magadha the paramount power in the east, but its westward growth was confronted by the kingdom of Avanti. It is not clear exactly who overcame this rival—the Purāṇas[23] assert that it was Śiśunāga, an official raised to power by the people of Magadha in disgust at having been ruled by a succession of patricides from Ajātaśatru down to Nāga-Dāsaka, but in any case Avanti was part of Magadha before the time of Candragupta Maurya and before Aśoka became the ruler of Magadha he was the Viceroy of Avanti at Ujjain.[24] In Magadha itself, the Śiśūnaga line, in turn, was brought to an end with the assassination of Kākavarṇa Śaiśunaga at the hands of his Nanda successor. The Purāṇas attest to the power of the Nandas when it refers to Mahāpadma, the first Nanda king, as the destroyer of all kṣatriyas and the sole monarch of the earth.[25] Raychaudhuri suggests on the basis of the Hathigumpha inscription mentioning the activities of Nandarāja that parts of Kalinga may have been under the Nandas.[26] If this was so, then it may have been lost in the course of a revolt during the reign of Bindusāra, and Aśoka's Kaliṅga expedition can thus be viewed either as the regaining of what had been Magadhan territory or as a fresh conquest.[27]

The Macedonian invasion under Alexander the Great in 326 B.C. played a very decisive role in simplifying the politics of Northern India and indirectly facilitated Magadhan growth. The welter of states in Northwestern India and the Punjab were quite unable to offer any coordinated opposition to the invader despite the stubborn resistance of the elder Porus, the Oxydrakai (Kṣudrakas), the Malloi (Mālavas), and the Kathaians (Kathakas, Katha, Kautha or Kratha and others in the Punjab).[28] By defeating these clans and kingdoms, what Alexander accomplished was not their replacement by Hellenic outposts—for even as he was retreating through Karmania in 324 B.C. he was informed of the murder of Phillipos, governor of the Upper Indus Province,[29] and it was clear shortly after that the Greeks could not hold on in India—but the creation of a political vacuum which was to be of great use to Candragupta Maurya. It enabled him, after the withdrawal of the Greeks, to gain a firm hold on the Northwest and the Punjab after defeating the Nandas.[30] The Junagarḥ inscription of Rudradāman[31] linking him with the building of the Sudarśana lake is clear evidence that he was in control as far west as Saurashtra, and thus makes him the first king of Magadha to rule from ocean to ocean. To the Northwest after the settlement with Seleucus, he came into possession of Herat, Kandahar, Makran and Kabul (Aria, Arachosia, Gedrosia and the Paropanisadae).[32] The evidence for Mauryan activity in the south is not as specific as one could wish, but the distribution of Aśokan edicts as far south as Raichur makes it certain that their control did extend south of the Vindhyas. K.A.N. Sastri maintains that Kannada inscriptions from Mysore and the Bombay-Karnatak of the 10th and 11th centuries A.D. preserve faint memories of Nanda rule in the Kuntala country, and although this is not confirmed by other sources, it does conform to the extent of Aśoka's empire as determined by the location of his inscriptions.[33] Further, the Tamil writer Māmūlanār, writing about four hundred years after the downfall of the Mauryas, mentions the latter taking a hand in the local politics of the Tamil land around the Salem and Coimbatore districts.[34] But this does not clarify under which Mauryan king this occurred, nor does it delimit the southern possessions of the Mauryas. Bindusāra, who succeeded his father Candragupta Maurya around 300 B.C.,[35] is not known to have added to his territorial inheritance, and the conquest, or re-conquest, of Kalinga by Aśoka in 260 B.C. marks the apex of Magadhan power and the culmination of the policy initiated by Bimbisāra with his conquest of Aṅga. The territorial extent of Aśoka's empire can be more precisely estimated than those of his predecessors on the basis of the distribution of his rock and pillar edicts which spread from Kandahar and Shahbazgarhi in the Northwest to Raichur in Mysore in the south.[36] Since Kalinga was Aśoka's only addition to the empire, and in view of the fact that Bindusāra undertook no expansionist activities, the establishment of a trans-Vindhyan kingdom must be seen as the work either of the Nandas or of Candragupta Maurya himself.

We have now come to the point where the two motifs mentioned earlier fuse into one, where the symbolic ideal of the world conqueror finds territorial expression. It is now proposed to study the other side of this process and to determine the extent to which administrative centralization paralleled geographical centralization, and to see, if possible, the extent to which the paramount power not only reigned but ruled. The Dharmasūtras, while supporting the royal duty of arms and in principle not opposed to conquest, stand opposed to the idea of a unitary administration. Thus Gautama: "the laws of countries, castes and families, which are not opposed to the (sacred) records, (have) also authority."[37] There is little doubt that both within the kingdom and in a newly acquired territory a considerable degree of autonomy persisted amongst the various regional and clan groupings involved, and although it is difficult to adduce concrete examples, the following instance may provide a degree of circumstantial evidence. We know that in the time of Prasenajit of Kosala the Śākyas formed part of his kingdom.[38] Now, the lives of Prasenajit and the Buddha were roughly contemporaneous,[39] and in the *Ambaṭṭha Sutta* of the *Dīgha Nikāya*[40] there is a discussion between the young Brahmin Ambaṭṭha and the Buddha, in the course of which the former explains why he considers the Śākyans to be mere menials. He mentions that having once gone to Kapilavastu on some business for his master, he ventured into the Śākyan congress hall where he was mocked and jibed at by the members of the assembly. Thus, despite the fact that it was part of a monarchy, the Śākyans still continued with their republican folk-moots to deal with administrative concerns, and it can be reasonably assumed that acceptance of Kosalan suzerainty did not imply direct rule from the Kosalan capital. At the same time, there are indications that attempts were made to establish a more cohesive and less diffuse administrative pattern, or at least to create a linkage between the king and the powers at the local level. An example of this is possibly furnished by the *Mahāvagga's* account of the time when Bimbisāra held an assembly of 80,000 gramikas or village head-men.[41] Nevertheless, the limited means of communication seem to have led to a kind of qualified delegation of powers; thus Aṅga was governed by the Magadhan Crown Prince as a separate province from its capital of Campā, while the king himself remained at Rājagṛha.[42] The next glimpse of the mechanics of the Magadhan government is provided by the Arthaśāstra work ascribed to Kauṭilya and the account of Megasthenes of the Mauryan administration.

There is a general consensus of opinion that although the *Kauṭilyan Arthaśāstra* may have to be dated as late as the 2nd century A.D.,[43] the material that it contains is considerably older, and can be taken as referring in general terms to Mauryan conditions. It must, however, be always kept in mind that what Kauṭilya is reputed to have composed is a 'śāstra', a treatise on the science of administration, and not a work descriptive of any concreate and given governmental system. His concern is with the ideal state, but, as is the case with all ideals, the elements of which it is composed undoubtedly reflect a fair degree of reality. A comparison of the *Kauṭiliyan Arthaśāstra* with the account of Megasthenes does not yield a one-to-one concordance in terms of details, but in the degree of administrative organization and control to which they both testify, they have a lot in common. It has been pointed out that Megasthenes was not in a position to talk about India as as whole in that his travels were limited in all probability to the Gangetic plain,[44] but as an emissary at Pāṭaliputra, he must certainly have gained some knowledge of the working practices of the central government. The observations of Megasthenes pertinent to the socio-administrative nature of the country are briefly summarized. He claimed that the population of India was divided into seven 'castes', and their enumeration makes it probable that he confounded caste with profession. These were the philosophers, husbandsmen, shepherds and herdsmen, artisans, the military, the overseers, and finally, the councillors and assessors.[45] City administration was in the charge of a body of thirty members divided into six boards of five each. These were in respective charge of the industrial arts, foreigners resident at the capital, census compilation and tax assessment, trade and commerce, supervision of manufactured articles and realization of taxes.[46] Collectively, they undertook programmes to ensure the upkeep of buildings, temples, ports and harbors, and were also responsible for the regulation of prices. The military was governed under a similar scheme, again with a board of thirty divided into six committees of five each supervising the admiralty, the commisariat, the infantry, the cavalry, the war-chariots and the elephants. Not much is mentioned of rural administration apart from a class of officers who appear to be in charge of irrigation and also possess cardastral functions. They are said to "measure the land . . . and inspect the sluices by which water is let out from the main canals into their branches, so that everyone may have an equal supply of it."[47] In addition, they collect taxes and oversee other occupations connected with the land such as wood-cutting and mining.

The characteristic feature of Megasthenes' account is the impression of bureaucratic centralization that it imparts, the idea of a steel framework within which the activities of the kingdom are compressed, and in this it accords perfectly with Kauṭilya. Further, although the schematic organization described varies, a comparison of the two accounts in functional terms affords a substantial agreement. The sixth class of Megasthenes, that of the overseers, is certainly closely linked to the spies and supervisors of the Kauṭilyan system. Of them Megasthenes says, "It is their province to enquire into and superintend all that goes on in India, and make report to the king . . .,"[48] while Kauṭilya divides these functions between the various superintendents of departments and the espionage system proper—which does not have any administrative duties but is solely concerned with keeping an eye on the state system at every level from the Crown Prince to the Commandant of the frontier fort.[49] The seventh category of Megasthenes, the councillors and assessors, are described as the smallest but most prestigious of all the 'castes' because from "these ranks the advisers of the king are taken, and the treasurers of the state, and the arbiters who settle disputes."[50] This is surely the ministerial and councillor circle of Kauṭilya, and both he and Megasthenes thus distinguish clearly between the policy formulating and executive branches of the government.

Regarding urban government, Kauṭilya makes no mention of the board of thirty divided into six committees that is to be found in Megasthenes, but the various administrative areas covered are also dealt with by him. The city is under the overall control of the City Superintendent aided by the Section Officer and the Divisional Warden.[51] The Section Officer, in charge of units of ten, twenty or forty families,[52] is charged with the duty of keeping a census and tax register noting numbers, castes, occupations, sex and income and expenditure. The functions of the City Superintendent are fundamentally municipal : sanitation, hygiene, security and fire prevention. The main sources of city revenues are listed as accruing from custom-duties, fines, the sale of weights and measures, the mint, the issue of passports, animal slaughter, yarn, oil, ghee, sugar, goldsmiths, markets, prostitutes, gambling, buildings, artisans and temples,[53] but beyond a blanket statement that the king is entitled to one-tenth of the commodities and a schedule of custom-duties which vary according to the goods from one-fifth to one-twenty-fifth of the price,[54] we are not given an idea as to the scale of taxation. The government took a direct hand in trade, not only for the sake of profit but also in the interests of price stabilization. The Director of Trade is asked to sustain the price of a glutted commodity by purchasing it,[55] and he is exhorted to avoid making a profit which would be harmful to the subjects.[56] State participation in industry was quite widespread, and mining and the establishment of connected metal and gem industries are laid down as the functions of the Director of Mines.[57] Another field of governmental endeavour was the textile industry, and the Superintendent of Yarns is asked to set up manufacturing units utilizing the labour of widows, crippled women and other socially disenfranchised females who are thus aided in eking out a livelihood.[58] The government was obviously alive to the necessity of a regular and uniform infrastructure, and as a basic prerequisite established factories for the manufacture of standard weights and measures.[59]

Once again, in the case of military organization, Kauṭilya makes no mention of the board of thirty, but as with the city, his organizational scheme covers the same ground and offers a greater depth of detail. The Superintendents of horses and elephants are provided with detailed instructions for training and feeding their beasts, and it is assumed that the state maintains its own extensive stables.[60] The Superintendent of chariots is charged with the establishment of factories manufacturing chariots, and is also responsible for the training and employment of charioteers.[61] The Superintendent of infantry is expected to be knowledgeable about various types of troops and their suitability for fighting in diverse terrains. It is also hinted that he may have to employ them in some non-military capacity if the occasion so demands.[62] The state maintained its own armament factories,[63] and the troops were armed from the government armories.[64] Some care appears to have been taken in keeping the populace unarmed, or at least in carefully supervising the issue of arms. Kauṭilya expressly stipulates that "People shall move about unarmed, except those permitted with a sealed license."[65] Elsewhere,[66] frontier officers are instructed to impound the weapons and armour of caravan traders, or to seal them.

Kauṭilya provides a far more intensive account of rural administration than Megasthenes. Revenue centres are to be set up for groups of ten (Saṃgrahaṇa), two hundred (kārṇaṭika), four hundred (droṇamukha), and eight hundred (sthānīya) villages,[67] and a revenue officer is to be in charge of groups of five or ten villages.[68] For purposes of administration, the countryside is divided into four sections, each quarter being under a divisional officer.[69] The administrator, in over-all command, "should cause to be entered in a register the number of villages, classifying them as best, middling and lowest, (recording) this much is (the revenue in) grains, cattle, cash, forest produce, labour, and produce in place of tax."[70] As in the case of cities, the register also notes census figures of population and income and expenditure.[71] The above stipulations would tend to indicate that the taxation system was a flexible one accepting multiple criteria and favouring a proportional scheme rather than a flat tax. Thus, while in general the king is said to be entitled to "one-sixth of the grains, one-tenth of the commodities as his share,"[72] taxes on crops would seem to have varied with the irrigational facilities involved, and the rates go up to one-third or one-fourth of the produce from a region "that is not dependent on rains and yields abundant crops."[73] Kauṭilya is keen on expanding the range of settlement, and his agrarian policies are oriented to this end. Exemptions are advocated as a means of attracting people to marginal lands,[74] and agricultural loans of grain, cattle and money are suggested with repayment at one's convenience.[75] Stockpiling is recommended to mitigate the effects of famine along with other public relief measures, and Kauṭilya strikes a modern note with the suggestion of instituting public works—forts and waterworks—in what would otherwise be a time of widespread unemployment.[76] The concern of the central government in agricultural affairs is further evidenced by the detailed instructions regarding the sowing time for various types of crops in the context of their water requirements which the Director of Agriculture is required to implement.[77] Considerable attention is payed to the question of irrigation, and the state is asked to "cause irrigation works to be built with natural water resources or with water brought in from elsewhere."[78] If the work is not directly undertaken by the government, it is at least required to aid those who are performing it with land, roads, implements and so on.[79] In fact it would appear that the bulk of irrigation projects were undertaken at the local village level and were primarily cooperative enterprises. A scale for exemption from taxes is laid down for newly constructed tanks and embankments, for those renovated, and for those cleared.[80] The Sudarśana lake testifies to the scale of state irrigation projects, but in general it would seem that the government acted as a kind of catalyst in irrigation projects, aiding with money and materials, and not as the sole irrigation agent. From what one can glean from Kauṭilya, Wittfogel's theory of the Mauryan state as a hydraulic despotism would not appear to hold true.

The structure outlined above makes it clear that the world of Kauṭilya is far removed from the theological, rural and largely self-contained units envisaged by the writers of the sūtras. In the first chapter an attempt was made to reveal that even within this framework there were, so to say, low-pressure areas which invited an increase in royal powers, but the essential note of the Dharmasūtras is certainly one of concern with societies which are, at least in principle, regulated by custom and usage rather than by positive law. And the social picture projected by them is one of decentralized agrarian communities living largely in isolation from urban concerns and pressures. Pluralism in social and legal norms was given the backing of Śāstric support so long as they were not totally antithetical to Vedic concepts. The ethos of Kauṭilya's work is opposed to most of these features of Śāstric thought. It upholds a centralized state against a loose conglomeration of virtually autonomous village units under a policeman-king; against the pluralism of the Sūtras it asserts an ubiquitous administration with uniform standards and codes of law so far as this is compatible with his general adherence to the scheme of the *varṇāśrama-dharma.* He does grant the higher castes certain privileges in law,[81] but the emphasis is far less pronounced than in the Dharmasūtras.

For the first time, a defined role is carved out for the king, and it is, moreover, accorded the highest validity. "A matter in dispute has four feet, law, transaction, custom and the royal edict; (among them) the later one supercedes the earlier one."[82] Further, "Where (a text of) the science may be in conflict with any edict in a matter of law, there the edict shall prevail; for there the written text loses its validity."[83] Even if, with regard to the second quotation, we translate *nyāya* as 'logic' as opposed to Kangle's 'edict', and take the verse to mean that the letter of the śāstra may be overruled when it conflicts with the spirit or 'logic' of Dharma, the king would still be important for purposes of interpretation. Despite this evidence supporting bureaucratic and legislative centralization, however, the actual extent to which organs of the central government replaced the various groupings of trade and occupation which intervened between the state and the people is not clear from Kauṭilya's work. We are, for instance, told very little about government at the village level beyond the functions of the revenue officer in charge of groups of five or ten villages,[84] and he is clearly a functionary of the government and not a village official. Nevertheless, we do gather elliptical evidence which testifies to the persistence of the old village councils, and Kauṭilya assigns the job of determining disputes concerning fields to the village elders.[85] Similarly, Kauṭilya makes mention of guilds[86] and labour unions,[87] but in both cases his concern is with laying down rules for the professional relations between these institutions and their clients; nothing is said to indicate that the state took an interest in their internal structure and organization, or that it took active measures to repress them. Kauṭilya's attitude towards republics[88] is symbolic in a limited way of his attitude towards all organizations which have a *raison d'être* independent of their position in, and their relation to, the state. He regards it as necessary to infiltrate and break them down for precisely that reason, but he is also intensely aware of the strength of loyalty and affection which can arise from local patriotism, family sentiment and parochial ties. Because these forces, in general, are antagonistic to the monolithic state, Kauṭilya is keen on dissolving them through duplicity or force, but he is very keen on them when they can be garnered in the interests of the king. He displays his awareness of the cohesiveness and solidarity of blood ties in his description of the kind of exhortation which the bards should bestow upon the soldiers about to enter battle—"sing praises of the caste, corporation, family, deeds and conduct of the warriors"[89]—and from this it would appear probable that these intermediary organizations were not only acknowledged, but may even have found a place in military organization.

Thus, the kind of centralization that Kauṭilya had in mind was not the rigid kind of bipolarity which isolates the state and the subject at opposite ends of the political spectrum with no intervening elements. The government appears to have acted in conjunction with local powers—where existent—as in the case of irrigation projects. In other cases, as with the guilds mentioned above, the main idea was to regulate and supervise their relations with the public. Nor, of course, did centralization and the existence of state capitalism mean total nationalization in production and distribution. None the less, the central concern of the work is with the extension and preservation of the king's welfare in the largest sense; the highest priority is accorded to the strengthening of the state and the means by which the obstacles in the path of this ideal can be disposed of. In the consideration of the work as a whole below, it will be the implications of this contrast, amounting perhaps to a contradiction—implicit in the nature of the work if not overtly and unambiguously expressed—which will draw most attention.

CHAPTER II

Section 2. The *Kauṭilīya Arthaśāstra*— An Attempt at Regnal Autonomy?

Of the fifteen books into which Kauṭilya's work is divided, the first six are devoted to essentially internal matters of administration of which some idea has been given above. The last nine are given over to issues of foreign policy and the crux of his thinking on the subject can be dealt with in terms of a few key concepts. Kauṭilya echoes the *Aitareya Brāhmaṇa* regarding the extent of the kingly realm and the uniqueness of the Cakravartin's status. "In that (i.e., the earth), the region of the sovereign ruler extends northwards between the Himāvat and the sea, one thousand yójanas in extent across."[90] And, "for the king . . . enjoys the earth (alone) without sharing it with any other (ruler) being devoted to the welfare of all beings."[91] The conceptual scheme of the maṇḍalas, or circles, which arises from this premise is necessarily, therefore, an imperialist one. Relations with foreign states are conceived of in circular terms, a series of concentric circles of which the conquering king constitutes the hub. The neighbouring country is axiomatically the enemy, while his neighbour is the conquering king's natural ally. The middle king is the one who is immediately proximate to both the enemy and the conqueror, while the neutral king stands outside the sphere of these three and is in a position to exert a decisive influence in moments of crises.[92] Kauṭilya outlines six measures of foreign policy, "Peace, war, staying quiet, marching, seeking shelter and dual policy,[93] but it is typical of him that all these policies are but modalities of the same aggressive impulse. Peace, for instance, is recommended only when it will result in ruining the undertakings of the enemy,[94] and it is axiomatic that any advantage of power should be promptly exploited—"When prospering, he should make war."[95] What is evisaged is a constant state of aggrandizement utilizing a variety of expedients with force as the last resort. It is suggested that the weak be won with conciliations and gifts, while the strong are overcome with dissension and force.[96] But moral restraints are not what are responsible for the relative reluctance with which force is espoused; the reason lies in the fact that peace, or for that matter, the other means short of war, are cheaper.[97] The effective utilization of the circular concept of states depends upon the formation of telling alliances which tilt the balance of power against the enemy of the conquering king, but these alliances are highly provisional as yesterday's ally might be today's neighbour, and Kauṭilya accordingly advises against taking such international obligations too seriously. He takes it for granted that pacts may be violated at one's convenience.[98]

Kauṭilya distinguishes between three kinds of conquests: the righteous conqueror demands no more than submission, the greedy one is content with the seizure of land and goods, while the demoniacal conqueror insists upon total acquisition of "land, goods, sons, wives and life."[99] In the light of his preference for expanionist policies, one would expect Kauṭilya to enthusiastically recommend the way of the demoniacal conqueror, or at least that of the greedy one, but he surprisingly advocates what is tantamount to an acceptance of ritual submission.[100] Even when, owing to the implacable hostility of the enemy, the king is forced to kill him, he is adjured not to take possession of his foe's land and property.[101] This is not merely an instance of clemency to the vanquished, but of a very particular type of attitude towards war as a political activity. No attempt is made at exterminating the enemy's line; on the contrary the king is asked to place on the throne the son of one killed in action.[102] Similarly, those who approach of their own accord are to be treated with exemplary courtesy, and, "after promising them safety, he should favour them like a father."[103] One begins to suspect that there is a very strong symbolic element in Kauṭilya's concept of the *Cakravartin*, that at the political level what Kauṭilya meant by universal dominion was not as concrete or absolute as he would normally lead us to assume. Thus Kauṭilya would appear to be nothing but his pragmatic self when he advises against Draconian annexation on the grounds that "the circle of kings, being frightened, rises to destroy one who were to kill or imprison those who have submitted and covet their land, property, sons or wives."[104] This implies that the lenient treatment of conquered foes is nothing more than an expedient in the face of an overwhelmingly strong coalition against one. But it is not mere caution which prompts this moderation; Kauṭilya in fact does not consistently follow the logic of political power to its final end, that of the establishment of absolute paramountcy with no other centres of authority except that of the king—a pattern of total centralization exemplified by the performance of Ch'in Shih Huang-ti in China. In Kauṭilya's view, even if the king were in a position to triumph over his assembled enemies, and not hampered by any fears of retaliation, the extirpation of his foes root and branch is not the ideal which he should seek to achieve. Thus, in summing up the chapter relating to the conduct proper for the king subjugating other kings by force, Kauṭilya provides us with the goal which he feels is desirable: "And therefore kings, protected in their own territories by means of conciliation, become favourably disposed towards the king, remaining obedient to his sons and grandsons."[105] It is not so much that Kauṭilya's reasons are not expedient, for they are, but what end do they expedite? Not the goal of unitary and monolithic power, but that of symbolic paramountcy—he seeks, so to say, not universal domination but universal acclamation. Overt in the above quotation is the fact that the conquering monarch, while certainly being more than a *primus inter pares*, does not seek to be the only locus of power. We do not have sufficient data on socio-political forms in this period of Indian history to justify statements about feudalism, nor does such evidence as we do possess testify to that pyramid of rights and obligations which the feudal order presupposes. Nevertheless, the relations of the dominant monarch in Kauṭilya to the other kings does bear some resemblance to that between a feudal overlord and his vassals. They acknowledge his superiority and remain linked to his line through the gratitude and loyalty inspired by his re-affirmation of their respective positions of authority. This means that war ceases to be an effective implement, or extension, of politics, it is not a measure aimed at procuring greater control but a mode of behaviour which befits kings, an activity which can result in fundamentally symbolic superiority. In other words, war is part of the Kṣatriya dharma, the warrior code, and is therefore a ritual, and not functional, activity.

If one regards Kauṭilya's work, as one is often prone to do, as a primarily secular and intensely realistic work, what has been said above appears exceedingly unlikely. So much of the work is so openly amoral and pragmatic that it seems to eschew not only ethical but even formalistic considerations. In other words, it so openly avows cynicism and duplicity, so clearly espouses the principle of acquisition of wealth and extension of power regardless of moral price, that its treatment of war—the archetypal means of achieving these—seems inexplicable. This is not to say that the actual act of war is reduced to a chivalric contest. On the contrary it is engaged in with a complete absence of scruple—although Kauṭilya does abide by the traditionally humane rules regarding the injured, the unarmed, the defeated and those surrendering.[106] Despite this, however, the contrast does remain between the callous ruthlessness of the means and the surprising modesty of the ends, a contrast which amounts to a contradiction when it is said, on the one hand, that the purpose of kingship, or rather the Rod wielded by the king, is "the acquisition of (things) not possessed,"[107] and, on the other, that the king is forbidden to take a dead enemy's land and property.[108] What is the reason for this curious restraint? Partly, no doubt, the shrewd awareness that any kind of extreme is self-defeating, but more than that, perhaps, is the possibility that Kauṭilya is struggling in the simultaneous grip of two distinct traditions.

Historically, as we have seen, the period under review is characterized by a series of inter-state conflicts which ultimately result in the emergence of Magadha as the paramount power. There is little doubt that the wars undertaken by

Bimbisāra and Ajātaśatru were not ritual exercises, a formalistic performance of their kingly function, but concrete and successful endeavors at increasing political power and territorial extent. We know, for instance, that when Bimbisāra as the Crown Prince of Magadha defeated and killed the king of Aṅga, he moved to Campā and resided there as the Viceroy.[109] There was no question of reinstating the line of the defeated monarch on the throne, and Aṅga was effectively ruled from Rājagṛha. It is also very probable, as Basham has pointed out,[110] that Bimbisāra's annexation of Aṅga was connected with the fact that Campā was an important entrepot centre for the southern trade in gold, jewels and spices, and that Bimbisāra sought to tap this wealth to finance his policy of internal consolidation. Similarly, the wars of Ajātaśatru with Kosala and the Vṛjjis may have been aimed at further securing a hold on the lower reaches of the riverine sysetm by gaining a foothold on the north bank of the Ganges.[111] These manoeuvres clearly testify to a sophisticated conception of real-politik strategy, and, as Basham goes on to say, transcend earlier Indian conceptions of statecraft.[112] But these new developments on the political front were lacking in theoretical frameworks, no dogmas existed to guide or instruct those now facing this new reality, nor to relate it to the established values and patterns of behaviour. It was this vacuum that Arthaśāstra literature sought to fill by prescribing, in duly hieratic fashion, a range of solutions and strategems to the strong prince who wished to become stronger, and the weak one who strove to save himself from annihilation. The Arthaśāstra tradition obviously enjoys considerable antiquity, and Kauṭilya's work, while being the first extant representative, is by no means the earliest. He himself makes mention of several predecessors,[113] and the work itself is regarded as being, fundamentally, a compilation of earlier śāstras written by those interested in the "acquisition and protection of the earth."[114]

The treatise, as has been noted earlier, is of an essentially theoretical nature, with dubious references to possibly historical personages being made very occasionally by way of illustration. Thus mention is made of Dīrgha Cārāyana[115] who may be the same as Dīgha Kārāyana, the minister of Prasenajit of Kosala who obtained revenge on the latter for the execution of his uncle, Malla Bandhula, by handing over the royal insignia to the heir, Viḍūḍabha, in the royal absence.[116] Although Kauṭilya does not say so, the correspondence between the methods outlined in the Eleventh Book for the treatment of republics and the technique adopted by Vassakāra in coping with the Vṛjjis is so close that one suspects the historical event to have provided a kind of archetypal example.

It is precisely because of its political and acquisitive orientation that the Arthaśāstra could undertake problems necessarily beyond the scope of the Dharmasūtras. To begin with, we have seen that although the Dharmasūtras cover both the temporal and spiritual realms, in the sense that no distinction is drawn between them, they are devoted to the status quo, and are thus incapable of constructively coping—as against merely reflecting—with a phenomenon which is essentially characterized by change. More fundamentally, the Dharmasūtras are primarily concerned with soteriological issues which afford very little or no room to politics as an independent realm. Where the Dharmasūtras see the king in an essentially policing function, the Arthaśāstra literature see him in a largely political one. Nevertheless, in a very important sense, both share a common framework, or perhaps it would be more accurate to say that the Arthaśāstra seeks to set itself within the overall perspective of the Dharmasūtras. It is our contention that the anomalies in Kauṭilya's work spring from the tensions engendered by this endeavour.

Kauṭilya's general philosophical approach to the state is very similar to that of the Dharmasūtras. He accepts the fourfold division of society,[117] and holds it as the king's particular duty to uphold and enforce the *varṇāśramadharma*.[118] The king is cautioned not to transgress the boundaries of his authority, for "Varuṇa is the chastiser of kings who behave wrongly towards men."[119] The ruler is the chief barricade against chaos, which act of protection is carried out with the aid of the Rod—the joint symbol of punishment and defence.[120] But it is to be used with circumspection and respect, for, "used unjustly, whether in passion or anger, or in contempt, it enrages even forest anchorites and wandering ascetics, how much more then the householders."[121] The role of caste is considerably less emphasized than in the Dharmasūtras, but the penalties laid down for criminal acts do nevertheless clearly reflect caste status and privilege. Against all this has to be set the encroachments, both specific and implied, which Kauṭilya made upon the traditional order. To deal with the latter first, it is clear that the sweeping rationalizations of administrative, economic and judicial procedures, that is to say, their bureaucratization, brought under the direct control of the state activities which had hitherto been undertaken by custom and community organizations. We have seen that castes, guilds and other intermediaries continued to exist, but the growth of a surrounding bureaucracy would necessarily alter both their nature and their relationships. Regardless of motive, therefore, the introduction of a bureaucracy cannot help but infringe upon the traditional order, or, rather, a central bureaucracy is envisaged at that point when the resources of the established mechanisms of social control have been outstripped by socio-political change. In itself, bureaucray tends to separate the idea of the state from its complete identification with the king by simply divorcing the administrative continuity of the kingdom from its ritual, ceremonial and dynastic continuity—which still inheres in the king and his line. Kauṭilya, however, was concerned with a centralized, monarchical bureaucracy, and could therfore afford to overlook, or even to be ignorant of, this disjunction. The bureaucratic apparatus in Kauṭilya's work redounds directly to the monarch's benefit, and it is fitting in this context to mention that Kauṭilya was at pains to ensure the payment of officials in cash[123] so that they were bound materially to the king. The increasing power of the monarch is buttressed by explicit provisions, the most important of which are the absolute validity accorded to the king's edict[124] and the acknowledgement of local laws and customs so long as they are not contrary to the interests of the treasury and the army.[125] The departure from the Dharmasūtras is significant, for Gautama qualifies this right by subjecting it only to a general compatibility with the sacred laws.[126]

What Kauṭilya confronts us with, therefore, is a conservative traditional framework imbued with a revolutionary content, and what remains to be determined is whether the old forms can withstand the injection of a new concept. Does, in fact, Kauṭilya succeed in emancipating himself from the old views on political power, or does he, in the final analysis, remain in thrall to them? The conservative elements in Kauṭilya's thought deserve to be taken seriously, and cannot be disregarded as being nothing more than mere sops to convention, traditional platitudes duly uttered prior to getting down to the basic business of strengthening the state. Nor will it do, contrarily, to ignore the desire towards political power as a paramount goal which permeates Kauṭilya's work, and see him in a primarily traditional light, a true representative of the Brahmanical theory of kingship. The main problem is to determine the extent to which the structure of the Dharmasūtras is compatible with a scheme which aims at absolute political imperium, that is, the absoluteness of the state as a political entity. To do this, we will have to revert briefly to the concept of power and its relation to the varṇa hierarchy. Dumont defines it accurately in dual terms,[127] those of territory and hierarchy. It is "the monopoly of legitimate force within a given territory."[128] It is, also, simultaneously, "force made legitimate by being subordinated hierarchically to the Brāhma and the Brahmans."[129] Moreover, this does not exist merely as a generalized abstraction—"actual caste systems, in contrast to the theoretical model, were organized within a fixed territorial area, were so to speak contained within a spatial framework.[130] Thus, symbolically and theoretically, power is legitimized by subordination to the Brahman, but as we have seen above, the hierarchy this implies is, in practical terms, a localized one, and the subordination which takes place must also be in a spatial context. Now Kauṭilya recognizes both the facts that actual caste systems are territorially conditioned and that legitimacy requires a subordination at the local level—something already recognized by Dharmasūtras. Thus he not only advocates, in terms of the pacification of conquered territory, that the customary rights and exemptions be granted to the local castes and their usages honoured.[131] but also that, "after conquering the world, he should enjoy it, divided into varṇas and āśramas, in accordance with his own duty."[132] This constitutes the subordinating act which establishes the legitimacy of conquest. In other words, the legitimacy of conquest hinges upon the acknowledgment of the structure of the conquered, or, in the cases where the scheme of varṇas is introduced, upon the ceding of precedence unto that institution. This is clearly antipathetic to the concept of conquest as an assimilation into a new frame-work and the imposition of new values. The conquering king remains dependent on sacrally ordained society. Nor does the fact that Kauṭilya allows the king to dispose of rights and customs which militate against the interests of the army and the treasury[133] substantially alter the basic reality that no scheme can simultaneously assert the priority of both the political and the socio-spiritual principle, of the king as well as the *varṇāśramadharma.* It is Kauṭilya's refusal to take congizance of this axial contradiction which vitiates the consistency of his work.

The same incongruity manifests itself from a different perspective. Dumont, in his chapter on the Jajmāni system,[134] reveals that the castes are inter-dependent and that the caste system does constitute a hierarchy—which is defined as "the principle by which the elements of a whole are ranked in relation to the whole.[135] He goes on to say that in the majority of societies the view of the whole is provided by religion, and that the ranking will therefore be religious in nature. This is largely the case with the Dharmasūtras where the holistic element is provided by the soteriological goal, but the valorization of the various ranks does not altogether follow the principle enunciated by Dumont above. The system of values exemplified by the various duties of the four varṇas is both relative and absolute. Externally, in terms of their contributions to the whole, they are relative, but internally, within each varṇa, they are absolute, and Kauṭilya overtly recognized this—as of course do the Dharmasūtras—when he says: "(The observance of) one's own special duty leads to heaven and to endless bliss. In case of its transgression, people would be exterminated through (the) mixture of (duties and castes)."[136] In a system where primacy is accorded to a concrete goal, say to the maximization of political power, a value system would not possess this duality, there would be no internal aspect, and ranking would be made purely externally, exclusively in terms of what is contributed to the whole. It is this fact which explains why Kauṭilya—as described at some length earlier—advocates such extreme measures to subdue a foe but then renounces the most substantial fruits of victory. It is because his acts are fundamentally varṇa-determined; the obligation of the king is to fight, he must undertake everything necessary to do so and spare no ploy or strategem, but this imperative to warfare and political might does not constitute an acceptance of the political principle as autonomous and fundamental—it remains subordinated in its secondary position in the overall hierarchy of which it forms a part. The strange paradox that the king is permitted, or rather encouraged, to engage in duplicity, intrigue, betrayal and cynicism in the interests of political aggrandizement while at the same time the putative goals of such endeavors are not granted the highest position in the hierarchy stems from this duality in the nature of the *varṇāśramadharma*. One fulfils the demands of the hierarchy best by regarding the values of one's class as absolute, whatever be its position in the general scheme. Thus endeavour and not achievement is the most important thing—and in fact the total attainment of any varṇa-duty would violate the necessary pluralism of values which the *varṇāśramādharma* expresses. In this sense, therefore, Kauṭilya is true to the injunction in the *Bhagavad-Gītā* which requires the performance of one's duty without thought to the reward.

In summation, what is being proposed is that Kauṭilya, while being urged in the direction of the establishment of political power as an independent realm, was yet unable to free himself from the traditional conceptions of the Regnum which ran contrary to it.

Two things can be said in conclusion. Firstly, because of this ambivalence, and also for reasons that, as we shall see, are implicit in the nature of the *varṇāśramadharma*, the Dharmaśāstra tradition was able to treat of Kauṭilya's work, or rather of Arthaśāstra literature, as essentially an elucidation of the king's role and not as a new conceptual scheme, and was able therefore to accept it. Thus, if Kauṭilya is restrained by Dharmasūtra precepts, Manu will show us the expansion of the same tradition to include Arthaśāstra concepts. Secondly, whatever be the case at the ideational level, we shall see the significance of the bureaucratic principle—the central core of Kauṭilya's work—in the context of Aśoka and his attempts to regulate and unite society.

CHAPTER III

Heterodoxy and the Primacy of the Regnum

CHAPTER III

Section 1. The Kṣatra in Early Indian Buddhism

A review of the Buddhist theory of kingship may be useful as an introduction to Aśokan innovations as it provides an earlier tradition—and one by which Aśoka was much influenced in his personal beliefs—of an individualized approach to the question of temporal authority and could thus enable us to demarcate specific Aśokan contributions more finely.

Buddhist legends in the *Dīgha Nikāya* and the *Mahāvastu*—the former dated by Winternitz as belonging to the 3rd century B.C. and the older strata of the latter to the 2nd century B.C.[1] —link the growth of political power to cosmic re-evolution and the increasing moral decay of man. There comes a time when this world passes away and beings are reborn in the World of Radiance, and, after another lengthy chronological spell, this world begins to re-evolve, in which process those who had deceased from the World of Radiance gradually come to life as humans.[2] At this stage beings were just 'beings' without distinction of sex who dwelt in a universe undifferentiated into sun and moon, stars and constellations.[3] The earth was like a vast lake of honey, and it was through tasting and eating this ambrosial matter that greed first became manifest. Then, however, 'beings' became corporeal and varied in degrees of beauty, while the cosmos was differentiated. In course of time, the lake of honey gave way to a sweet excrescence on the surface of the earth, this to an edible creeping plant, and the latter to a fragrant huskless rice that grew in a day. Each of these changes is seen as being causally related to increasing avarice, as is the emergence of distinctive sexual characteristics. This engendered lust and immorality, while sloth led to the hoarding of the marvellous grain—whereupon it lost its magic properties, developed husk and no longer grew in a day. It was then suggested[4] that the rice fields be divided and apportioned amongst them, and with this establishment of private property, theft was not slow to arrive. And, "it is when theft and falsehood make their appearance in the world that wrong and injustice are known."[5] In this situation, and urged by dire necessity, the people gathered together and chose one of their number, distinguished by character, authority and virtue, to be the Mahāsammata—the Great Chosen One. In recompense for reproving those who needed reproof and approving those who deserved approval,[6] he was to get one-sixth of the crop. The king thus attains to his dignity through a universal acclamation of his superior virtue and not through any divine right, and at this level the institution of kingship is a human compact. It is also to be noted, however, that society gains its cohesion through the king; in contradistinction to the Brahmanical scheme, society itself appears to have no centripetal, unifying force, and it is this which necessitates the existence of the Mahāsammata.

To continue, the legend—in the *Dīgha Nikāya* though not in the *Mahāvastu*—then goes on to trace the evolution of the caste system, and gives an essentially functional interpretation of it.[7] The Kṣatriyas were the first to emerge with their function of protection, the Brahmins next with their devotion to meditation, and then the Vaiśyas who established the various trades. Those who were left took to hunting, and these then constituted the Śūdras. It is emphasized that these are men like any other, they are not established in their positions through divine ordinance—and in this the Buddha is specifically arguing against the Brahmanical notion that the Brahmins are the particular chosen ones through being born from the mouth of Brāhma.[8] The analysis so far is therefore consistently utilitarian and republican—a position further buttressed by the assertion that the iron law of *karma,* by which we reap in the next birth the fruits of the actions performed in this one, operates irrespective of birth and caste.[9] But side by side with this belief in voluntarism and the view of the king as a jointly elected figure can be discerned a more determinist vein, It has been mentioned above that the legends concerning the origin of kingship—both in the *Dīgha Nikāya* and the *Mahāvastu*—link it with the re-evolution of the cosmos. While it is held that natural changes are induced by moral decay, we are also told that the process of universal dissolution and re-evolution are part of the necessary order of things. If this is so, then moral degeneracy has to be seen as an integral part of the evolutionary process, and the institution of kingship which seeks to stem this advancing tide cannot be seen purely as a human artifact depending on mutual consent, but as something interwoven with the unfolding dialectic of re-evolution. In this sense, even if the Buddhist myth of kingship is a parody of an original Brahmanical one—now lost—which attempted to establish the king as a divinely ordained personage, it would not seem to succeed in making it a purely human institution. What is more important, however, are the functions ascribed to the king. As we shall see in Manu, the deification of the monarch is very closely linked with his function of staving off chaos. Now, as we have seen the Buddhists do not deify the king, but their kind of cosmic determinism, operating through the moral fallibility of man and resulting in the necessity of a king, makes their position functionally not very different from that of Manu. In both cases, the king is vital in holding chaos at bay. There is, however, a very significant difference. The Dharmasūtras, and Manu largely carries on the same tradition, see the king not only as a guardian in a general sense, but specially as the protector of a very distinctive kind of order, that of the *varṇaśramadharma*, and it is the disturbance of this that truly constitutes chaos, while the king's special glory arises from the fact that he prevents this confusion of castes. The Buddhist myths, on the other hand, while dealing with caste, do not make it the foundation of the institution of kingship. In the Brahmanical scheme, therefore, the king is necessary for the maintenance of a pre-existent society, while for the Buddhists he is the necessary agent through whom a viable social life can come into being. Now, if the Buddhists regard man as tending inescapably towards chaos—and it is clear from the concensus regarding the necessity of the Mahāsammata that personal virtue alone was incapable of preventing the fatal drift—and consequently see the king as functionally irreplaceable, it would seem that, far from stemming temporal power, such a perspective would lead to absolutism. Such a trend would be mitigated if it could be shown that the Buddhists accepted the structure of castes, thus acknowledging a self-regulatory social mechanism which could act as a counter-balance to the monarchy and the state. We have already seen that the Buddhists do, in fact, provide a somewhat fanciful etymology for caste, but their version of it bears little resemblance to the Brahmanical model. To begin with, it is not juxtaposed against the king and is not seen as a complete and autonomous entity in its own right. Instead, it seems to merely portray what may be called the four basic conditions of man after the fall from grace. They constitute less a hierarchical and interlinked organism than a statement on the origin of four archetypal modes of human activity. That being so, it seems to lack any autonomous dynamic of its own, and this is reflected in the fact that the attainment of salvation is completely divorced from caste considerations. This is not only to say that complete egalitarianism prevails so far as seeking emancipation is concerned,[10] but also that the rigorous performance of caste duties, for the Buddhist, has no soteriological import. Thus the Buddhists reduce caste to essentially nothing more than a sequence of social divisions, and it is within this secularized hierarchy that the Buddha, in outlining his view of the caste structure to the Brāhmin Vāseṭṭha in the Aggañña Suttanta of the *Dīgha Nikāya*, gives the Kṣatriya pre-eminence over the Brahmin so far as those who "put their trust in lineage" are concerned.[11] The same verse goes on to say that the best of all are those clothed in wisdom and virtue.[12] The point being made is that although the Buddhists did talk in terms of caste and place some importance on giving the Kṣatriyas pride of place therein, their concept of it, pragmatic and utilitarian as it was, devalorized it in religious terms, stripped it of its internal interconnections, and reduced it to little more than social classes.

This being so, it is difficult to see how a weakly existent system of castes such as the Buddhists acknowledge can constitute a check to the growth of executive power. Implicit therefore, in the very secularization and rationalization of the Buddhist attitude, is the potential for increased political might. Society exists as a loose agglomeration of people, the Mahāsammata is chosen to give them stability and order and, as in this pursuit royal power increases in proportion to social need, it is difficult to put a limit on the former. This paradox, which lies at the heart of all utilitarian political thinking, is particularly ironic in the case of the Buddhists where the desire for a compassionate society and a benign ruler are transparently present. This is particularly clear in their conception of a decent administration—symbolized by the presence in the sky of a "wheel gem" during a virtuous reign.[13] This celestial phenomenon was induced if the king conducted himself in an "Aryan" manner by being just, protecting the people, granting financial aid to the indigent and constantly seeking out advice from the *śramaṇas* and Brahmins who were tolerant and mild. Another text in the *Dīgha Nikāya*,[14] reflects their thinking on the importance of economic life. Agricultural grants and advances of capital are recommended as a means of activating agrarian and commercial activities—and these would occupy those who would otherwise turn into brigands and harass the state.

Basically, however, it is difficult to see how socio-political concerns are essential to Buddhism at a strictly doctrinal level. Its emphasis on emancipation, on release from the ephemerality of the given world, makes it difficult to render concerns of political power or social reform substantive. Its views on government and administration are sane, compassionate and rational, but this does not render them integral to its fundamental dogma of salvation. The strength of the Brahmanical position lies in the fact that society itself is made a vehicle for liberation. Emancipation is possible through the strict observance of the obligations of the four-fold order. Thus it succeeds in being most soteriological when it is being most secular; salvation is attendant upon assiduity in fulfilling social duties. Whatever penchant Buddhist thought may have for administrative and social issues, it cannot similarly link them to its primary aim of emancipation. There is no organic link between soteriology and society in the way in which the Brahmanical order achieves it. This, however, has its advantages. Through this dichotomy, Buddhism escapes from being tied to a specific social system as the Śāstras are. This dictinction between the spiritual and temporal spheres enables the existence of a moral autonomy capable of freely criticizing temporal events, and may go some way towards explaining why, while the integral nature of the Dharma drove the Brahmin into intimate contact with politics, the Buddhist was in a position to remain quite detached from the concerns of the Arthaśāstra, at least in the sense of contributing to them.

In relation to the next section, what Aśoka shares with the Buddhists will be seen to be firstly, the view of society as a group of individuals and not as something sacred and immutable, and secondly, and inseparable from the first, the idea that the king is responsible for the integrity and stability of society which, indeed, would be bereft of these qualities in his absence. We shall also see that, with the most altruistic of motives, he is drawn into the inescapable consequence of such attitudes—the magnification and extension of royal power. Where he differs from them is in sharing their perspective and yet simultaneously living in society, an attitude whose social and political fruits we shall review below.

CHAPTER III

Section 2. Aśoka and the Universalization of Values

The previous chapter considered the problem of power as it presented itself to the theoretician working essentially within the tradition of the Dharmasūtras, the attempt to allot a formal place within that ideological tradition to the Realpolitik ethic which was so amply manifest in the historical scene from at least the times of Bimbisāra and Ajātaśatru in the 6th century B.C. We have tried to argue that the *Kauṭiliyan Arthaśāstra* fails, in the ultimate analysis, in the attempt at establishing the autonomy of the political power and extricating it from its subordinate position in the Darmasūtra framework—a failure which stems from the incompatibility between the *varṇāśramadharma* concept and the notion of temporal authority as absolute and independent.

The importance of Aśoka in these considerations is that he contributes to these issues as a practising monarch—and not solely as a writer of treatises—and also that his policies constitute by implication a considerable increase in the realm of monarchical concerns. As we shall see, the very fact that he confronts the problem of power and the role of king as an administrator and ruler is of primary significance. Implicit in his edicts is the question of not only how the king acts, but why he does as he does. This pondering over the functions and duties of the throne means that they are no longer organically taken for granted, but have become matters for deliberation and conscious decision.

This is not to argue that the concept of individualism which this implies was singularly Aśokan, or that it became socially significant only in his time. It is not our purpose here to study the history of individualism in Indian thought or to delineate its various forms, but to touch upon it only in so far as it is germane to the development of political doctrines. The idea of personal responsibility for one's destiny is implicit in the notion of *karma,* that is, in the linking of metempsychosis with individual behaviour—and this doctrine finds expression as early as in the times of the *Śathapatha Brāhmaṇa.*[15] Heesterman,[16] in his analysis of the evolution of Brahmanical ritual, traces another dimension of individualism, and a brief excursus discussing this may be useful in displaying a model of individuation in contrast to which Aśoka's may be more clearly defined.

Heesterman sees the steps leading to the interiorization of the sacrifice—and subsequent individualization—as a three-phase progression the first of which is a situation of complementarity in which the patron (*yajamāna*) and the officiant periodically renew life by rendering each other reciprocal service in the form of alternatively accepting the impurity of the other—the impurity of death.[17] Thus the officiant, in accepting the sacrifice of the patron, purifies him by accepting his impurity, but sullies his own purity in the process, and, in order that his inferiority not be made permanent, the position is then reversed. A paradigm for this kind of relationship is the instance when Prajāpati wishes to undertake a *dīkṣā*—a purificatory ceremony—and invites the seasons and the months to officiate. Having done so, the latter begin to feel "heavy", and they, in turn, undertake the *dīkṣā* and have Prajāpati officiate for them. Thus mutually dependent, "they become firmly established in each other."[18]

This cyclical dependence for the periodic renewal of life has obvious elements of conflict and strife. The *Pañcaviṃśa-brāhmaṇa*[19] says that "he who, having accepted many gifts, feels as if he had swallowed poison should perform the punaḥstoma", i.e., offer a feast in his turn, and this indicates the risks attendant upon being an officiant. The urge to escape this dependency, to avoid being the officiant, finds mythical expression in the story of the Ādityas and the Aṅgirasas[20] in which the two compete for possession of the heavenly world. It was agreed that the party which officiated at the ritual of the other would be left behind on earth while the other would win heaven. The Aṅgirasas then invited the Ādityas to their ceremony, but the latter avoided the trap by preparing a ceremony which would be performed in one day (the *sādyaskra*) and could therefore take place before that of the Aṅgirasas—thus winning the contest.

Heesterman sees the next step emerging as the result of the quest for a means to deal with the issue of recurrent death—the impurity—outside the ambit of this complementarity tense with competition and dependence. The fruition of this search is described in the *Jaiminīya-brāhmaṇa*.[21] Prajāpati and Death compete with each other through rival sacrifices. Prajāpati finally supervenes through his discovery of symbolical and numerical equivalences which could neutralize the value of Death's weapons. This means that the forces of the opposing moiety, referred to by Heesterman as the Rival, no longer have any particular power of their own, and the structure of complementarity loses its validity. Thus the *Jaiminīya-brāhmaṇa* adds at the end of the tale, "now there is no ritual competition; . . . the sacrifice is only one; Prajāpati alone is the sacrifice." Heesterman goes on to make the very telling point that Prajāpati now becomes the prototype of the single Patron who performs alone and for his sole benefit. He contrasts this with the earlier situation in which the ritual was performed by rival groups[22]—and, of course, what is pertinent here is not only the rivalry but the conjoint participation, the participation in groups on both sides, as opposed to the later individualized performance.

This is, however, not the final stage of individuation, for it still required the services of the officiant—even if the latter was needed now fundamentally as an expert in matters of liturgy, a ritualist technician, a knower of the equivalences. The culmination of the process lies in the internationalization of the ritual when the sacrificer "offers only in the self."[23] All the obstacles of duality have been overcome, and "He sees himself (or: the self) in all creatures and all creatures in himself (or; in the self)."[24] The individual thus emerges through the awareness of monistic unity, all the oppositions constituted by phenomena are reconciled within the universal life. Given a perspective in which all things are but the manifestations of the One, the only kind of socialized behaviour possible for such an individual will be one based on objective obligations—such as that of the *varṇāśramadharma* order. All actions are essentially the same, moral distinctions are fundamentally invalid, only duty remains, the fulfillment of caste obligations. And duty becomes an imperative because living in society involves some sort of commitment or pattern of action, and where moral differences are not obvious and valid enough to constitute a motive for endeavour, the divinely ordered and obligatorily absolute varṇa duty becomes paramount. In other words, the amorphousness resultant upon the unreality of moral distinctions is redeemed, in terms of the impulses to action, by the stringent nature of the *varṇaśramadharma* requirements—and this is superbly illustrated in the theme of the *Bhagavad-Gītā*. The situation for Aśoka, as we hope to demonstrate, is quite different. He shows no evidence of participating in the oneness of all things, and his remorse over the slaughter in Kaliṅga is in striking contrast to the passage in the *Bhagavad-Gītā* which argues that there is neither slayer nor slain.[25] Further, without the conviction of noumenal identity, moral values become important in their own right, and do not flounder in the vacuum of ontological invalidity which would surround them if they were regarded as the mere epiphenomena of the one underlying entity of the monistic scheme.

Aśoka, however, and it is in this that his contribution lies, does not share in the sense of monistic unity, does not accept the dictates of a sacred society nor yet succumb to the values of the market-place, those of power and property—which normally rise in proportion to the collapse of social values. It could be argued from the statecraft and political attitudes of Bimbisāra and Ajātaśatru that they too had broken away from the social moorings of the traditional state, and in that sense shared the ethos of Aśoka. But even if this were so—and it is to be remembered that the traditional Brahmanical attitude towards territorial acquisition was by no means a negative one—their psychological uprootedness took refuge in the primary and elemental drive towards possession and conquest, while Aśoka strove to create a framework of values which he tried to imbue with an intrinsic worth and thus establish a system of relationships which were not dependent on force alone. It is necessary to emphasize, however, that when we talk of Aśokan individualism we do not mean that he regarded himself as the creator of the values that he espoused. The ethic in itself was no doubt regarded as a transcendent one, but, as we hope to show, its nature is such that its application to the terrestrial realm, its social and political form, has to be determined by the monarch himself. In other words, the question confronting him is: what kind of organization, what form of social structure, will embody the ethical code to which he subscribes most fully? And this, of course, is a question which a king within the confines of the *varṇāśramadharma* would find redundant, for there the social form is given.

To pursue the contrast with the perspective of the Dharmasūtras, this search for an adequate socio-political form implies that the monarchical function cannot be one of mere protection. And further, the problem of attempting to reify his ethical code brings the entire question of determining the direction of the thrust of temporal authority into fresh review. At the level of implementation—the determination of categorical social ends—avenues of choice are therefore seen to exist. And it is precisely this awareness of alternatives that is absent in the sacred Brahmanical Sacerdotium-Regnum syzygy that was described in the first chapter. This particular syzygy is a modality of the fundamental system of the union of opposites on which all creation depends, another link in that chain of copulatory pairs which extends from the Sky-Earth archetype to the husband and wife The sacred social scheme, the *varṇāśramadharma*, is the material embodiment of the spiritual principle, and the Regnum fulfills its *raison d'etre* by subordinating itself to it and pledging itself to its defense and protection. In doing so, it conforms to the fundamental cosmological principle which sustains all and simultaneously fulfills its own duty. The Regnum therefore, in the *varṇāśramadharma* scheme, has no independence, no freedom, and no choice. This is, however, not to claim that the Regnum was empirically compelled to subordinate itself to the Sacerdotium. Disobedience was always possible, and in that sense it was never denied an option. What is being stressed here is that the subserviance to the Sacerdotium was the only way in which the otherwise brute and unhallowed nature of temporal power could be spiritually valorized, its validity could only be established through supporting—or furthering—the concretely detailed structure of the *varṇāśrama-dharma*. Doubtless, in periods of social flux, the ideal Brahmanical king was also faced with the problem of implementation, but he was never in any doubt as to the precise social forms which constituted his given end. The difference between him and Aśoka lies in the fact that the minutely detailed order of castes and stages of life constitutes an objective correlative to his ethical imperative, whereas Aśoka lacks any such defining concordance. And it is because of this that Aśoka bears the burden of greater freedom.

At the same time, being outside the system of castes also implies that acts which found a ready justification within that system would now have to be viewed differently, and this point can best be illustrated in terms of the approach to force. Thus Aśoka, after the conquest of Kaliṅga, expresses his remorse at the suffering that the war has caused and says that "even if the number of those killed, who died, and who fell captive during the conquest of Kaliṅga were a hundred or a thousand times less it would still weigh very heavily on the mind of Devānampriya,"[26] and he goes on to say that he desires security, control of the senses, equanimity and kindness for all men.[27] As against this, the Dharmasūtra attitude toward war, although not explicitly stated, is an extension of the duty of the king to protect all beings,[28] and as such is part of his *Kṣatriya* function in the performance of which "those learned in the sacred laws declare that to be free from fear and pity is, indeed, a life-long sacrificial session (sattra, to be performed by the king)."[29] Even the *Kauṭilīyan Arthaśāstra*, in some respects such a secular work, considers force, not entirely pragmatically, but as a metaphysical and integrative agent which draws the various ends of life together.

"The means of ensuring the pursuit of philosophy, the Vedas

> and economics is the Rod (wielded by the king), its administration constitutes the science of politics, having for its purpose the acquisition of (things) not possessed, the preservation of (things) possessed, the augmentation of (things) preserved and the bestowal of (things) augmented on a worthy recipient."[30]

As can be seen, the quotation breaks down into two separate statements. The second half deals with the fundamentally material aspects of the Rod—its power to acquire, protect and bestow. The first portion is more significant in our context as it establishes the Rod as the main dynamic behind both spiritual and mundane activities. It supports philosophy and the three Vedas because the "people of the four varṇas and in the four stages of life, protected by the king with the Rod, (and) deeply attached to occupations prescribed as their special duties, keep to their respective paths."[31] What is being stressed here is obviously not the glorification of force *per se*, since Kauṭilya himself emphasizes the dangers to the king consequent upon the unjust use of the Rod,[32] but the fact that the Rod attains a cosmological significance and becomes the power which ultimately underwrites the sacred social order--any forceful violation of which is both unjust and doomed—a point on which Manu, too, is emphatic. Taking this a step further, it means that the utilizer of force, so long as he does not use it for personal ends which are, of course, *ipso facto* unjust, is only an impersonal agent of a cosmic imperative—and the recourse to violence, undertaken in the interests of the sacred order, is legitimized by supernal sanction. In the Dharmasūtras, therefore, and also, as we have tried to argue, in the *Kauṭilīyan Arthaśāstra*, the king fights and defends independent of his own personal will; his duty lies in the nature of things, not to be discussed or repented but simply to be performed. That is why the Dharmasūtras hold that pity and fear are not part of the royal lot. Aśoka, on the other hand, provides no evidence that he felt any superior and overweening justification for the use of force; his acts do not derive any strengthening support from higher sanction. This is not to say that Aśoka therefore eschewed the use of force. As the 13th

Rock Edict testifies,[33] he was prepared to forgive a wrong only to the extent that it could be forgiven, and he cautions the forest tribes to repent lest they be killed,[34] but the resort to force was now a rational decision, it had become secularized. Its use now hinged upon political expediency, necessity or feelings of compassion, but in every case the salient feature is that Aśoka bears the entire responsibility on his own shoulders; he is no longer the instrument of tradition or of sacred dogma. Although he too acknowledges a higher order, it is for him to determine the compatibility of force and the extent of its application with that order. In fact, he reveals a certain reluctance to use force and a strong desire to limit its use, but what we are trying to stress here is the change in the complexion of actions when they are viewed from a non-*varṇāśramadharma* perspective. The painful conquest of Kaliṅga need have provoked no heart-searching at all in the mind of a ruler who felt with Manu that he ought to "make all creatures subject to himself even by the employment of force."[35]

Before proceeding to deal more fully with the Aśokan ethic, the concept of *Dhamma*, it may be useful to mention that although the term *Dhamma* is the Prakrit equivalent of the Sanskrit *Dharma*, it refers to a very different body of ideas. *Dhamma* is a generalized code of humane morality which is quite distinct from the hierarchic and integrated structure of castes, stages of life and the duties appertaining thereto which the term *Dharma* involves in the Dharmasūtras. As stressed earlier the individualism of Aśoka does not imply that he regarded the Dhamma as his own creation, but only as something which he serves. He says in the 7th Pillar Edict, for instance, that the kings of time past have sought means for making the people progress in Dhamma.[36] In this respect, like the orthodox king of the Dharmasūtras, he acknowledges a transcendental imperative. The difference—and it is a critical one—lies in the fact that the Dhammic code, unlike the Dharmic one, is not socially specific. There is no concept of a sacred society when the king must guard, nor, in categorical terms, is there any description of the ideal society such as is set forth in the Dharmasūtras. It is up to the king to induce a society in which Dhammic values will flourish, its exact configuration is his responsibility, and this obviously affords him a far freer hand in the domain of socio-political concerns—with all the burden for the evaluation of ends and means that this entails. For a king within the *varṇāśramadharma*, the social goals are very precisely pre-determined, for one like Aśoka they are not, and it is in this context that his individualism—that is, the increased burden of his personal responsibility—is to be seen.

Having argued that Aśoka is no longer within the bounds of an organic and integrated order wherein his role is predicated in defined terms, the issue is now what use Aśoka made of his freedom in terms of defining afresh the nature of the monarchical function—a question which is not answered in direct terms but is implied in his attempts at utilizing *Dhamma* as a new principle which would serve to unify society. To some extent, the relative immobility of the Dharmasūtras, their noted inability to cope with socio-economic flux, would inevitably have led to the growth of monarchical power to deal with current exigencies, and it is precisely the problem of accommodating increasing temporal authority within the *varṇāśrama-dharma* scheme that we shall see Manu dealing with in the next chapter. Had, therefore, Aśoka been primarily concerned with reintroducing stability into the Brahmanical scheme shaken by the vast growth of the empire, he could have attempted a synthesis between Arthaśāstra doctrines and a reaffirmation of the *varṇāśramadharma* structure. He is, however not concerned with adapting the Dharmic scheme to changed conditions, but seeks instead to provide a different foundation for society and the state. This does not in the least imply that Aśoka deliberately attacked the old Brahmanical forms. The more significant arguments in favour of a covert persecution of Brahmins by Aśoka advanced by Haraprasad Sastri[37] on the grounds of the ban on sacrificial animals, the Śūdra origin of the Mauryas, and the Dhamma-mahāmattas destroying the prestige of the Brahmin class have been effectively countered by Raychaudhuri.[38] He has pointed out that the ban on animal slaughter was not absolute, that the Purānic statement referring to all the kings following Mahāpadmananda as being Śūdras applies only to the Nandas, and that, finally, part of the functions of the mahāmattas lay in safeguarding the welfare of the Brahmins themselves.

On the other hand, while it is true that Aśoka never attacks or condemns the Brahmanical structure, it is equally true that he does not look to it either for salvation or as a satisfactory form of social organization. The gist of his Dhammic message, generously repeated, is to be found in the following statement taken from the 3rd Rock Edict at Girnar:[39] "Obedience to mother and father is meritorious, meritorious is liberality towards friends, acquaintances and parents, to Brahmaṇas and Śramaṇas. It is meritorious to refrain from killing animals. Frugality in expenditure and the possession of goods is meritorious." To this may be added suitable courtesy to slaves and servants.[40] There is no evidence of any kind of doctrinal partiality here, and what Aśoka is clearly trying to do is to formulate certain basic ground rules which will alleviate social tensions and provide a *modus-vivendi* for the various groups involved. This is particularly stressed in his 12th Rock Edict: "Devānampriya attaches more importance to the promotion of the essentials of all sects than to liberality or honours."[41] And this goal is to be attained by "restraining one's speech, so that one abstains from praising one's own sect or denigrating those of others; and if one is to do this on occasion, it should be done with moderation,"[42] and, "In doing this, he promotes his own sect while serving those of others."[43] Basham[44] has indicated in his work on the Ājīvikas that there was considerable rivalry and tension between the Buddhists, Jains and the Ājīvikas in the social realm, a tension which sprang not only from dogmatic differences, but from conversionary zeal. Thus, a group of Buddhist monks are sadly dismayed at being mistaken for Ājīvika ascetics,[45] while the Ājīvikas besiege the home of the wealthy banker Migāra when he agrees to entertain the Buddhist Sangha and thus opens the prospect to the Ājīvikas' losing "so wealthy and influential a convert."[46] The pressures engendered by such sectarian rivalries are also no doubt partially responsible for Aśoka's dislike of festivities (although he may also have objected to the drunkenness, licentiousness and animal sacrifices which could possibly have accompanied them): "Devānampriya Priyadarśin sees great evil in festival meetings"[47]—occasions on which factional strife could so easily erupt. Presumably, his animus was aimed more against specifically sectarian festivals and not against festivals as such, for he concedes that "there are also some festival meetings which are considered meritorious by Devānampriya Priyadarśin,"[48] and we get an idea as to what these may be when he says later, "the sound of drums has become the proclamation of the Dhamma, showing the people representations of celestial chariots (palaces ?) and elephants, masses of fire and other marvellous spectacles."[49] Such exhibitions, both harmless and edificatory, combining entertainment with instruction, was an effective way of expressing his message. Viewed socially therefore the content of Aśoka's Dhamma is an appeal for reconciliation and harmonious coexistence. He is not as concerned with establishing the predominance of any one given scheme, social or theological, as with finding a foundation common to all, and his Dhamma is a distillation of those essential tenets which he feels constitute the substratum of all faiths. Everyone is free to cleave unto his own beliefs so long as these do not infringe upon the rights of others to do the same.

The expression of a generalized universalistic ethic in the form of Dhamma implies, not so much an acknowledgment of historical and social changes, as a new way of looking at society. It is true that the situation of Magadha, outside the true pale of Brahmin orthodoxy defined by the conservative and nostalgic Manu as the area between the rivers Sarasvatī and Dṛśadvati,[50] made it easier for such a perspective to manifest itself, but it could not be taken for granted. The appearance of dissident sects, for instance, was hardly a new phenomena in Aśoka's day, but those who worked within the Brahmanical framework did not regard this as a mark of social divisiveness. The king, for reasons of state, would acknowledge the local usages of communities—even if opposed to Brahmanical precepts—and, while hoping that they would Brahmanize their customs by a process of adaptation and osmosis, did not regard them as a threat to the very stability of the social order which he existed to support. On the contrary, he saw any attempt at their suppression as tending to lead to a discontent which could result in a turbulent and dangerous disordering of the realm.[51] Thus, Aśoka's view of society as a fragmented assemblage of discrete and disparate faiths, beliefs and conditions was possible precisely because he was outside the organic and interrelated structure of the Dharmasūtras—within which such a perspective could never have arisen. At the same time the feature of the *varṇāśramadharma* which intertwined society and dogma so that they were indistinguishable made it impossible for Aśoka to use it, even mechanically, as an instrument with which to unify society, for it would mean leaving heretical sects outside it. These, like the local customs which were in disaccord with Brahmanical modes, would, so to say, be politically acknowledged but socially unintegrated. But the abandonment of the Brahmanical order also meant the abandonment of the belief in the integrative capacity and cohesiveness of society which was that order's greatest functional asset. The idea of Dhamma provided, perhaps, a framework of values which was more extensive—and hence inclusive—than that of caste, and thereby a broader common denominator for the meeting of divergent faiths, but it could not draw upon what we have elsewhere termed the sacro-social nexus of sanctions and injunctions of the old order, elements possessed of great consolidatory power. In other words, a generalized ethical code had replaced sacred dictates, and this ethical secularization was now dependent upon the secular use of power for its implementation. Thus the essential problem facing Aśoka was: given the breakdown of traditional and organic integrative forms, is it possible to create a common social consciousness by positivistic means? The vast majority of the Aśokan edicts, with the exception of the purely religious ones,[52] are concerned with this endeavour.

Before proceeding to trace this attempt, it is important to note that such an enterprise far transcends anything conceived of by Kauṭilya, staunchly though he upheld the power of the Regnum. His espousal of the state was fundamentally at the quantitative level, at the level of increasing its practical responsibilities. He favoured a greater role for the state in the economic and administrative life of the society, and for this purpose bestowed upon it powers and obligations which made it far more important than it had hitherto been. Nevertheless, as noted above, in terms of its final values the *Kauṭiliyan Artha-śāstra* remains faithful to the Dharmasūtra position, and the true sanction of the Regnum lies in its support of the *varṇāśra-madharma*. No attempt is thus made to render the state responsible for the creation of a new centre of gravity, a new centripetal principle in society. The bureaucracy which Kauṭilya envisages is fundamentally, in theory at any rate, the servant of an existing order, but in Aśoka—as we hope to show below —it is intended to become the creator of a new one. This is, of course, not to suggest a serious contradiction between them; once the principle of bureaucracy has been established, there is no reason why it should limit itself to material goals and not extend its sway over the minds of men. Aśoka is, in this sense, merely developing what is already inherent in Kauṭilya's thought.

The close link between increasing bureaucratization and the propagation of the Dhammic message is fairly manifest in the edicts. The 3rd Major Rock Edict imposes on the Yuttas (sub-ordinate officers), Rājukas (rural administrators), and Pādesi-kas (heads of districts), obligations to undertake quinquennial tours for the purpose of instructing the people in Dhamma in addition to their other duties. After he had been consecrated thirteen years (c. 255 B.C.), Aśoka instituted a new bureau-cratic order specifically created for the purpose of spreading Dhamma. "In times past, Dhamma-mahāmattas did not exist. They were appointed by me thirteen years after my consecra-tion."[54] He goes on to say that they were active among all sects in teaching the Dhamma, amongst the Brahmins and those devoted to the Dhamma as well as among the old and the destitute. In brief, they were involved at every level with all that pertained to the domain and the establishment of Dhamma and the administration of charities.[55] The 6th. Major Rock Edict urges the prompt dispatch of business and demands that Aśoka be kept informed of events at all times. "At any moment, whether I am eating, in the harem, in my apartments, at the cow-pen (privy?), in the palanquin or in the parks, reporters are to keep me informed as to public affairs."[56] This tightening of the lines of communication is for the purpose of promoting the welfare of all men, than which no duty is more important.[57] It is significant that this edict, whose substantive portion is a bureaucratic ordinance, should be seen as a Dhammic document: "This text of Dhamma has been written for the purpose that it may last long and that my children, grand-children and great grand-children may conform to it for the good of the entire world."[58] It tacitly exemplifies the notion that the welfare of his subjects is inseparable from the bureaucratic means adopted to that end, or, more precisely, that these means create, rather than subserve, the welfare of his people. The 12th Rock Edict[59] stresses the importance that Aśoka lays on harmony between the various sects, and outlines the extensive participation of the bureaucracy in bringing about this end. "Many officers are employed towards this end, the Dhamma-mahāmattas, the mahāmattas controlling women, the inspectors of cow-pens, and other classes of officials."[60] The Separate Edict[61] is of importance on two counts—Aśoka's estimate of the strength and influence of his officials, and his own attitude towards government. The edict is directed to the city officials of Tosali. "You are in charge of thousands of persons. Gain, therefore, the affections of men. All men are my children. As I desire for my children that they will enjoy goodness and happiness in this world and in the next, so I desire for all men." The king and his subjects are no longer united within the bounds of a common framework which transcends them all, instead the king himself has become the critical agent of exemplifying Dhammic values and the arbiter of behaviour. Here again the main sanction which underlies the universalistic ethic of the Dhamma is the status and power of the king himself—a status subject to hypertrophic growth in the light of the fact that it constitutes the only common ground for an otherwise discrete and fragmented society. It is true that eschatological rewards—the winning of Heaven[62]—are also an inducement to Dhammic behaviour, and in that sense it is not temporal might alone which buttresses the desired social conduct. But—apart from the fact that eschatological rewards or sanctions are much less developed as a system of incentives than in the Dharmasūtras (a fact which may be linked to the absence of caste and karma causality)—the significant point is that it is the king who determines the social content of Dhamma, and therefore the rewards of the after-life are consequent upon conforming to a code established by him. Thus, the dependence of society upon the king for its unity and integrity can open the way to the untramelled growth of royal power because it lacks any adequate counterpoise of its own. The importance thus accruing to the monarch has an echo in the Minor Rock Edict addressed to the officers of Isilā:[63]

> "It is necessary to scrupulously obey the orders of the king. The Rājukas receiving the order will proclaim the following to the population and to the chiefs of the districts to the sound of the drum, 'Obey mother and father, and the masters. Be merciful towards human beings. Speak the truth. These are the Dhammic values to be practised.' "

The Pillar Edicts carry on the same themes in sustance, but Thapar[64] is probably right in discerning a new and imperious note creeping into what had hitherto been an enthusiastic and earnest endorsement of a basic and simple moral creed. Thus, the first Pillar Edict speaks of the need of "extreme vigilance, extreme obedience (and) extreme circumspection" in the search of people for happiness in this world and the next."[65] He goes on to assert that his agents, whether high or low or of middle station, sufficiently conform to the law and apply it to persuade the hesitant. Similarly, in the 2nd. Pillar Edict, after enumerating his own acts which were beneficial to society and to living beings, he counsels that "He who conforms will do well."[68] The 4th. Pillar Edict grants independent authority to the Rājukas to judge and punish so that "they can procure goodness and happiness for the people in the provinces and give them assistance. They (i.e., the Rājukas) will learn what makes for happiness and unhappiness, and, along with those faithful to Dhamma, will guide the people of the provinces to the way in which they can gain this world and the next."[67] There is in this a somewhat ominous tendency to bureaucratically manipulate the people in order to achieve a desired positive result—and not just as a measure of restraint. The 7th. Pillar Edict is perhaps the most remarkable of all. It sums up what Aśoka has done by way of concrete actions to spread the Dhamma, but more importantly, it also poses the question of how people can be made to conform to Dhamma, and considers the efficacy of direct state action in this respect.[68] He begins by saying that the kings of the past searched for means whereby to make the people progress on the path of Dhamma, but that this progress never occurred. How was it to be achieved? By sermons on the Dhamma and prescriptions regarding it. Further, numerous officials with extensive jurisdiction were appointed to instruct the people and provide them with explanations, and the Dhamma-mahāmattas arose as part of this project. These officials were concerned with all people, with the householders and the ascetics, and with all the sects and communities, the Brahmins, Ājīvikas and Jains. So far the emphasis has all been on the positivistic endeavours of the state to promote Dhamma, but in conclusion he states that "the progress of the law among men has been obtained by only two means: by regulations and by meditation. But on this point regulations have not been of much avail and meditation has gone further."[69] This is a touchingly candid appraisal of the powers of positivistic action to alter ethical consciousness, and it stands to Aśoka's lasting credit that he realized the fundamental impotence of the state, *qua* state, in creating a desired moral climate.

Prior to discussing certain objections to the analysis which has been offered above, it may be useful to sum up the main points of the argument. What is being said is that Aśoka's concept of kingship constitutes a radical departure from what we have encountered in the Dharmasūtras and the *Kauṭiliyan Arthaśāstra.* In these latter, the role of the king emerged, so to say, from society, which was the existent, the primordial and God-given, and which the king subserved through his function of protection and punishment—symbolized by, and embodied in, the Rod. This does not mean that the royal power never intervened in society, but this intervention was always, in theory, in order to keep the faithful to duties and obligations which formed part of a hierarchy in which the Regnum too had its allocated place. The *varṇāśramadharma* constituted a whole which enveloped both the ruler and the ruled within its folds of status and obligations. Within this, the kṣatriya duty was to fight, and not to debate whether the act of war was intrinsicaily right or not. When Aśoka, therefore, becomes concerned with questions of compassion and the suffering consequent upon wars, he is clearly not seeing war as a given but as something which needs to be evaluated on its own terms. War is no longer regarded as an inescapable duty, a function attendant upon his status as a monarch, but as an act which is eluctable and can be judged as condemnable. Aśoka has thus taken a stand quite different from the network of injunctions and associated justifications which constitute the *varṇāśramadharma.* In the now necessary act of establishing his own *raison d'être,* he has to evaluate and judge acts on his own responsibility. But this freedom, this choice, is closely linked with the issue of social atomization. It has been pointed out earlier that the appearance of dissident sects considerably pre-dated Aśoka's time, but he nevertheless appears to be the first king to view society as a hostile group of divergent interests needing reconciliation. His edicts, with the steady appeal for harmony between sects and mutual tolerance, bear witness to this. And it is argued that this social perspective, this sense of standing outside any social order is the necessary corollary to his individuation. It is in this context that Aśoka is closest to the Buddhists, of whose organization, in a private capacity, he formed a part. Dumont has pointed out that the Buddhist theory of society—reviewed above—"is given as a mere aggregate of individual men."[70] And he goes on to say that "the individual in that sense appears in India only through the man who abandons life in the social world, the renouncer, and it is plain that the Buddha as well as the Buddhists monks are renouncers."[71] Now, given this fragmented view of society, and granted too that the king did not abdicate his responsibilities as a ruler and turn his back on the world, his function lay clearly in trying to introduce a common principle into society in terms of which it would gain a new cohesion, and this, as has been argued, was the role of Dhamma.

Similarly, granted the loss of self-regulatory power on the part of society, the state, the Regnum, had to assume the responsibility for instilling the new values and creating a fresh synthesis. By a paradox which has become commonplace in our times, therefore, the very act of trying to breathe new life into society, to restore its integrative powers, gives a greater role to the state and political authority, which, as the endeavour becomes more pressing, themselves increase in scope and power. The main point to be stressed is that Aśoka does not aim deliberately at increasing royal power, he does not seek to oppose the resources of a bureaucratic state against a disorganized and atomized society in order to achieve maximum control. Such an analysis would doubtless be open to a charge of anachronistic modernism, but the point is that the perception of society as being fragmented and the consequent need to impart to it a new unity leads by an inescapable logic to the increase of state power. The moral that Aśoka would seem to exemplify is that social fissiparity, if it is not to end in total distintegration, will at some point invite greater political control. This becomes particularly clear if one remembers that Aśoka did not really try to reorganize society on principles and ideas uniquely his own. On the contrary, he regarded Dhamma as being comprised of the essentials of all sects, nor did he attempt to get rid of the sects but merely to establish harmony between them and thus preserve the status quo. This nevertheless was sufficient to draw in the bureaucratic resources of the state in an attempt at remedying the situation. Similarly, what is vital is not so much the fact of sectarian dissent and turbulence as Aśoka's view of it as a symptom of a lack of social cohesion—a view which is reflected in his concern for harmony between the sects and in the activities of the Dhamma-mahāmattas spreading the Dhammic message throvgh every level of society so that no strata would remain untouched by it. We have argued that if he had been securely ensconced in the *varṇāśramadharma* tradition he would not have seen it as such, and thus a crucial element is the change in social perspective that Aśoka represents—that is, the king looking at society through the eyes of a renouncer.

It is also necessary to add that the existence of sects cannot in itself be taken as a sign of social integration. Admittedly, it does signify that the individual was not left to confront the awesome power of the state in his isolation for the sects acted as intermediaries, but the significant factor, as Aśoka appears to have seen it, is that they had no system of inter-linkage, they shared nothing in common—unlike the mutually connected hierarchy of the Brahmanical structure—and in this sense they were atomized. Society could be seen, therefore, if not as a discrete body of individuals, still, as a collection of diverse bodies lacking a rationale bringing them together.

Like the Buddhists, and unlike the adherents of the Brahmanical scheme, Aśoka does not regard society as sacred, he does not see it as an embodiment of a sacred principle. But unlike the Buddists, he is concerned with injecting an ethical principle into society, not just preaching the good life to society, but making social life, as social life, an ethically viable pursuit. Thus the pursuit of Dhammic values bears its fruit both in this world and in the next.[72] Clearly social values, practised and realized by those in and of society, can also have salvationary power. The Buddhists also, of course, propagate the same values, but the difference lies in the fact that for them the critical act for emancipation is not the practice of these values in society, but the turning away from the world. The moral agent behind this ethical transformation is to be the monarch, and this constitutes his special claim to fame. He is the one who causes the gods to come down to earth and mingle with men.[73] Aśoka's position in the attitudes towards kingship that we have studied so far is therefore unlike both the Buddhist and Brahmanical ones. Like the Buddhists, his individualism leads him to see society as an agglomeration of particular units, but rather than turning away from it he engages in the task of imbuing it with a common moral purpose—an endeavour which is intended to save, edify and unify. In his attempt at making social behaviour bear soteriological rewards, however, he is close to the Brahmanical spirit. Nevertheless, despite the use of his title "Beloved of the Gods," there is no attempt at deifying the king or regarding him as the guardian of a sacrosanct order. What is attempted is to make an essentially secular creed the vehicle of salvation—a creed which operates in and through society which is not a 'given' in the Brahmanical sense, but one created through the good-will and tolerance of men. In the means through which these admirable aims are to be realized, however, Aśoka reveals himself as a partisan of the Arthaśāstra spirit, if by that we understand not an amoral cynicism but a belief in bureaucracy. Judging by the brevity of the life of the Dhammic message and the recrudescence of Brahmanical forms as manifest in the post-Mauryan period of the Śuṅgas, the experiment does not seem to have been successful, but the enduring historical importance of Aśoka is surely linked with his attempts at fostering a moral soteriology through bureaucratic means—an attempt which, albeit in modified forms, endures into our times.

CHAPTER IV

Manu and the Regnum

CHAPTER IV

The *Manusmṛti* is a work which fits into the same generally religious genre as that of the Dharmasūtras both in terms of its genealogy and its concerns. Bühler[1] has argued on the basis of the greater organization that the work displays—its scheme of dealing with civil and criminal matters under the eighteen titles of the law—that it is posterior to the Dharmasūtras, but since it still confuses between the morally reprehensible and the legally actionable, it is anterior to the works of Nārada and Yājñavalkya.[2] It sums up and organizes the contents of the pre-existent Dharmasūtras, but it also, as will be seen below, contains a far stronger political element, and this, along with its penchant for the more grandiose Brahmanical forms such as the horse-sacrifice,[3] makes it similar in ethos to the period of the Śuṅgas in the post-Mauryan epoch.

The main theme of Manu's work, as of the Dharmasūtras, is the search for salvation within the structure of the *varṇāśrama-dharma*, but although in this sense the chapters on matters of political import are not the heart of the work, the attitudes toward temporal authority reflect a very important change from those of the Dharmasūtras. Manu follows the latter in seeing the king as a supportive instrument defending a pre-existent social order; thus, "The king has been created to be the protector of the castes (*varṇa*) and orders, who, all according to their rank, discharge their several duties."[4] But it now appears that the presence of the king is vital for the existence of the sacrosanct structure and not just for its protection: "For, when these creatures, being without a king, through fear dispersed in all directions, the Lord created a king for the protection of this whole (creation)."[5] And, stemming from this function of being a bulwark against anarchy comes greater glory than was accorded to him by the Dharmasūtras: "Taking (for that purpose) eternal particles of Indra, of the Wind, of Yāma, of the Sun, of Fire, of Varuṇa, of the Moon, and of the Lord of Wealth (Kubera)."[6] Further, "Because a king has been formed of the particles of those Lords of the Gods, he therefore surpasses all created beings in lustre."[7] Finally, "Even an infant king must not be despised, (from an idea) that he is a (mere) mortal; for he is a great deity in human form."[8] The king's role is still protection, but protection in a rather extended sense; not only is he the watchman of a given order, but it now seems that the given order can only come into being under his aegis. Increasing deviations from the sacred norm are doubtless responsible for the shift from the king as instrument of protection to the king as the forger of order, and his deification can perhaps be seen as a symbolic acknowledgment of this transition. The means for the re-establishment of order, or, what amounts to the same thing, its re-creation, are seen to lie in coercion, and the weakness of a self-regulatory system of penances to cope with this problem is manifest in the increasing weight given to punishments—identified henceforth with the king. "Punishment is (in reality) the king (and) the male, that the manager of affairs, that the ruler, and that is called the surety for the four orders' obedience."[9] For without him, "All castes would be corrupted (by intermixture), all barriers would be broken through, and all men would rage (against each other) in consequence of mistakes with respect to punishment."[10] And in the event of this happening, we get the classic statement on *matsyanyāya*, "If the king did not, without tiring, inflict punishment on those worthy to be punished, the stronger would roast the weaker, like fish on a spit."[11] In the light of this, it is not surprising to find that the *Manusmṛti* is far more organized in matters relating to *vyavahāra* than the Dharmasūtras. It is not only, as Bühler asserts,[12] a matter of greater specialization leading to a more precise and cohesive handling of civil and criminal law, but rather, by seeing the king as the only element which can fend off encroaching chaos with the aid of punishment, Manu is compelled to pay greater heed to the positive aspects of executive rule. Nowhere is this more clear than when Manu is dealing with the rules and proscriptions concerning administrative matters such as were outlined under the fifth category with regard to the Dharmasūtras in Chapter I—the category which implied the necessity of an executor and thus presaged an increase in royal functions.

It was then noted that although the Dharmasūtras did have rules regarding cattle trespass, for example, it was not at all clear how, or by whom, the sanctions, if specified, were to be imposed. With Manu, on the other hand, all matters likely to give rise to litigation are dealt with under eighteen titles ranging from the non-payments of debts through non-payment of wages, reneging on agreements, boundary disputes, defamation, theft, robbery, and adultery to partition of inheritance and gambling and betting. In addition, the king's connection with justice, both as judge and as the final executor of sanctions, is firmly established. He is given the task of "Daily (deciding) one after another (all cases) which fall under the eighteen titles (of the law) according to principles drawn from local usages and from the Institutes of the Sacred Law (i.e., the Dharmasūtras)."[13] The sequence of punishments to be followed by the king is clearly noted, "Let him punish first by (gentle) admonition, afterwards by (harsh) reproof, thirdly by a fine, after that by corporal chastisement."[14] In the section on *vyavahāra* eschatological punishments are reserved only for those bearing false witness, and, seen primarily as a means of enforcing honesty, are not incomparable with the testifying on oath in law-courts today. The scale of fines is precisely detailed: "Two hundred and fifty panas are declared (to be) the first (or lowest) amercement, five (hundred) are considered as the mean (or middle-most), but one thousand as the highest."[15] The increase in legal definition is well illustrated by comparing Gautama's punishment for theft with that of Manu. Whereas the former[16] is content with stating that a thief must present himself to the king to be clubbed by him, Manu deals with thirteen categories of thefts and lays down specific punishments for each.[17]

Similarly, Manu is more specific than the Dharamasūtras in

affording a place to the state in matters of socio-political administration. Indeed, in this respect he draws close to Kauṭilya, and although we do not find the same degree of bureaucratic specialization, there are many points of resemblance. Kauṭilya's scheme of rural administration in which revenue centres are to be set up for groups of ten, two hundred, four hundred and eight hundred villages[18] is paralleled by a similar hierarchical system of groups of ten, twenty, hundred and thousand villages[19] in which each unit will report to the one above. Further, in both the works[20] the state is given the responsibility for the purchase and sale of marketable goods, as also for the collection of tolls and duties.[21] Again, there is common testimony to a fairly developed economic infra-structure in the emphasis on standardized weights and measures as part of the responsibility of the king.[22] We have noted the existence of monopolies and state enterprises in Kauṭilya, and Manu too makes mention of the former.[23] It is, however, in his attitude towards political power that Manu is most Kauṭilyan. In words which virtually echo those of Kauṭilya[24] the king is told, "What he has not (yet) gained, let him seek (to gain) by his army; what he has gained, let him protect by careful attention; what he has protected, let him augment by (various modes of) increasing it; and what he has augmented let him liberally bestow (on worthy men)."[25] A new spirit of calculation enters into the old chivalric Kṣatriya ethic of warfare. "Let him be ever ready to strike, his prowess constantly displayed, and his secrets constantly concealed, and let him constantly explore the weaknesses of his foe."[26] Expansionist policies are encouraged for the just king, "A king who thus duly fulfills his duties in accordance with justice, may seek to gain countries which he has not yet gained, and shall duly protect them when he has gained them."[27] The essential elements of the Arthaśāstra machinery for espionage are to be found in Manu,[28] as are the concept of the maṇḍalas[29] and the cliché regarding the four basic policies of statecraft: *sāma* (conciliation), *dāna*) (bribery), *bheda* (creating dissensions) and *daṇḍa* (force).[30]

And it has been noted that, *pari passu* with this, there is a move towards greater internal organization with the countryside being divided into units of ten, twenty, hundred and thousand villages arranged in a hierarchic order of responsibility. A degree of centralized control is exercised by having the village officials supervised by another minister of the king who is to be "loyal and never remiss."[31] The king's right to dues has been touched upon above, but it may be added that he is entitled to a day's labour a month from mechanics, artisans and those Śūdras who subsist by manual labour.[32] As regards taxes, he is entitled to a fiftieth part of the increments on cattle and gold, and the eighth, sixth or twelfth part of the crops.[33]

These aspects of the *manusmṛti*, the Realpolitik ethic of force, the greater emphasis on centralization and state activity, do mark it off from being nothing more than a mere extension of the Dharmasūtras, although it has been noted that the latter also contained certain areas with potential for a positive monarchical role. There is little doubt however that Manu pays greater attention to questions of temporal authority and state power than the Dharmasūtras, and this impression is strengthened by the calculations of Bühler[34] establishing that one-third of Manu's work is devoted to topics concerning the duties of the king, the administration of justice and civil and criminal law, whereas the portion normally allotted to these subjects in most Dharmasūtras is one-fifth. Working on the basis of Bühler's table, Trautmann has composed a set of concordances between the *Manusmṛti* and the Dharmasūtras of Gautama, Baudhāyana, Āpastamba and Vasiṣtha expressed in terms of percentages.[35] The findings show that, with the exception of Chapters 1 and 12 which deal largely with accounts of creation and transmigration respectively—themes not dealt with by the Dharmasūtras and exclusive to the smṛti—a median percentage of nearly 50% of the verses covered in Chapters 2-6 and 10-12 have counterparts in the Dharmsūtras. These are the sections dealing with the rules for initiation and studentship, the obligations of householders, marriage, domestic sacrifices, purification and similar matters of religious concern. For Chapters 7-9, however, the median percentage falls to rather below 20%, reflecting the greater emphasis in Manu on matters concerning the king and civil and criminal law than is found in his predecessors—these being the topics dealt with therein. It would therefore seem reasonable to assume that the *Manusmṛti* assigns a higher priority to executive concerns than do the Dharmasūtras. Taken in conjunction with the marked ideological similarity with Kauṭilya's work, it would further imply that the science of Artha—of worldly profit—already existed in its own right, and that Manu was aware of, and drew from, this genre when he composed his sections on the king and administration.

It is of course to be remembered that problems of power and questions regarding the position of the king occupy only a part of Manu's work, the greater portions of which deal exclusively with issues concerning the duties and obligations of those within the social fabric of the *varṇāśramadharma*, whereas the *Kauṭiliyan Arthaśāstra* is entirely devoted to political concerns. Nevertheless, within the political section itself, Manu's standpoint is hardly to be differentiated from that of Kauṭilya. He thus stands somewhere between the Dharmasūtras and the *Kauṭilīyan Arthaśāstra*, nearer to the former in terms of the general tenor of his work and to the latter in the context of his political views. It can perhaps be said that while Kauṭilya struggles with the problem of allowing political power an autonomous position within the Dharmasūtra structure, Manu attempts to reconcile the growth of monarchical power within the essentially static nature of the *varṇa* scheme. While Kauṭilya's penchant is in the direction of increasing political might, Manu leans towards the maintenance of the sacred social pattern. This distinction however should not be construed as an opposition, for we have seen a strong *varṇāśramadharma* element in Kauṭilya's scheme. His espousal of power as a formative agent is negated by the necessity—as Dumont puts it—that force be made "legitimate by being subordinated hierarchically to the Brāhma and the Brahmans."[37] Thus Kauṭilya advocates compliance with local usage and custom and even the setting up of the *varṇāśramadharma* scheme in conquered territories, which implies that the road is blocked to the independent creation of any socio-political structure by the Regnum alone. The exercise of legitimate Regnal power is always contingent upon being authorized by a pre-existent system, one which was not created by the king, and hence the nature of kingly power prevents it from innovation, from creating an order for which it alone is responsible and which gains its form from the will of the political agent.

Now, it is precisely because Aśoka is outside the role allotted to the king in the caste structure that he is in a position to formulate the universalistic ethic of Dhamma which he feels is applicable in all places and at all times. This has a two-fold significance. Firstly, it constitutes a value-structure which is not spatially limited and is thus unlike the Dharmasūtras, Kauṭilya and Manu. The most striking proof of this is that he holds the doctrine of Dhamma to be applicable not only within his kingdom but even to the Greeks beyond.[37] Secondly, and this is inextricably connected with the first, the social configuration of Dhamma gains its sanction from the political power and not from any relation to a given archetype. It may in parenthesis be stressed again that the king's responsibility for the behavioural implications of Dhamma remains true even if the Dhamma itself is seen as a transcendental ethic. In Aśoka, therefore, the political power is freed from the necessity of being legitimized by subordination to an existent order and of recognizing a given social archetype as being absolute. The example of Aśoka makes it clear that political power can become independent only if it succeeds in abandoning the system of castes and its implications. And this in turn implies greater centralisation on two levels. At the level of values, the pluralistic ethic of the caste system gives way to a unified and universalistic code, while at the administrative level the authority hitherto inherent in local bodies no longer possesses a sanctity which has to be respected by the king. Bureaucracy exists with centralization in a symbiotic relationship in which each needs to grow in order to strengthen the other, and while Kauṭilya is the first to offer us the bureaucratic model, its efficacy is impaired because he is unable to accept the full implications of centralization, namely the abandonment of the *varṇāśramadharma* scheme. It is Aśoka who, by the adoption of this step, offers bureaucracy its fullest scope. It is unfortunate that we cannot trace the exact degree of administrative centralization under Aśoka, but, as we have tried to show, the attempt at what might be called the centralizatton of values—and the role of the bureaucracy therein—is readily apparent. In the context of temporal authority, this type of centralization —in which the king undertakes to establish the basic principles which will underlie the state—is perhaps more significant than the one in which bureaucratic centralization simply applies to material tasks. And this could well be said to be the difference between Kauṭilya's use of the bureaucracy and that of Aśoka.

Reverting to Manu, the interpretation to be placed on his according a more prominent place to the power of the Regnum involves the larger context of the compatibility of the sacrosanct Brahmanical scheme with historical change. Manu shows himself to be aware of this dimension when, utilizing the *yuga* concept—the four basic divisions of time between the evolution and dissolution of the world—he says "One set of duties (is prescribed) for men in the Kṛta age, different ones in the Tretā and in the Dvāpara, and (again) another (set) in the Kali, in proportion as (those) ages decrease in length."[38] Lingat[39] has argued very persuasively that this refers not to a change in the Dharma over the course of years, but to a concession to the increasing moral frailty of men. Thus whereas in the Kṛta age the duty par excellence was that of austerities, in the Kali age it has been simplified to a mere liberality. It is not the Dharma which has changed—for Manu does not say that austerities lose their value in the Tretā age—but the ability of men to conform to it, and the various duties are prescribed taking into account the steadily increasing moral turpitude of the world. At the same time, as Lingat also concedes,[40] there are occasions where Manu engages in quite flagrant contradictions. Thus, for example, he regards it as a sin to eat meat,[41] but a *snātaka* (one who has just completed his studentship and is on the eve of becoming a householder) is asked not to refuse meat offered to him.[42] It is clear that a case like this results from Manu's attempt at accommodation with a custom which he regards as retrograde. Similarly, he condemns the marriage of any of the three higher castes with Śūdra women,[43] but then fixes the share of the paternal estate which will devolve on the issues of these unions.[44] Here again he is coming to terms with customs, which, though antithetical to Dharmic precepts, were now too widespread to be ignored. It is certainly true that his acknowledgment of these customs is grudging, but the very fact that he includes them amongst his precepts grants them a measure of Śāstric prestige and sanction. Other examples of this kind of contradition are to be found in his dictums regarding *niyoga*[45] and widow remarriage.[46] In cases such as this, Manu does not attempt to rationalize these aberrant customs but contents himself with stating which practices he regards as pure while at the same time describing the unorthodox forms. The two are simply juxtaposed in such a manner as to justify the suspicion that the Dharmic code, at least peripherally, is historically conditioned despite its claim to an eternal immutability.

Nevertheless, the universal reverence in which Manu's work has been held by those jurists and commentators who followed him makes it clear that its dictums are not regarded as being of only temporary validity but enjoy a near-absolute authority for all times. In other words, Manu is seen not as legislating only for his period, but as expressing dogmas of eternal verity which stem from the Vedas. Thus Parāśāra says of him, "The Veda is without an author, it is (simply) recalled (for the world of men) by (the god) with four faces (Brāhma); in the same way, at the commencement of each kalpa, Manu puts (men) in mind of their duties (dharmas)."[47] In this sense, therefore, the Dharma remains unchanged whatever the concessions made to change and fluctuating customs. We have seen that Manu himself does not offer a methodology by which the two—Dharma and custom—can be satisfactorily reconciled, and for this we have to turn to the commentatorial literature, a subject which is outside the strict purview of the present work but recourse to which may be justified for coping with the problem posed above.

Lingat provides an excellent example of attempting to make inconsistencies arising from the occasional discrepancies between Dharma and custom seem merely apparent when he deals with the attitude of Mādhava toward the question of cross-cousin marriages.[48] Manu[49] is opposed to the marriage of a boy with his maternal uncle's daughter or his paternal aunt's daughter and holds it to be a great sin on the grounds that they all share a common ancestor—thus violating the *sapiṇḍa* rule. As Lingat goes on to say, Mādhava is a South Indian for whom such marriages were not only permissible highly but desirable through immemorial custom. In order to justify this usage, therefore, he first quotes Vedic passages which, according to him, refer to marriage with the maternal uncle's daughter or the paternal aunt's daughter and argues that these passages are injunctive (*vidhi*) and not merely descriptive (*arthāvada*). Such a position could claim validity on the grounds that Vedic injunctions are *Śrutiś* (what is heard) and can thus overrule the *smṛti* (what is remembered), but this would be to completely disregard Manu's precepts, and Mādhava's regard for him is such that he has no desire to contravene them. He thus further argues that Manu's point of view is justified, but only in instances where this type of union is conducted in an inferior form of marriage, and not in those where the marriage is of an approved and superior form. Therefore, despite the fact that cross-cousin marriages are rejected in general by the śiṣṭas (learned and pious men) of North India, Mādhava argues that they are accepted by those of the South—and this cannot be attributed to mere license as it is practised by pious people learned in the sacred texts. Thus, by a process of legalistic finesse and interpretative agility a heterodox custom is shown to have links with śruti and is justified. The actual authority or consistency of the Vedas or of the smṛti is never questioned, the endeavour being not to oppose the validity of custom against that of the *Śāstras* but to see the former as in some way derived from the latter and as attaching to it. In this way the religious law remains above, and untained by, historical reality while at the same time it maintains a linkage with custom—in so far as the latter has to justify itself in Śāstric terms. In the event of an unbridgeable gulf between Dharma and custom, a solution is still found by making them both operative in different ways. We have seen custom to be acknowledged by Manu,[50] but as Lingat points out in the context of latter commentators and jurists, even if a man who follows customs antipathetic to the Śāstras is not socially culpable, he may still be guilty of sin,[51] and in this way the transcendent authority of the Śāstras is maintained while allowing custom to be operative at the level of social behaviour. The distinction between Dharma and custom is thus still made to hold. "In sum," as Lingat says, "this suggests that the rule of Dharma and the rule of custom has each its own level of application. If the rule of Dharma cannot abrogate the customary rule, the latter certainly cannot abrogate the rule of Dharma as such, that is to say as instrument of the law of karma."[52]

A similar logic pertains when it comes to the duty of the king to maintain intact the customs of countries, castes, families and other groups. Bṛhaspati[53] argues that "otherwise the public would revolt, the subjects would take an aversion to (their king), and the army and the treasury would be destroyed." In other words, customary usages are to be upheld for reasons of simple expediency. It is not that Dharma—to which such customs may well be opposed—is wrong or outmoded, but simply that its full-scale application would lead to internal disorders the avoidance and rectification of which should be the king's main concern. It is doubtless in this context that Manu's deification of the king should be seen. It is a symbolic reflection of the need for order; it is because the social order is so sacred that he whose job it is to defend it assumes the stature of a god. And that this attribute of divinity belongs to the function of protection and not to the person of the king is attested to by Manu's statement in the context of the utilization of the Rod that "Punishment (possesses) a very bright lustre, and is hard to be administered by men with unimproved minds; it strikes down the king who swerves from his duty, together with his relatives."[54] The increased emphasis in Manu on political might, therefore, is not aimed at establishing a parity between royal power and the Dharma. On the contrary, executive power is extolled solely in order that the social scheme be fortified, the latter always retains its primacy. Thus temporal authority has no more power than the force of custom to shake the ultimate validity of the Dharma.

In purely empirical terms, however, the opposition between the Regnum and the Sacerdotium which was dealt with in the first chapter—and which was seen to be essential to the complementarity of the syzygy scheme—still remains true. Leaving aside the consideration—dealt with above—which distinguishes

Dharma from both custom and royal power, the contradiction between these must still receive congnizance. Political acts, intrinsically, are valueless unless guided by spiritual force. But the existence of a stable realm is indispensable to the Sacerdotium, and if the price of this stability is the violation of certain aspects of the Dharma—such as the acknowledgment and protection of possibly heterodox customs—this is a price which has to be paid (always keeping in mind that the recognition of such customs does not imply their elevation to the rank of Dharmic precepts). Viewed pragmatically, therefore, it can be said that the Dharma does contradict itself insofar as its existence may involve an infringement of some of its tenets. To gloss over this contradiction would in fact be doing harm to the central core of Brāhmanical political thought which stresses the intrinsically opposed natures of the Regnum and the Sacerdotium so that paradoxically, the latter is dependent on its 'enemy' for its protection. The partial sacrifice of its purity by the Sacerdotium—and its violation—in entering into a relationship with the Regnum is the central contradiction upon which the fecundity of the syzygy scheme depends. As we saw in the analysis of the Brāhmaṇas, there is no attempt at making spiritual and secular power synonymous; their necessary opposition is succinctly expressed in the observation: "that which is of Mitra is not of Varuṇa."[55] The noumenal natures of the two are opposed, but this opposition is a prelude to their cooperation through which the Regnum is validated. This does not mean that the Regnum is rendered autonomous, but only that its essentially brute nature is redeemed through serving the Sacerdotium. Moreover the complementarity between the two is a complementarity between unequal partners—for Mitra can do without Varuṇa[56]—and the Regnum can never be allowed to determine ends, this being the role of the Sacerdotium alone. This is what explains the seemingly strange phenomenon of the king never being asked to totally abrogate forms alien to the Dharmasūtras. We have seen that even Kauṭilya shies away from what we have termed Draconian annexation and the imposition of a structure erected by temporal might, for this would involve the king exceeding his caste-duty. Similarly, in the quotation from Bṛhaspati above, the king is asked to tolerate aberrant customs for the purpose of political stability but the possibility of this being achieved through a rigorous exercise of regnal authority which would sweep away heterodox forms is not countenanced, again, it is argued, because this would be to make the king exceed his authority. It is true that in this endeavour the king would be seeking to impose orthodoxy, but the Dharmasūtras and Manu seem to prefer that this be done through a process of emulation fostered by the desire to ascend the hierarchy of purity rather than through state action. It is not the king's role, in other words, to determine social forms; to the extent that these are contrary to the Śāstras, they will be modified gradually by the power and prestige emanating from the Śāstric norms and from those who adhere to them.

The ambiguity implicit in Manu's espousal of royal power thus reflects the dialectical tension expressed in the Brahmanical view of kingship. The king is necessary to the extent that the *varṇāśramadharma* needs protection, but the danger that this function may spill over into innovation is zealously guarded against. Political power is necessary, but it is not to become autonomous. However much the importance of the Regnum may be stressed, it is never allowed to become its own master.

CHAPTER V

Hierarchy and Emulation

CHAPTER V

Section 1. Confucius

A study of Chinese attitudes towards political authority in our period must, necessarily, start with Confucius (c. 551-479 B.C.), for, in addition to its intrinsic importance, Confucian ideology can also serve as a model in contrast to which succeeding dogmas may be more clearly defined.

For Confucius, a distinction between the private and the political is untenable; the public sphere is the extension of the private one, and the virtues of the former spring from the latter. Confucius thus argues that filiality and the fulfilment of fraternal obligations in themselves constitute the exercise of government, and that such exercise is therefore not contingent solely on being formally installed as a functionary in government.[1] The absence of a private-public dichotomy is matched by a similar absence of distinction between the religious and the secular—we shall see that the rules of propriety, for instance, play both a social and a religious role. In general, however, it would be reasonable to assert that Confucius prefers to lay greater emphasis on social and ethical issues rather than on metaphysical and cosmological questions.

The keynote of the Confucian attitude is therefore its integrated nature, and this is the inevitable outcome of the fact that legitimate political power is always seen to be a manifestation of personal virtue, an attribute of a particular quality of being, and not just a skill, a facile trade capable of being learnt and wielded as an instrument. Should the ruler possess this quality, acts conducive to orderly administration will follow as a necessary consequence: "He who exercises government by means of his virtue may be compared to the north polar star, which keeps its place and all the stars turn towards it."[2] The ruler thus does not need to actively exercise control, but simply and profoundly to be the ruler. When this is truly achieved, the ruler may give the appearance of quietism or indifference—"How majestic was the manner in which Shun and Yü held possession of the empire, as if it were nothing to them!"[3] This concept of effortless governance resultant upon the ruler's harmony with virtue is a constant thread in Chinese thought and will be met with again when the Legalist school comes under review. The point that it is the quality of personal being which is of fundamental importance finds succinct expression in a celebrated passage from the Great Learning:[4]

> "The ancients who wished to iilustrate illustrious virtue throughout the kingdom, first ordered well their states. Wishing to order well their states, they first regulated their families. Wishing to regulate their families, they first cultivated their persons. Wishing to cultivate their persons, they first rectified their hearts. Wishing to rectify their hearts, they first sought to be sincere in their thoughts. Wishing to be sincere in their thoughts, they first extended to the utmost their knowledge."

And therefore, ". . . from the Son of Heaven down to the multitude of the people, all considered the cultivation of the person to be the root (of everything besides). It cannot be, when the root is neglected, that what should spring from it will be well ordered."[5]

The first necessity of government—both on the part of the ruler and the ruled—is thus the development of one's inner nature, the rooting of oneself in virtue. What Confucius is attempting to assert is a form of rule which depends as little as possible on external restraints and hinges on the belief that the self-cultivation of each will ensure the harmony of all. The ruler's own behaviour will constitute the model, and the Li-chi states, in the context of the ruler ruling through the effulgence of his virtue and not through positivistic means, that "the people imitate the ruler, and we have their self-government."[6]

Similarly Confucius, when once asked about how to cope with the number of thieves in a state, replied, "If you, Sir, were not covetous, although you should reward them to do it, they would not steal."[7] The ruler should exist primarily, not as an executive agent, but as a moral paradigm. The basic issue, however, is the nature of the discipline to which men should condition themselves, that is, the kind of self-cultivation which they should undertake. It is here that the Confucian doctrine of *cheng-ming* or the Rectification of Names gains its significance. When Confucius was asked by his disciple Tzu-lu what the first step was to be in governing, he replied, "What is necessary is to rectify names," and he went on to amplify, "If names be not correct, language is not in accordance with the truth of things. If language be not in accordance with the truth of things, affairs cannot be carried on to success."[8] The world of words exists in direct and concrete correspondence to the objective world, and misuse of the one will necessarily entail confusion in the other. The social and political corollaries of this doctrine are seen to be that words denoting status and rank must find concordances in the moral and ethical values which they imply if they are not to breed disorder and chaos. Thus, in answer to a question from Duke Ching about government he says, "There is government when the prince is prince, and the minister is minister; when the father is father and the son is son."[9] These categories are fundamental to Confucian thought, and they are, as the above quotation indicates, both social and moral. They fit into the five basic Confucian relationships, those between ruler and minister, father and son, husband and wife, elder brother and younger brother, and the intercourse of friend and friend.[10] These categories, and the values they embody of loyalty, filiality, compassion and fraternal affection, are seen to be ordained by Heaven and thus immutably ingrained in the texture of social life. Their violations, in a sense, are not simply violations of a social code or political order but are sacrilegious.[11]

Self-cultivation for Confucius therefore resides in the assimilation by people of the values implicit in their respective stations, an endeavour which—if successful—will result in government becoming like "an easily growing rush."[12] The values to be cultivated are the terrestrial manifestations of heavenly norms, and the aim is to render social life in harmony with principles which exist on high and which are to be reified by the ruler in his own behaviour. The basis of the entire structure is therefore the fundamental categories of relationships which, in hierarchical fashion, both distinguish and unify the various elements of the social scheme. It is this function of distinction which imparts to *li*—a term best left untranslated but combining the meanings of etiquette, ceremony and ritual—its cardinal importance. "Thus, rules of ceremony are the embodied expression of what is right . . . (The idea of right makes the distinction between things, and serves to regulate (the manifestation of) humanity."[13] The rules of propriety, again, are the exemplification of heavenly distinctions, ". . . those rules are rooted in Heaven, have their correspondences in earth and are applicable to spiritual beings."[14] The rites are the formal expressions of celestially ordained differences both in physical nature and in the moral nature of man and so "They change with the seasons; they agree in reference to the (variations of) lot and condition. In regard to man they serve to nurture (his nature)."[15] Confucius is, however, more concerned with the utilization of rites in the establishment of an orderly society than with their cosmological significance—although he is not unaware of the latter.

> "The object of all ceremonies is to bring down the spirits from above, even their ancestors; serving (also) to rectify the relations between ruler and ministers; to maintain the generous feeling between father and son, and the harmony between elder and younger brother; to adjust to relations between high and low; and to give their proper places to husband and wife. The whole may be said to secure the blessing of Heaven."[16]

The correct utilization of rites is thus seen to exemplify and confirm the notion of the hierarchy in which each performs his allotted task in order to establish the harmony of the whole. It is perhaps in order to stress the point that the categories of the Confucian hierarchy are not only not exclusive of each other but actively overlap. The ruler is himself a son, and the minister is ruler to his subordinate officers and so on. In a way therefore, the values implicit in the hierarchy are common to all, and it is for this reason that Confucius holds that a government based on emulation is possible.

At the same time, the performance of the rites has also to be the objective expression of inner virtues. Confucius is very, stern in stressing this: "It is according to the rules of propriety' they say—'It is according to the rules of propriety' they say! Are gems and silks all that is meant by propriety? Are bells and drums all that is meant by music?"[17] And elsewhere he amplifies this disgust at the rules of propriety being confounded with mere empty formalism by stating that "With a superior man the use of ceremonies is to give proper and elegant expression to the feelings. Would it not be empty form to go and condole and wail with others while wearing the three years mourning?"[18] Seen objectively, *li* is operative at two connected levels. At the most basic one it is a terrestrial exemplification of Heaven's order. At the social level it transforms the brute emotional propensities of men into forms of elegance and rectitude appropriate to a civilized human community. At this level, Confucius seems to assert that no social graces or values can exist without *li*—for without its refining power even impulses which one would normally regard as good remain crude and extreme.

> "Respectfulness without the rules of propriety becomes laborious bustle, carefulness without the rules of propriety becomes timidity, boldness without the rules of propriety becomes insubordination, straightforwardness without the rules of propriety becomes rudeness."[19]

What *li* endeavours to do is to morally valorize social life so that the main forms of human activity become objective correlatives of inner states of mind, and we gain an idea as to the extent of this attempt when the *Li-chi* tells us that the rules of ceremony "are practised by means of offerings, acts of strength, words and postures of courtesy, in eating and drinking, in the observances of capping, marriage, mourning, sacrificing, archery, chariot-driving, audiences and friendly missions."[20] Music always played a prominent role in the rites, and the *Li-*

chi precisely defines its function in the context of the rules of propriety: "Music served to give the interior cultivation; the rules to give the external. The two, operating reciprocally within, had their outward manifestation, and the result was a peaceful serenity."[21] And later the same work makes the same point in the whole context of government.

> "And so they—i.e., the ancient kings—instituted ceremonies to direct men's aims aright; music to give harmony to the voices; laws to unify their conduct; and punishments to guard against their tendencies to evil. The end to which ceremonies, music, punishments and laws is one: they are the instruments by which the minds of the people are assimilated, and good order in government is made to appear."[22]

The point can bear reiteration that all these external forms are of value only infosar as they reflect an internal state of virtue. Confucius stresses this when he asks, "If a man be without the virtues proper to humanity, what has he to do with the rites of propriety? If a man be without the virtues proper to humanity, what has he to do with music?"[23] And the virtues proper to humanity are those of *jen*—commonly translated as human-heartedness—which the following passage from the *Great Learning* may roughly define.

> "What a man dislikes in his superiors, let him not display in the treatment of his inferiors; what he dislikes in inferiors let him not display in the service of his superiors; what he hates in those who are before him, let him not therewith precede those who are behind him."[24]

Without this attitude as a fundamental pre-requisite nothing is of any avail. At first glance, the ceremonial aspect of the Confucian ethic is very conspicuous, but Confucius himself is very much aware of what might be called their 'reflective' character, that is, their essentially symbolic function. He gives a striking expression to this while dealing with "the three points that have no positive existence" which are 1) "the music that has no sound, 2) ceremonial usages that have no embodiment, and 3) the mourning that has no garb."[25] There could be no greater testimony to the fact that all aspects of ritual have, in essence, an internal function; the ritual can be completely internalized. Thus the first is seen to correspond to profound virtue, the second to an impeccable deportment and the last to a great solicitude towards the people.[26] Now, if rituals can only be validly practised when they act as external expressions of an inner state of being, it can be understood that such practices will re-inforce inner virtue, but they cannot, in themselves. create it. Confucius does not deal directly with the problem of how such inner virtue—summed up in *jen*—can be initially, created but the answer is implicit in his overall outlook. For him man constitutes a ternion with Heaven and Earth,[27] and the ruler-sage —as also all good men—exemplifies cosmic order in his deportment. At the social level, as we have seen, this order manifests itself both externally, as the five basic relationships, and internally, as the values appropriate to the relationships. Thus the various aspects of *jen*, the attributes of filiality, loyalty and compassion, are seen to be immanent, implicit in the very idea of man who is possessed of these virtues as noumenal qualities.

In answer to the question as to how the inner values can be brought into existence, therefore, Confucius would argue that they are already there, it is only a question of granting them cognizance. It is in this context of recognition that the rites would appear to play their greatest role. They are possessed of a kind of archetypal power which recalls men to themselves and the greater order of which they are a part. Thus the road to sagehood is open to all or nearly all. Confucius does admit that there are a few, "the wise of the highest class and the stupid of the lowest class,"[28] who cannot be changed, but in general it remains true that "By nature, men are nearly alike; by practice they get to be wide apart."[29] It would perhaps be erroneous to see this as meaning that men are infinitely conditionable. We have noted that certain values are seen to be innate, and those who act contrary to them are doing so because they are unaware of their true nature. Evil thus becomes a concommitant of ignorance, and what Confucius would appear to be saying is that while all men are capable of sagehood, they are all equally prone to error arising through ignorance. Here again it is *li* that serves to protect and guide men. "Thus it is by the universal application of the rules of propriety that the lot and duty (of different classes) are fixed; thus it is that men, (acting contrary to those rules) would all have to account death a boon and life an evil."[30] What *li* does is to affirm and clarify distinctions which are intrinsic to social life and are thus quite different from externally imposed laws which depend primarily on the power of state sanctions. The emphasis in Confucius on self-realization—aided by *li*—as the basis of all good government is particularly manifest in his attitude towards punitive law.

> "If the people be led by laws, and uniformity sought to be given them by punishments, they will try to avoid the punishment, but have no sense of shame. If they be led by virtue, and uniformity sought to be given them by the rules of propriety, they will have the sense of shame, and moreover will become good."[31]

Confucius is not satisfied with mere behavioural emendation, but wants external acts to be the outward and visible symbols of inner virtue—hence the importance of shame as indicative of an inner evaluation of an act as distinct from the purely reflexive fear of punishment which does not morally weigh the act as such at all. The same spirit is manifest in Confucius' answer to a question relating to the killing of the unprincipled for the good of the principled.

> "Sir, in carrying on your government, why should you use killing at all? Let your evinced desires be for what is good, and the people will be good. The relation between superiors and inferiors is like that between the wind and the grass. The grass must bend when the wind blows across it."[32]

This does not mean that Confucius altogether dispensed with the use of punishment, rather, it was an assertion that the aim of government is directed towards the nature, and not just the external acts alone, of the subjects. Punishments too, if they had to be used, should be utilized with this goal in view and not as a formal method of control.

Since what is desired is the interior cultivation of man, the role of the ruler necessarily becomes an exemplary one. His function is not primarily just to change the ways in which men behave (although that will automatically occur as the reflection of an internal transformation) but, so to say, to lead them back to themselves, to become a moral archetype through the force of whose example men would understand themselves. There is thus an axiomatic distrust of positive government, a government which seeks to control men through direct action, for this implies according a significance to external power which properly belongs to inner virtue alone. In fact, the positive exercise of power can be seen as a confession of failure, an admission that the harmony which assures an automatic and effortless excellence of rule has not been attained. The ideal ruler "did nothing but gravely and reverently occupy his royal seat."[33] A passage in the *Li-chi* further illustrates the irradiative—though seemingly passive—power of the ruler who is rooted in virtue and the needlessness, indeed danger, of overt governmental action.

> "Hence the ruler is he to whose brightness men look; he does not seek to brighten men. It is he whom men support; he does not seek to support men. It is he whom men serve; he does not seek to serve men. If the ruler were to seek to brighten men, he would fall into errors. If he were to seek to nourish men, he would be unequal to the task. If he were to seek to serve men, he would be giving up his position. Therefore the people imitate the ruler, and we have their self-government . . . ."[34]

It would be a mistake to conclude from what has been said above that Confucius advocates a literal passivity on the part of the ruler. On the contrary, he urges Tzu-lu, in response to a question about government, to "Go before the people with your example and be laborious in their affairs."[35] What he intends, rather, is that if the ruler be assiduous in cultivating his own virtue, he will establish himself in harmony with the overriding principle of order in the world which, in turn, will ensure good government. It is not the will of the ruler in his personal capacity which is the determining factor, but his reverential subordination to the superior principle on which all accord depends. There is a dynamic force in the very nature of things which assures order, and what is meant by passivity in this context is the subordination of the individual will to this force in such a manner, and to such an extent, that the ruler himself becomes nothing more than the transmitter of its dictates.

Granted this attitude, it is not surprising that Confucius does not regard the brute strengthening of the state—an increase of its wealth and power—as an end in itself, and, as may be expected, this is an extension of the same perspective at the individual level. "A man should say, I am not concerned that I have no place, I am concerned how I may fit myself for one. I am not concerned that I am not known, I seek to be worthy to be known."[36] And, "The mind of the superior man is conversant with righteousness; the mind of the mean man is conversant with gain."[37] The following passage from the *Great Learning* in the context of the catastrophe which will befall a ruler who regards his revenues as his main concern makes the same point with regard to the state: "In a state, gain is not to be considered prosperity, but its prosperity will be found in righteousness."[38] Confucius manifested his own dislike of such cupidity when he gave permission to his disciples to assail one of their fellows who aided the already wealthy family of Chi to augment their riches through further impositions.[39] Confucius' disdain for purely utilitarian motives can be further attested to by other incidents in which he makes it plain that he does not place any great store on specific abilities *per se*—that is, on attainments of an essentially technical character[40]—but this does not mean that he spurned practical skills *in toto*. What he is concerned with stressing is that without interior cultivation all such proficiencies are worthless. When, however, such capacities are utilized with reference to virtue, they are acknowledged, and he takes note of the fact that pure learning —important though it is—is of little worth unless it is capable of being practically utilized.

"Though a man be able to recite the three hundred odes,

> yet if, when entrusted with a government charge, he knows not how to act, or if, when sent to any quarter on a mission he cannot give his replies unassisted, notwithstanding the extent of his learning, of what practical use is it?"[41]

It would therefore be inaccurate to characterize Confucius as being anti-utilitarian as such; what he is against is the viewing of utility as an end in itself. He is far too pragmatic not to realize the importance of material factors in the issues of government, but he does not see them being sufficient unto themselves. When asked once by Tzu-kung about the basic requisites of government, he said that they were sufficiency of food, sufficiency of military equipment and the confidence of the people in their ruler, but their relative importance was stated to be in reverse order to the presentation. Military equipment and food could somehow be dealt with, "but if the people have no faith in their ruler, there is no standing for the state."[42] And this faith is, of course, contingent upon the self-cultivation of the ruler. The unremitting emphasis that Confucius lays upon the ethical referent of any given act, on its interior aspect, does not mean that he found himself confronted with the choice of inner virtue on the one hand and practical efficiency and success on the other. He seems to have felt that, both on a personal and a political level, ethical forces were functionally vital to strength and power; far from being antagonistic, power was the overt expression of virtue.

A brief summary of what has been said above may help further clarification. The highly cohesive, interrelated and integrated nature of Confucian thought defies any attempt at exploring it in strictly logical sequence, for what it offers is less a system of thought than an ontological model. It is for this reason that its ramifications and implications are best expressed through a polyvalent medium such as poetry. As has been mentioned above, it is difficult to establish any distinctions within it between the religious and the secular, the political and the personal, for in few other philosophies is the fundamental unity of man, his attributes and his concerns, so firmly and inextricably woven. Effective political power is seen to be the manifestation of total being, and by this is meant the internal realization—and external exemplification—of the principles of cosmic order. This order is manifest socially in an essentially hierarchic form—the five basic relationships, and these in themselves are the externalizations of the values of loyalty, filiality and compassion which are thus seen as being intrinsic to human life. These values, and the distinctions which they imply, are, so to say, made to shine forth through the utilization of the rites which in themselves are formalistic trivia unless conducive to this purpose. Another aspect of the same endeavour involves the Rectification of Names so that terms correspond with the values and obligations which constitute their inner nature. The cardinal strength of Confucian thinking, particularly on the social level, arises from the fact that there is no such thing as a 'value-free' act; everything is seen as the expression of an ethical imperative. Consequently, in the political sphere, the mere regulation of social behaviour through punitive systems can never be an end in itself. Order could really only be attained through guiding men to an awareness of the values latent in them. This could be done, apart from the example set by the ruler, through the rules of ritual —the rules of propriety serve as dykes to keep the passions of the people, whether arising from pride or poverty, within bounds.[43] The idea of order for Confucius is inseparable from the idea of hierarchy. "Thus it is that there are the grades of the noble and the mean, the distinctions of dress, the different places at court; and so the people (are taught to) give place to one another."[44] But although men were characterized with reference to their position in the hierarchy, it did not mean that the hierarchy existed as brute force coercing each individual into a niche. The hierarchy was a whole, and it was vital to its efficient working that each member of it interiorized—and not just obeyed—the values appropriate to his condition, and, as we have seen earlier, the overlapping nature of the categories of the hierarchy mean that the same individual belonged to more than one at the same time so that the fundamental imperatives were common to all and ran through the entire scheme. It is precisely because of the existence of this level of uniformity that the ruler can set an example to all, irrespective of individual condition. That Confucius did not intend the hierarchy to operate through overwhelming power alone is apparent in his awareness of the autonomy of individual volition: "The commander of the forces of a large state may be carried off, but the will of even a common man cannot be taken from him."[45]

The role of the hierarchic principle in acting as a buffer between the individual and the state, and the severe consequences resultant upon its abandonment, will be dealt with in greater detail in the chapter on the Legalists. Moreover, certain aspects of Confucius' thought, notably those connected with the espousal of the meritocratic principle and the departure from the feudal scheme which this implies, will be covered in the section devoted to the historical development of Legalist theory.

CHAPTER V

Section 2. The Confucian Perspective: Mencious and Hsün-tzu

This section will consider the two major exponents of the Confucian School, Mencius and Hsün-tzu in our period; though Mencius does not alter the direction of Confucian thought, his dictum regarding the basic goodness of man is of some significance in that it constitutes a thesis in opposition to which Hsün-tzu, by way of an antithesis, asserts the fundamental evil of man and thus establishes a link between Confucian and Legalist thought.

The overall structure of the thought of Mencius (c. 372-289 B.C.) is almost identical with that of Confucius, and in matters of politics, like the latter, he eschews the idea that a government should seek only utilitarian profit—not only because inner cultivation is more important than external success but also because an exclusive concern of each with his own profit would lead to the endangering of the state.[46] Thus, even at a practical level, he does not accept the principle that the good of the society as a whole can be seen as a sum of the good of individuals. This is obviously not to argue that he regards the state as a transcendent entity or that, conversely, he regards the principle as being false at a purely economic level—here he would argue that the good of each can indeed be the basis of the good of all—but simply that, in perfect keeping with the tenor of Confucian thought, he regards *jen* and *yi* (benevolence and righteousness) as more important than mere expedient gain.[47] When asked what virtue was required to attain to the royal position, Mencius answered, "The love and protection of the people; with this there is no power which can prevent a ruler from attaining to it."[48] In general, Mencius devotes considerably more attention to the material forces in government than Confucius. He repeatedly advocates low taxes,[49] and asserts that with the common run of mankind a stable livelihood is vital to virtue:

> "if they have not a stable livelihood, it follows that they will not have a fixed heart. And if they have not a fixed heart, there is nothing which they will not do in the way of self-abandonment, of moral deflection, of depravity, and of wild license. When they thus have been involved in crime, to follow them up and punish them; this is to entrap the people."[50]

Evil for him is thus basically materially rooted—

> "Notwithstanding good years, their lives are continually embittered and, in bad years, they do not escape punishing. In such circumstances they only try to save themselves from death, and are afraid they will not succeed. What leisure have they to cultivate propriety and righteousness?"[51]

The road which the ruler ought to follow in order to ensure harmony is not one of mere suppression, but on the other hand he is not asked to be impossibly good; Mencius acknowledges that men require pleasure and he asserts that "if people generally are not able to enjoy themselves, they condemn their superiors."[52] The ruler himself is not asked to abandon his love for valour or wealth as such, but he is exhorted, perhaps rather optimistically, to indulge his fondness for these values in such a way that the people too can gratify similar urges.[53]

Mencius sees the clue to good government as lying precisely in this kind of reciprocity, and it constitutes his universal imperative. On one occasion when there was a clash between the states of Lu and Chou, the Duke Mu was enraged that his people had watched thirty-three of their officers being killed and had not stirred to their defense. Mencius pointed out that when the people were starving although the state granaries were full, none of the officers sought to mitigate their distress and so "now at length the people have paid back the conduct of their officers to them. Do not you, O Prince, blame them."[54] The reciprocity principle with its implied attitude of an eye for an eye and a tooth for a tooth is in somewhat incongruous contrast with his basic belief in the goodness[55] of man and the esssentially compassionate nature of humanity,[56] but the statement regarding the innate worthiness of man gains its full significance only when seen in the context of what it implies for government—and this is seen most clearly in his dialogue with the philosopher Kao.

> "The philosopher Kao said, 'Man's nature is like the Ch'i willow and righteousness is like the making of cups and bowls from the Ch'i willow.'[57] Mencius replied, 'Can you, leaving untouched the nature of the willow, make with it cups and bowls? You must do violence and injury to the willow before you can make cups and bowls with it. If you must do violence and injury to the willow in order to make cups and bowls with it, on your principles you must in the same way do violence and injury to humanity in order to fashion from it benevolence and righteousness. Your words Alas! would certainly lead all men to reckon benevolence and righteousness to be calamities.' "[58]

He goes on to specify—"From the feelings proper to it, it is constituted for the practice of what is good. This is what I mean in saying that the nature is good.[59] Thus commiseration, shame, dislike, reverence, respect, approving and disapproving are common to all men, and from these spring the complementary virtues of benevolence, righteousness, propriety and knowledge—and all these are intrinsic and not extraneously imposed.[60] In this respect the Sage and the common run of mankind are made of the same clay, and what differentiates one from the other, or good from evil, are the circumstances involved.[61] Mencius is asserting, not the practical and existent goodness of men, but their latent virtue—which he characterizes as their noumenal and true nature. Here again, as we saw implied in Confucius, evil is seen not as a basic quality but as a consequence of material deprivations, the result of an ignorance rooted in poverty and hardship. Because man has a beneficent noumenal nature, Mencius is opposed to the kind of conditioning suggested by the philosopher Kao which assumes that the original nature of man would never of itself move to the good. Both from the point of view of moral cultivation and from that of virtuous behaviour the main necessity is the rediscovery of this primordial goodness, and this is an end to which positivistic means are obviously not oriented: "Good government does not lay hold of the people so much as good instructions."[62] Education rather than efficient rule is what is important. True to the basic tenets of Confucian thought, there is very little difference in Mencius between excellent government and the personal elucidation by the ruler of his virtue—which display acts as an educational force. Good government and empire accrue automatically upon the blazoning forth of virtue[63] owing to the vast power of example.[64] The differentiation made between mere conditioning force and the moral power which characterizes the true ruler finds succinct expression in the distinction made between the institutions of the Hegemon (*pa*) and the Sovereign (*wang*). It is true that in doing this Mencius is probably making an adverse comment on his times in which the strength of the legitimate house of Chou had been severely eroded, but it will suffice for present purposes to point out that the *pa* is defined as one who "using force, makes a pretence to benevolence (and) is the leader of the princes,"[65] while "He who, using virtue, practises benevolence, is the sovereign of the kingdom."[66] Mencius not only stresses that the rule of force is based merely on the passive helplessness of others while that of virtue is founded on a sincere and pleased submission,[67] but he also sees, in purely empirical terms, that the attempt to conquer through force is ultimately doomed to fail because it pits a minority against a majority who are bound to triumph in the end.[68] Thus, not only is violent conquest wrong, it is also futile—like "climbing a tree to seek for fish,"[69] while virtue is both correct and effective.

In this context, the attention that Mencius pays to the

question of legitimacy is worthy of some note. Based on the notion that the manifestion of virtue was the determining mark of the sovereign, Mencius offers a guarded defense of usurpation. He argues that the killings of the last ruler of the Shang, Chou, by King Wu was not an act of regicide and could not be construed as violating the just relations which ought to prevail between a ruler and a minister. "He who outrages the benevolence proper to his nature is called a robber . . . The robber and ruffian we call a mere fellow. I have heard of the cutting off of the fellow Chou, but I have not heard of the putting a sovereign to death, in his case."[70] Mencius further holds that it is not in the power of the sovereign to hand over the throne to the person of his choice; thus Yao did not give the throne to Shun but Shun acceded to the throne by the will of Heaven,[71] by which is not meant that Heaven issues specific injunctions on the matter, but that Heaven makes its will felt through the virtue and ability of the one that it has chosen.[72] In other words, the virtue of an individual is an indication that he is Heaven's chosen one, and his virtue enables him to deserve and win the throne. But the criterion of virtue in itself is not paramount. Thus, for example, Confucius was deserving of the throne by that standard, yet he failed to gain it, and apropos of this Mencius inserts another condition: "In the case of a private individual obtaining the throne, there must be in him virtue equal to that of Shun or Yü; and moreover there must be the presenting of him to Heaven by the preceding sovereign. It was on this account that Confucius did not obtain the throne."[73] The legendary sovereigns obviously possessed both these qualifications, but the tyrant Chou lacked virtue while Confucius lacked the introduction of a previous sovereign. Mencius thus ingeniously contrives to combine the principle of virtue with that of continuity. So far, the principle of blood ties has been ignored and Mencius would appear to be outside the feudal ethic in this respect. But the idea does assert itself rather elliptically in the context of what should be done by the ministers when a prince has faults but refuses to countenance remonstrances. Mencius distinguishes between those ministers who are noble and relatives of the prince and those who are of a different surname. In the former case, if repeated remonstrances fail, they are given the right to dethrone the prince, but in the latter all they can do is to leave the state wherein their advice is endlessly neglected.[74] Thus the right to revolt, and by implication, the notion of legitimacy, is conditioned not only by virtue and the necessity of introduction but also by the factor of blood. In fact, Mencius is sometimes reluctant to let even merit and virtue prevail over familial connections: "The ruler of a state advances to office men of talents and virtue only as a matter of necessity—since he will thereby cause the low to overstep the honourable and the distant to overstep his near relatives, ought he to do so but with caution?"[75]

To revert to the doctrine of human nature, Mencius is not altogether consistent on this score. Sometimes it is assumed that men are, in fact, good, and sometimes that they are good only "by nature" and that this pristine worthiness has been sullied by circumstances and needs to be refurbished. Further, contrary to the postulate that all men are good, and therefore, in potential at least, equally capable of realizing their virtue, he states apropos of the sons of Yao and Shun that they were inferior to their fathers and this "was from Heaven, and what could not be brought about by man"[76]—in other words the differences were decreed once and for all by Heaven. In politics he gives considerable importance to the people,[77] and states that they are best qualified to judge of the virtues of a potential officer.[78] Now, if men were good in practice and cognizant of the true values, this would be perfectly reasonable. but Mencius does not have too much faith in the actual moral stature of the average man. "That whereby man differs from the lower animals is but small. The mass of the people cast it away, while superior men preserve it." This being the case, it is difficult to see why democratic opinion is so recommended. It can be argued that even corrupted men, once they are actually confronted by virtue, will be compelled to acknowledge it—and this is implicit in the thought of Confucius and his belielf in the power of example. Mencius too holds to this idea[79] but again somewhat ambivalently, for he says, "Virtue alone is not sufficient for the exercise of government; laws alone cannot carry themselves into practice."[80] An external system is therefore vital for rule; men cannot be expected to govern themselves.

It may also be mentioned that the doctrine of innate goodness is in no way to be mistaken for egalitarianism although it may appear occasionally in that light. "It is in the nature of things to be of unequal quality" says Mencius in the context of objects, but this is obviously valid for government as well. The equalitarian principle taken seriously would violate the five basic relationships so dear to Confucian thought, and the awareness of this point emerges in Mencius' diatribes against the egalitarian and utilitarian Mohists. For Mencius as for Confucius these relationships and the rituals which symbolize them are not extraneously imposed but immanent in the basic nature of human sentiments—and their hierarchical structure reflects the fact that sentiments necessarily move in the realm of distinctions. The love of a man for his brother's child is different in kind from his affection for the child of his neighbour,[81] and equally, the desire for a ceremonial funeral for one's parents does not derive from social pressures but from the simple inability to countenance their death indifferently.[82] The goodness of human nature thus in no way implies the breakdown of the hierarchy, but rather that it is within the power of each man to realize the values implicit in it. "Mo ti's principle is—to love all equally; which does not acknowledge the peculiar affection due to a father. But to acknowledge neither king nor father is to be in the state of a beast."[83] In political terms, therefore, the doctrine of basic goodness implies neither the belief that man can rule himself without the aid of external regulatory forces nor that a horizontal equality can exist between men. It simply means, as was said above, that people have the intrinsic ability to recognize and respect the internal complements of the forms exemplified by *li*.[84] This had already been implied by Confucius, and Mencius cannot be said to have utilized it to impart a new dimension to Confucian thought. But by taking a definite line on the issue of fundamental human nature—an issue which Confucius had left open[85]—he was to provide a stand in opposition to which Hsün-tzu was to clarify his opposite doctrine. And this shall be our next concern.

Hsün-tzu (c. 300-237 B.C.), the last major figure in Confucian thought in our period, will be dealt with in terms of two major themes: firstly, his defense of *li* and the hierarchy that this implies and, secondly, his view of human nature which, in polar contrast to Mencius, he regards as irretrievably evil. His attitude towards specifically political concerns will then be considered in the light of the two foregoing topics.

Hsün-tzu advocates the necessity for hierarchy on the same grounds that Confucius had adopted, namely, not for reasons of innate differences between men *per se*, but because of the paucity of goods in relation to the infinity of desires.[86] But the fundamental similarity between men that this implies does not mean, as we have already seen with Mencius, that social differences, the differences implicit in the five basic relationships, are not valid and immutable. This fusion of the idea of fundamental similarity with the principle of basic social divisions finds expression in the maxim "Irregular but uniform, oppressive but favourable, unlike but alike—these are the human relationships."[87] Divisions are seen to be imperative for rule—"when everyone's powers are equal, there is no unity in the state; when everyone is equal, there is no one to employ the people on public services. . . . For two nobles cannot serve each other; two commoners cannot employ each other—this is a law of nature."[88] The nature of hierarchy is the nature of order, and it is this principle which enables man to compensate for his intrinsic weakness as compared to the beasts.[89] Unity derives from hierarchy, for if there were no divisions and all were equal, strife would ensure and the great power which derives from unity, and on which civilization depends, would not exist.[90] *Li* and *yi* (righteousness, natural justice, the virtues appropriate to one's status) are the foundations of all social life and thus of all specifically human life.[91] This hierarchy, however, is not automatically manifest; it requires the powers of a sage, a good man, to render it clear and definite, and one of the curses of unbridled egalitarianism is that such a man will not be able to arise and separate the multitude into their proper ranks.[92]

But it is not only in terms of their social status and obligations that people vary; although they may be noumenally the same, considerable variety exists in the amount of knowledge they possess.[93] Here again, the rules of *li*, amplified and expounded by a teacher, are the sole instruments by which one may be educated to a greater degree of virtue. Education in this very fundamental sense is what distinguishes the sage from the ordinary mortal—"He is different and superior to ordinary people (only) in his acquired training."[94] As with Confucius and Mencius, education, the exemplification of *li* by the teacher, is a reflexive activity in that it internalizes the objective social distinctions at the same time that these distinctions are seen as being intrinsic to human nature. He says thus that every man on the street is capable of knowing benevolence (*jen*) and natural justice (*yi*) and recognizes the relations between father and son and prince and minister.[95] The contradiction that this constitutes with his cardinal doctrine of the unworthiness of human nature will be dealt with below, but for the present our main concern is with the importance that Hsün-tzu lays on the question of self-cultivation. A necessary corollary of the belief that it is in the degree of acquired training that men differ is the belief in the power of human will and autonomy. And indeed the status that Hsün-tzu accords to the human *Tao* is more sharply and explicitly differentiated from that of Heaven and Earth than any of his Confucian predecessors. "The Way (*Tao*) is not primarily the Way of Heaven; it is not the Way (*Tao*) of Earth; it is the way (*Tao*) man acts, the way (*Tao*) the superior man acts."[96] This attitude was, of course, implicit in Confucius' own preference for ethics as opposed to metaphysics, and Mencius too had held that men and not Heaven determine calamity or happiness, but the primacy of human will and endeavour gains a new importance when considered in the context of man's fundamentally evil nature, for it becomes the only way of explaining why virtuous acts are, in fact, possible. If man is seen as being part of an over-arching cosmic harmony it is impossible to describe his nature as fundamentally evil, but by a singular paradox Hsün-tzu insists on devalorizing Heaven and making man, with his base nature, not the expression of cosmic harmony, but responsible for that harmony. Thus,

"Heaven and Earth unite and all things are born; the Yin and the Yang meet and mutations begin; original nature and acquired characteristics unite and the country is ruled. Heaven can bring things to birth, but cannot discriminate things; the Earth can support man, but cannot rule men; under the canopy of Heaven the ten thousand things bring humankind to birth, but wait for the Sage and then only are separated in their proper classes and uses. The Ode says:

He has attracted and pacified all spirits
Even the spirits of the River and the loftiest mountain—

this expresses what I mean."[97]

Here, therefore, Hsün-tzu sees *li*—the discriminatory power—not as a cosmological entity, or even as the expression of a cosmological structure, but as a specifically human form. The paradox which confronts us here is that man, irremediably evil, is raised to a position of preeminence as the entity on which *li* depends. Both Heaven and Earth are reduced to principles of fertility and bounty lacking in a distinctively moral nature —and by moral we mean nothing more than the cardinal faculty of making distinctions. And it is perhaps because he has thus devalorized Heaven that he objects to the Taoist philosopher Chuang-tzu on the grounds that he was prejudiced towards Nature (*T'ien*) and was therefore concerned only with the brute, almost mechanistic sequence of cause and effect.[98]

The dilemma which appears to confront Hsün-tzu is how to explain the existence of the Sage given the postulate of a noumenally evil nature. If man is an expression of a harmonious cosmic order he cannot be evil. If that cosmic order is irretrievably bad, then he cannot possibly become good. As such some division becomes necessary, and he therefore impersonalizes Heaven and Earth and constitutes man as the moral entity. By establishing the autonomy of man, his separation from transcendental and pre-given orders, Hsün-tzu is in a position to explain his potential for good despite the fact that he may not be spontaneously urged in that direction. But this, as we shall see, still does not prove that virtue can emerge from a basically evil stratum. For the moment it may be noted that in adopting this scheme he does not abandon the archetypal trinity of Chinese thought, that of Heaven, Man and Earth; his point is to establish that this triad is not a given but depends on the self-cultivation of man and an unremitting concentration on virtue—it is only when this has been done that he is able to establish a triad with Heaven and Earth.[99] Thus, stemming from the idea of human autonomy, self-reliance is constantly stressed; the notion that Heaven's order in itself neither guarantees nor condemns anything.[100] But while, on the one hand, he makes the human *Tao* responsible for engendering distinctions in the otherwise gross and undifferentiated realm of phenomena and thus reducing it to order, he also assumes on the other that Heaven does have an order and that man's role is simply to accord with it. When talking of *li* he says, "this social structure exhibits the same principles as Heaven and Earth; it is of equal permanence with the universe."[101] The contradiction between these statements, implying an innate scheme in the universe which is accessible to man, and his earlier statement making man responsible for such an order, is obvious. Elsewhere Hsün-tzu attempts to blur this distinction by differentiating between the origin of the order and its application to the terrestrial realm:

> "The code of proper conduct (*li*) has three sources: Heaven and Earth gave birth to it—this is a source; the princes and teachers formed it—this is a source. Without Heaven and Earth, how could it be born? Without our ancestors, how could it be produced? Without princes and teachers how could it be given form? If one of these were lacking men would be without peace."[102]

But the contradiction still persists.

The concept of a non-deterministic order was implicit in both Confucius and Mencius, and they both accordingly regarded evil, not as a noumenal quality, but fundamentally as the result of ignorance. The question which is posed by the contradiction in Hsün-tzu is thus not the facile one of how evil can exist when an overriding principle of harmony prevails but, rather, why, if there is a generic similarity between man and Heaven, and Heaven is, so to say, a neutral principle of fecundity, man should be regarded as noumenally evil. Seen from a different angle, it can be said that Mencius was concerned with the problem of evil whereas Hsün-tzu is involved with the problem of good. By saying that man introduces a new dimension of distinctions into the world, he makes man free, since, being responsible for this new principle, he can no longer be regarded simply as a determined expression of cosmic forces. In establishing the principle of freedom he is in a position to explain the possibility of virtue although men may not be naturally good—it becomes a matter of will, discipline and training, and the importance he places on self-reliance and education is thus entirely reasonable. But he then violates the idea of autonomy by laying very assertive stress on the irrevocably base nature of man. And in so doing he is ensnared once more in the fundamental contradiction between the human *Tao* being *sui generis* and at the same time being identical in its inner nature with the *Tao* of Heaven and Earth. If the latter, he cannot ascribe a noumenal nature to man in view of his perception of Heaven as a non-distinctive entity, and if the former, the Heavenly order cannot be regarded as similar to the human one.

A closely related dilemma arises from the consideration of his doctrine that man is basically bad. It is important to stress that this fundamental evil nature is by no means disproved by the fact that man can become virtuous. It is precisely on these grounds that he firmly denies the contention of Mencius that the educatability of men reveals that their original nature is good.[103] For Hsün-tzu, "the nature of man is evil; his goodness is only acquired training. . . . Man originally is envious and naturally hates others."[104] The main difference between the age of the Sage-kings and his own day is not that in the times of the former the original nature of man was good, but simply that the Sage-kings were aware of man's truant nature and thus wholly cognizant of the need to discipline and form him through the forces of *li* and *yi*, laws and ordinances.[105] Mencius' doctrine, according to him, implies that the evil of man is the result of a fall from grace, but if one were to accept the postulate that man is naturally good then it should follow that "without growing away from his first estate, he becomes admirable,"[106] but since his primary urges are Hobbsian, since they are aimed at biological survival and the gratification of natural needs, it is obvious that the rules of courtesy which involve restraint, the granting of precedence and self-control, are opposed to his original nature.[107] All the rules of proper conduct, the codes of *li* and *yi* are therefore not from his original nature but from his acquired training, and he illustrates this with the following striking, if fallacious, example: "The potter pounds and moulds the clay and makes the vessel, but the vessel comes from the potter's acquired skill, not from the potter's innate character."[108] The flaw in the argument, of course, is that it would be quite impossible for the potter to acquire the necessary skill if in some way his innate nature did not possess the ability to acquire that skill. His tenet that "the original nature of man is the beginning and material; acquired characteristics are the beautification and glorification of the original nature"[109] necessarily assumes that the foundations of human nature must, in some fashion, be opposite to the edifice of self-cultivation which is to be reared upon them. And if this is so, then human nature cannot be unmitigatedly bad. In fact, Hsün-tzu does concede this point, without however seeming to be aware that this concession weakens his central postulate. He says, for instance, that "the teacher considers himself to be the measure of all things and honours that which nature has implanted within him. The Ode says:

> He has not learned, he did not know,
> But he followed the laws of God.—

this expresses what I mean."[110] And further he argues that every man on the street can know the difference between father and son and that between the prince and minister—"Thus it is evident that the man on the street possesses the power of knowing and the ability to practise these virtues."[111]

The first of the last two quotations is as Confucian as Taoist, and, in point of the latter, echoes the statements he makes elsewhere,

"For great skill consists in knowing how to do a thing

> without striving; and great wisdom consists in not needing to reflect about things. . . . If a man who has a responsible post attends to what belongs to Nature (*T'ien*), the people of themselves will keep to the right way of life (*Tao*)."[112]

Here again it is assumed that the structure of human life is identical to the structure of the universe, if not formally, at least qualitatively in the sence of a primordial rhythm and sequence. But how can this be made to jibe with the concept of a specifically human *Tao* which introduces distinctions into an undifferentiated world? With regard to the second quotation above relating to the intrinsic abilities of men to recognize and practise distinctions, he goes on to say that the reason why they did not go on to display these powers and become like Yü is the gulf between possibility and ability—

> "For it is true that the man on the street can become a Yü, but it is probably not true that the man on the street has the ability to become a Yü. . . . Then there is a great difference between whether a person has the ability and whether he has the possibility of being so and so. Thus the impossibility for them to exchange places is evident."[113]

By establishing a dichotomy between possibility and ability, and reducing possibility to a mere abstraction, he makes ability the cardinal factor. And, as regards ability, he is willing to countenance the most diverse inequalities between men. His dictum that "the Sage has his original nature in common with ordinary people; he is not different from ordinary people in this respect. He is different and superior to ordinary people in his acquired training,"[114] may lead one to suppose that this is a statement of qualified egalitarianism in its emphasis on the common basic nature of all men, and since they differ only in their acquired characteristics, the emphasis he places on education—the process whereby they acquire these characteristics—is quite justified. If one asserts that all men are equal, then, theoretically at any rate, it is legitimate to ascribe all existent inequalities to external factors, education, environment and so on, and to this extent Hsün-tzu is consistent. But, by bringing in the idea of ability, i.e., the reason why some are able to cultivate themselves better than others, he introduces another internal factor which is not externally explicable. The notion of ability introduces a gratuitous element which detracts from the idea of an attributionally uniform nature. His view of hierarchy then must be seen as deriving not only from the problem posed by limited means and unlimited wants but also from a basic inequality between men. It would perhaps have enabled Hsün-tzu to be more consistent if he had acknowledged this inequality, but in doing so he would have been compelled to give up the definition of human nature as being uniformly depraved. And this in turn would necessitate a less stringent emphasis on discipline and authority than he feels is needed.

Judging from the general tenor of his work, it would appear that Hsün-tzu differs from his Confucian predecessors not so much in terms of fundamental tenets, beliefs or dogmas as in the uneasy conviction that the exemplary power of virtue alone was not as great as was requisite for the ordering of mankind. In this, he was not far removed from Mencius who also felt that virtue alone was insufficient for rule. It is therefore not so much in specific details that his positivism is revealed as in subtle variations of emphasis. He is in agreement with all the basic political doctrines of Confucius and Mencius and says that although there has been bad government under good laws, there has never been bad government under a superior man[115]—and the *pa* is defined as the one who depends on laws.[116] He further distinguishes between a *pa* and a true sovereign on the grounds that the *pa's* benevolence was a pretense aimed at profit and that although they were able and efficient they were not truly virtuous, while the true kings were genuinely worthy and thus able to manifest their virtue throughout the empire.[117] He condemns the rampant power politics of his time by pointing out that "when a ruler does not exert himself to follow the way (*Tao*) but instead enlarges his power, he puts himself in a dangerous position."[118] And for this reason, when his student Li Ssu pointed out that the power of Ch'in was based not on *jen* and *yi* but simply on taking advantage of the course of events, Hsün-tzu attempts to counter the argument on the same grounds as used by Mencius. He points out that precisely because Ch'in's eminence was based on power alone, it lived in perpetual fear of being crushed by its enemies in concert. Thus Ch'in's advantage is an "unadvantageous advantage."[119] Like Mencius again, he offers a qualified justification of usurpation but, significantly, for a rather different reason. While Mencius had supported usurpation primarily on the grounds of the ruler's lack of virtue, Hsün-tzu justifies it on grounds of his inability to control the empire—a far more empirical criterion.[120] It can be argued that in the framework of Confucian thought ability and virtue are synonymous, but as Hsün-tzu's remarks regarding Duke Huan of Ch'i reveal, he was only too aware of the fact that genuine executive ability could go hand in hand with moral depravity—"Alas, Duke Huan of Ch'i had the greatest talents in the world; who could destroy him?"[121]

Perhaps the most significant aspect of Hsün-tzu's thought is his acute awareness of the principle of *shih* or power, a doctrine commonly associated with the Legalist Shen Tao. This we shall meet with again in the chapter on the Legalists and we shall, for the present, consider only Hsün-tzu's own appreciation of it. The idea is intimately connected with the notion of what might be called instrumentality, the idea that external forms have a power of their own with its covert implication of the insufficiency of virtue and the need for objective structures. He puts this tenet into the mouth of Confucius :[122] "If he borrows a horse and carriage, it does not aid his feet, yet he can travel a thousand *li*. If he borrows a boat and oars, even though he cannot swim, he can cross rivers or seas. The nature of the superior man is no different; he needs to use implements."[123] The importance of this doctrine, and its fundamental incompatibility with the essence of Confucianism lies in its emphasis on externality. Confucius himself did not underestimate the importance of external forms—it would have been impossible to do so given the importance he laid on *li*—but his kind of externality was one which constituted only an outward and visible token of inner distinctions and sentiments; it did not see objective structures as having a potency all their own and qualitatively different from that of man himself.[124] To be more graphic in terms of Hsün-tzu's example, the boat is an external facility whose efficacy has nothing whatsoever to do with the nature of the one who utilizes it, except of course in terms of his manipulative ability. With regard to the principle of *shih*, external agencies are no longer the objective correlatives of inner states of being and their power, but substitutes for them, and the fact that they can thus function indicates that they possess a validity and efficacy of their own which is independent of the nature of those who employ them. This opens the way to the possibility of rule through technique as against virtue, and technical ability can replace moral worth. The ruler in himself becomes unimportant save in the context of how skillful he is at manipulating the mechancial causality of pleasure and pain, rewards and punishments. This impersonality of government is, as will be seen, an important aspect of Legalist dogma, but as the resurgence of Confucianism under the Han was to prove, the cold technocratic sophistication of Legalism had to be tempered and assimilated with the belief in the inner man before a viable and stable system of government could be secured. In brief, the acknowledgment (and utilization) of the intrinsic independent power of external agencies detracts from the primacy of the individual, and the importance of the concept of self-cultivation which this implies. Government becomes the conditioning of the individual from the outside rather than the formal expression of the self-cultivation of various but similar individuals.

It would, of course, be quite erroneous to impute this attitude full-grown to Hsün-tzu, but his awareness of the principle must find a place in the history of the intellectual development of Legalist thought wherein it plays a most important role. In fact, even Mencius exhibits a somewhat shadowy awareness of this idea and mentions how much more virtue would shine were it to be placed in a prominent position,[125] but the basic dynamic of his argument is in the direction of self-cultivation.

The other aspect in which Hsün-tzu again draws very close to the Legalists is when he says: "That a man's virtue should not correspond to his rank; that his ability should not correspond to his official grade; that rewards should not fit merit; that punishments should not fit the crime—there is no misfortune greater than this.[126] This attitude is, in a sense, already implicit in the Confucian doctrine of *cheng-ming* or the Rectification of Names, but while Confucius still seems to be thinking in terms of the five basic relationships, and the duties and obligations which they imply, as the foundation on which good government depends, Hsün-tzu would appear to be using the doctrine in a more technical sence, particularly appropriate to administrative ends, that is, he utilizes it in a bureaucratic spirit. Here too the Legalists were to be far more explicit, but in his stress on the importance of punishment he reveals a very similar attitude towards political positivism, "Hence in good government the punishments are severe; in bad governments the punishments are light.[127]

In conclusion, Hsün-tzu's work reveals a somewhat split spirit divided between faith in the basic Confucian dogmas and the conviction that nevertheless virtue had to be prompted by more assertive means. More than his predecessors he gets involved, perhaps despite himself, in the actual mechanics of power—as his concern with (what was later to become, in Legalist thought, the principle of) *shih*, the doctrine of equipoised function and reward and his ideal of punishment avow. Further, the doctrine of the unmitigatedly evil nature of man, a nature which allowed virtue not through intrinsic change but simply through educational grafting that left the basic substratum untouched, cannot but be seen as conducing to the behavioural conditioning of the Legalists. If human nature cannot be altered, one can only limit the problem to assuring acceptable political and social behaviour. Mencius had also acknowledged that men were often bad in practice, but his belief that men were fundamentally good allowed him to retain his faith in the power of example and to avoid the temptation of external control. By regarding them as evil, Hsün-tzu abandons this optimistic hope and starts down the despairing road of control through the reflexes of pleasure and pain.

CHAPTER VI

Political Power and the Taoist Way

CHAPTER VI

Our purpose in this Chapter will not be to give a critique of Taoism in general—however possible or desirable that is—but simply to concentrate on those aspects of it which are pertinent to issues of political power. The two works which are to be discussed are the great classics of Taoist thought, the *Tao Te Ching* and the *Chuang-tzu*, both of which are known to have existed in some form since the 3rd centary B.C.[1] There is a perceptible difference between them in terms of philosophical emphasis and, in general, the latter is more gay and dazzling in its verve and freedom than the former. Nevertheless, in the context of their views which have important political implications, there is little which distinguishes them. Since the *Tao Te Ching*—as D.C. Lau has pointed out[2]—was largely written, or compiled, on the assumption that the Sage was also a ruler and is to that extent somewhat more temporally oriented, we shall devote the bulk of our attention to this work.

The cardinal principle of Taoism is, as has often been pointed out, that of *wu-wei* or non-action rather than inaction. In Lao-tzu this axiom does not imply the total absence of political structure. As indicated above, he often sees the Sage as being synonymous with the king, and he admits the king to be one of the four great things—"Hence the way is great; heaven is great; earth is great; and the king is also great. Within the realm there are four things that are great, and the king counts as one."[3] In this Lao-tzu is not far from the

Confucian spirit, and like them he lays great stress on the importance of the teacher:

> Not to value the teacher
> Nor to love the material
> Though it seems clear, betrays great bewilderment.[4]

The true performance of the kingly function is seen, in fact, as a way to return to the infinite:

> If you are a model to the empire,
> Then the constant virtue will not be wanting
> And you will return to the infinite.[5]

Here it is clear that it is not action *in toto* that is condemned but only that which does not conduce to "constant virtue." Again, he lays great stress on the importance of government in its more pragmatic form:

> In government it is order that matters;
> In affairs it is ability that matters.[6]

And the same attitude is evident in his concern with corruption and the disparities of wealth as well as in his castigation of those in power who take "the lead in robbery."[7] He is equally cognizant of the importance of the economic factor in rule, and admonishes the Sage-king to a liberal and lenient policy: "Do not constrict their living space; do not press down on their means of livelihood. It is because you do not press down on them that they will not weary of the burden."[8] And for the same reasons he deplores war:

> Where troops have encamped
> There will brambles grow;
> In the wake of a mighty army
> Bad harvests follow without fail.[9]

In all this there is little that is not in common with Confucius and Mencius, and this is even true regarding Lao-tzu's antipathy towards positive rule. "Whoever takes the empire and wishes to do anything to it I see will have no respite. The empire is a sacred vessel and nothing should be done to it."[10] Confucius too, as we have attempted to argue, believes in a kind of non-rule to the extent that good government is seen to accrue spontaneously from the fulfillment of the five basic relationships, and it is not so much in terms of the practical political implications of their doctrines that they vary as in their conceptions of virtue *per se*. Lao-tzu undermines the entire Confucian edifice by regarding its cardinal tenets as being signs of a fall from grace, or, more precisely, as a degeneration into the realm of polar opposites from the undifferentiated unity of the true way. He thus says:

> When the great way falls into disuse
> There are benevolence and rectitude.[11]

Even the hallowed virtues of filiality and loyalty are seen to be the result of the same decay:

> When the six relations are at variance
> There are filial children.[12]

and

> When the state is benighted
> There are loyal ministers.[13]

The major categorizations of the Confucian school, no less than the rites and rituals which exemplify them,[14] are all thus seen as springing from a lack of virtue – that is, an effortless and harmonious accord with the Way. It is perhaps important to note that what Lao-tzu objects to is not the existence of the six relations *per se*—he obviously regards them as desirable—but the fact that the people have become conscious of the moral desirability of these relationships. It is the pharisaic self-consciousness of this type of virtue that he deplores, the fall from a spontaneous natural probity to a synthetic and a structured one. Although, at a certain level, Lao-tzu also uses categories, they are provisional and very far from being rigid—

a set of stepping-stones on the way to the great unity within which differences are subsumed and which itself is incapable of being formulated verbally owing to the incapacity of speech to transcend the limitations of opposites.

> Man models himself on earth,
> Earth on heaven,
> Heaven on the way,
> And the way on that which is naturally so.[15]

Thus even the Way, to the extent that it has been formulated, should not be taken as a tangible entity but only as a pointer to that intangible potency which permeates all. To revert to the contrast with the Confucians, they too had regarded the formal paraphernalia of rites and ceremonies only as an external sign denoting internal states of mind, but what Lao-tzu seems to be at pains to point out is that even the Confucian inner values are polarized, they move within the opposed limitations of filiality and disobediency, loyalty and betrayal, merit and unworthiness, so that the very assertion of virtue implies the existence of vice. Man in the Confucian world, so far as Lao-tzu is concerned, has been alienated from virtue precisely to the extent that he has become aware of it. Thus, "The whole world recognizes the beautiful as the beautiful, yet this is only the ugly, the whole world recognizes the good as the good, yet this is only the bad."[16] And it is the same when it comes to merit, for, talking of the way which provides for all facelessly without seeking either gratitude or possession, he points out that:

> It is because it lays claim to no merit
> That its merit never deserts it.[17]

The very fact that the Way, in contrast to the Confucian values, transcends the realms of opposites, makes it impossible to describe. One can deal with it only in terms of its attributes, and the gap ever yawns between its manifestations and its being. In terms of its main qualities then, for that is all that is accessible to speech, it is the force which harmonizes bipolarities—those of the something and nothing, the difficult and the easy, the long and the short, the high and the low and the before and the after.[18] Perhaps it is more accurate to say that from the perspective of the Way these contrasts stand revealed as illusory.[19] To continue, the Way effects all things, nourishes all beings, accomplishes all tasks and yet does so without establishing any claim.[20] "Do that which consists in taking no action, and order will prevail."[21] But it is not action as such which he opposes but only that type of action which seeks to impose on the Way. If, on the other hand, one should "act from knowledge of the constant," one's actions will lead to impartiality and a return to the Way.[22] Action, therefore, has a certain circularity—if it arises from the Way then it will reaffirm one in the Way. What is inveighed against is simply what may be termed linear action arising from mere wilfullness or from a dogmatic or narrow idea of virtue. This circularity of action is, of course, a device to escape from the Manicheism implicit in all acts, the polarization that Lao-tzu is most anxious to avoid. And this attempt to evade the action-reaction pendulum contingent upon all deeds is a very important feature of Taoist thought. The possible avenues out of the dilemma are either a literal non-action in the social and political field or the performance of action in such a way that the personal deliberative aspect of it is toned down to the maximum point. There are traces of both these approaches in Lao-tzu, but in general it would perhaps be fair to say that whereas Chuang-tzu inclines towards the former, Lao-tzu aims largely at the latter. This point, that is the desire to remove the reaction which is latent in every action, can be illustrated with the help of his views on war. One of the points, and by no means the least important given the background of non-action, is that war is "something which is liable to rebound."[23] Being an example par excellence of assertive action it entails a response, an endless systole and diastole of attack and counter-attack. Therefore war, if it has to be fought, is to be scaled down as much as possible—"One who is good aims only at bringing his campaign to a conclusion and dare not thereby intimidate."[24]

In the context of rule, the specific form that this attitude invokes is one of detachment and non-specialization. With the empire, as with all else, personal volition must make way for something greater.

> Have in your hold the great image
> And the empire will come to you.[25]

The ideal emptiness of the ruler whose power yet manifests itself finds a magnificently succinct expression in the statement:

> Thirty spokes
> Share one hub.[26]

And the main question which the ruler ought to ask himself is:

> Can you love the people and govern the state
> Without resorting to action?[27]

A truly effective ruler—as in the case of genuine virtue—is so inconspicuous as almost to escape notice. "The best of all rulers is but a shadowy presence to his subjects."[28] The Sage-king, embodying as he does the nebulous but pervasive potency of the Way, must not be accomplished in specific tasks, for particular skills, like the virtues of the Confucians, are exclusive and imply dichotomies. Hence although he must utilize them, he himself transcends them and relegates their mastery to his subordinates. Thus, "When the uncarved block shatters, it becomes vessels. The Sage makes use of these and becomes the lord over the officials.[29] This is a significant point as it goes against the general tenor of Taoist thought—that of an anarchic dislike of external control and its preference for a bemused, unself-conscious efficacy arising from what may be termed an effortless oceanic sense of unity with the world. As D.C. Lau points out, the infant is a frequently used symbol in Lao-tzu for this state and that because "Its bones are weak and its sinews supple yet its hold is firm."[30] Given this condition it would appear that there would be no need for external control. The existence of an institutional framework is both an index of moral decay and a contributing cause to that decay, and the road to purity should therefore lie in the destruction of such rigid schema.

> Exterminate the Sage, discard the wise;
> And the people will benefit a hundredfold;
> Exterminate benevolence, discard rectitude,
> And the people will again be filial.[31]

But how is one to reconcile this kind of unwitting harmony which is totally independent of political structure with his remark above that the Sage needs his "vessels"—his technical subordinates—and, moreover, what role can those who are externalists by the fact of the partiality and exclusiveness of their skills play in this context? The point can of course be made that Lao-tzu has in mind two distinct stages, that of the tutelage of the people and that of the period when people have matured sufficiently to become "babes." But apart from the fact that the text affords no basis for this conclusion, it ignores the more significant point that the unheeding harmony of the Taoist ideal is not merely a quantitative development and a result of technocratic manipulation but a qualitatively distinct phenomenon. It is difficult to see how mechanical manipulation can lead to a unitary consciousness. This point will be reverted to later in the context of the affiliations between the Taoists and the Legalists. Somewhat distinct from this, Lao-Tzu offers two guidelines for the governance of the people. These are not mutually exclusive, but one has a stronger authoritarian flavour than the other. "Therefore in governing the people, the Sage empties their minds but fills their bellies, weakens their wills but strengthens their bones. He always keeps them innocent of knowledge and free from desire, and ensures that the clever never dare to act."[32] The other approach, like that of the Confucians, stresses the importance of models.

> The way never acts yet nothing is left undone.
> Should lords and princes be able to hold fast to it,
> The myriad creatures will be transformed of their own accord.[33]

In parenthesis it may be noted here that Lao-tzu obviously tacitly accepts the formal hierarchical structure of his time, but his ideas of hierarchy have little in common with the accepted notions of social stratification. To continue, the potency of the Tao is made manifest through personal example. And it is also this force which will prevent moral retrogression, for:

> After they are transformed, should desire raise its head,
> I shall press it down with the weight of the nameless uncarved block.
> The nameless uncarved block
> Is but freedom from desire,
> And if I cease to desire and remain still,
> The empire will be at peace of its own accord.[34]

Here again one comes upon the emphasis on the ontological quality of the ruler—and just as the *Tao* itself is undifferentiated and incapable of being truly formulated in specific terms, so with the ruler himself. We have earlier noted the distinction drawn between the Sage-king—the uncarved block—and the "vessels" who have categorizable skills, and the importance placed upon the absence of desire on the part of the ruler is because desires imply dislikes and thus once again draw one into the futility of infinite polarities which lead to the spiral decline of dogmatic virtues and an increasing decadence.

The best example which illustrates the Taoist penchant for the yielding over the strong, the flexible over the rigid, water and the baby against the rock and the soldier, is perhaps his view of conquest which might as well be called his doctrine of subordination.

> The female always gets the better of the male by stillness.
> Being still, she takes the lower position.
> Hence the large state, by taking the lower position, annexes the small state;
> The small state, by taking the lower position, affiliates itself to the large state.
> Thus the one, by taking the lower position, annexes;

The other, by taking the lower position, is annexed.
All that the large state wants is to take the other under its wing;
All that the small state wants is to have its services accepted by the other.
If each of the two wants to find its proper place,
It is meet that the large should take the lower position.[35]

The idea of conquest, far from being one of imposition, is one of subordination. By taking the lower position one is both the annexer and the annexed. This dissolution of traditional opposites is not just a clever play on words but constitutes the very quiddity of Taoist thought. What Lao-tzu has done is to dissolve the vertical stratification commonly associated with hierarchy while at the same time retaining the idea of subordination, which, along with the allegiance to a common ideal, is the essence of any hierarchy. This springs naturally from the idea of the merger of opposites; thus, even the idea of a political hierarchy becomes meaningless when strength is equated with yielding and the yielding are the strong. But it is still possible to retain the idea of subordination since the parties between whom this takes place are not formal classes or castes in the final analysis but the *Tao* itself and the Sage-king. In this sense one can say that the Way subordinates itself to the Way. Conquest is now a competition in yielding, as indeed is rule:

Therefore, desiring to rule over the people,
One must in one's words humble oneself before them;
And desiring to lead the people,
One must, in one's person, follow behind them.[36]

It will be clear, in the light of what has gone before, that what is meant is not the idea of the ruler merely articulating the aggregate sum of disparate desires of the people and formulating his policies on the basis of popular demand. That this is not so, despite appearances, is suggested by the use of the "uncarved block" in pressing down upon desires. In this sense it is possible to establish an opposition between the ruler—himself without desire—and the people—whose desires are to be eroded. But such an opposition would not be able to explain the above quotation, and what Lao-tzu would seem to mean is that the unity between the ruler and the people really springs from the fact that they are co-dwellers in the *Tao*. But we have seen that the essence of the *Tao* consists in yielding, in being like water, so that it is perfectly in keeping with it to say that the ruler must follow the people. Thus the relation between the ruler and the ruled is not based on greater and lesser power but precisely on the opposite, the more and the less yielding, with the ruler always constituting the paradigm of the former. It is because of his capacity for subordination, for yielding, that the ruler is ruler. "It is because he does not contend that no one in the empire is in a position to contend with him."[37]

Having surveyed the major political tenets in Lao-tzu's thought, it may be well—in anticipation as it were—to say a few words about the affiliations between Taoist and Legalist thought. Taoism evisages an automatic order in the world, an order which manifest its efficacy without ratiocination and without conscious effort. The Legalists have the same idea but with the cardinal difference that the ends of the axis on which their universe smoothly revolves consist of rewards and punishments. Pleasure and pain were elevated into nearly cosmic principles whose interaction would inevitably entail order and stability. Thus the heedless and fluid potency of the Taoist Way was replaced by an essentially mechanical dynamic. In doing so, the very spirit of Taoism was violated, for Lao-tzu no less that Confucius is emphatic on the point that

> The better known the laws and edicts
> The more thieves and robbers there are.[38]

At the same time, however, Legalism clung tenaciously to the Taoist ideal of impersonality. For the Taoists, impersonality was the logical corollary of the fact that the *Tao* was faceless, and from this sprang the necessary emphasis on secrecy:

> The fish must not be allowed to leave the deep;
> The instruments of power in a state must not be revealed to anyone.[39]

As D.C. Lau has pointed out,[40] the supposedly sinister aspects of Lao-tzu are generally open to an innocent explanation, and this would seem to be so of secrecy. The instruments of power in a Taoist state are adherence to the mysterious promptings and rhythm of the Way, and their disclosure would not be the revelation of a secret in the ordinary sense but a formulation of the Way—a dangerous distortion in that the *Tao* has been seen to be unformulatable. Thus disclosure of the *Tao* would mean its death, its need for secrecy—that is, its need to remain uncategorized—is like the fish's need for the deep.

It is nevertheless difficult to deny that in certain other aspects Legalism appears as a logical development of ideas implicit in Taoism. We have frequently noted above the mention that Lao-tzu makes of "vessels," and to the extent that they are "vessels" the uncarved block has been shattered. In other words, Lao-tzu acknowledges the existence and the importance of specialization, of those who are—by the very fact of their specialization—separated from the Way. The ruler himself may emboby the ideal of Taoist unity, but this will not be true of those technocrats whom he manipulates and utilizes. At the same time, we have noted that Lao-tzu does not specifically attack the social structure of which he was a part. He does not argue against filiality or fraternal affection as such but only against the awareness of these values. Similarly he does not inveigh against the feudal structure *per se*—he acknowledges lords and princes and indeed requires that they constitute the archetype of the Way. Now these two disparate points are connected by the fact that they both seem to be extraneous to the basic values of Taoism, and we shall consider them in turn.

The manipulative attitude implicit in the use of the "vessels" may be seen in the light of the essential impersonality of the universe, an impersonality shared by the Sage: "Heaven and earth are ruthless, and treat the myriad creatures as straw dogs; the Sage is ruthless and treats the people as straw dogs." This somewhat chilling utterance stresses the fundmental indifference of the *Tao* and its total independence of men and things. The Way uses things in the sense that it flows through all without particular respect or consideration for the concrete forms which it activates in the course of its passage. In this respect there is a parallel between it and the attitude of the ruler towards his "vessels." At the same time it is difficult to deny that the division between the ruler and the specialists establishes a form of polarity which, in general, Lao-tzu is so keen on avoiding. The problem is that the *Tao*, as an indivisible totality, cannot be reduced into being merely the sum of its separate parts—and yet this is precisely what happens when the attempt is made to make the *Tao* manifest through the utilization of specialists. The holistic nature of the Way makes it imperative that the *Tao* be exemplified in its ambiguous entirety—by the power of being—or not at all. The minute that specialized agencies are utilized the *Tao* is fragmented and order can be maintained only by a mechanical equilibrium of checks and balances as opposed to the effortless harmony engendered by a common dwelling in the Way. It is thus necessary to separate the idea of impersonality from that of the utilization of specialists. Impersonality *per se* only establishes the total independence of the *Tao* from all specific phenomena, while the utilization of the "vessels" on the contrary establishes the dependence of the Sage on specialized organs. The ruthlessness of the *Tao* is simply another way of affirming that it can never be captured in terms of phenomena and that any attempt at its reification is self-defeating. The same logic holds good at the level of using technicians—the ruler himself may be unified with the *Tao*, but as soon as he uses his virtue to activate specialized agencies to transmit his potency what is transmitted is not the synthetic and unitary power of the *Tao* but mere legislative injunctions which bear all the defects of polarity. We return, therefore, to the point that the *Tao* can only be transmitted ontologically and not through a bureaucratic technocracy, and while this contradiction is not central to Lao-tzu's thought as a whole, it is crucial to the Legalists as it is this that enables their ideal ruler to be mysterious, elusive and unmoving while still constituting the source whence specialized functionaries derive their power. Similarly, the non-divisible nature of Taoist thought makes it difficult to see why familial and feudal values should be of any importance whatsoever. Taoism has no room for divisions because they are all regarded as so many impediments in the path of the Way and yet Lao-tzu does not follow the social implications of his stand and declare, like Mo Ti, the necessity of abolishing all social distinctions. This is precisely what the Legalists did in attacking the aristocracy and even in attempting to break down—as we shall see—the family unit. Here once more one is confronted with the peculiar congruence of two very dissimilar philosophies: Taoism desires an absence of social structures since it sees them as polarizing influences, while Legalism accepts the same logic for very different reasons—the destruction of intermediaries between the state and the individual in order to maximize centralized authority.

One of the main difficulties in attempting to establish a distinction between the Taoists and the Legalists on the basis of the mechanical and manipulatory nature of the latter is that the Legalists can always assert that all they are interested in doing is in formulating a methodology by which the Taoist goal can be attained. In this Lao-tzu himself had given a clue when he spoke of the extermination of the Sage and of benevolence and of the importance of discarding rectitude for the sake of returning the people to the Way. Further, the Legalists were sophisticated enough to stress that the aim of punishment was the ending of punishment and thus they cannot be accused of loving punitive measures for their own sake. The differentiation of the two doctrines has thus perhaps to be sought on a different plane. The answer possibly lies in the almost simplistic point that Taoism is not a doctrine open to social institutionalization and that the disturbing similarities of theory and differences of tone between Taoism and Legalism both derive from the fact that Legalism is an attempt at making Taoism a socially applicable dogma. And we have already dealt with the kind of problems created by this misguided and necessarily futile attempt.

In the foregoing analysis of the political aspects of Taoist thought the *Tao Te Ching* has been consistently in the forefront and the reason for this is not an underestimation of the *Chuang-tzu* but simply that from the point of view of political perspectives, as opposed to the philosophical, there is not much to distinguish them. The main features of Taoist thought, its dislike for the rigid virtues of the Confucians and the Mohists,[42] its antipathy towards categorizations,[43] its penchant for the harmonization of opposites,[44] the idea of the impersonlity of the Sage[45] and the primacy of the Way[46] are all held in common. The main differentiating point perhaps lies in the emphasis laid on matters of temporal import. Whereas *Lao-tzu's* Sage is, however inconspicuously, normally a king, Chuang-tzu with effervescent good humour disregards the worldly stage altogether. "This man, with this virtue of his, is about to embrace the ten thousand things and roll them into one. Though the age calls for reform, why should he wear himself out over the affairs of the world?"[47] Lao-tzu and Chuang-tzu alike proclaim the importance of remaining as obscure and nebulous as possible, but the latter revels in the security which ensues from the fact of being functionally useless[48] in addition to realizing that "virtue takes no form."[49] It is from this spritely and acerbic lucidity and blithe disregard for the wearying burdens of this world that his work derives its unique poetic vitality. And this delightful reclusive independence allows him to avoid the problematic issue of the Sage-king and the "vessels" which Lao-tzu faces us with. Chuang-tzu implicitly accepts the fact that the Way cannot be institutionalized and contents himself, quite consistently, with gambolling happily along it. He does not believe in man helping out Heaven,[50] and simply asks that each thing be true to its own capacities and nature.[51]

CHAPTER VII

Mo Ti and Transcendental Utilitarianism

CHAPTER VII

Mo Ti, c. 479-381 B.C., offers a polar contrast to the Taoists—with him we revert firmly to the realm of governmental and administrative concerns. Nevertheless, one of the most interesting features of his thought is the intriguing co-existence of the most thorough-going utilitarianism with an equally profound belief in transcendental and extra-terrestrial verities.

Mo Ti is categorical in affirming the importance of the material and economic factors as the vital elements of governance. "Now, the five grains are the people's mainstay and the source of the ruler's revenue."[1] and a careful husbanding of resources is what enables a country to maintain its equilibrium despite natural calamities; the way lies "in diligent production and thrifty consumption."[2] Material shortages are particularly abhorred because they result in a breakdown of order,[3] and it is primarily the abundance of grain which guarantees the well-being of a state[4]—"Supply is the treasure of a country, armament its claws, and the city walls are the stronghold of its self-defence. And these three items are the essentials to the existence of a state."[5] It follows that Mo Ti is relentless in his attack on the conspicuous and futile consumption of his time in which the insatiability of the ruler's taste for luxury exhausted the people without satisfying their needs and thus left the country open to the threats of famine and external attack.[6] But it is not only the economic and military factors which are important in the establishment of order; equally significant is the necessity of centralization, the doctrine of Agreement with the Superior, and it can be said that the latter is vital for the existence and growth of a stable material base in Mo Ti's scheme.

Like Hsün-tzu, Mo Ti is very much aware of the diversity of human desires and the chaos which will ensue if each is allowed to pursue his own inclinations without let or hindrance. This is expounded cogently in his famous analysis.

> "In the beginning of human life, when there was yet no law and government, the custom was 'everybody according to his own idea'[7] Accordingly each man had his own idea, two men had two different ideas, and ten men had ten different ideas—the more people the more different notions. And everybody approved of his own view and disapproved the views of others, and so arose mutual disapproval among men."[8]

From this sprang filial disaffections, violence and economic catastrophe because the spirit of sharing and cooperative aid did not exist.[9] The way out of this bedlam and mutual discord was the selection and appointment of a virtuous man by Heaven as the emperor.[10] The emperor, confronted with the vastness of his task, in turn chose virtuous men to aid him in his enterprise of establishing order and these men became his ministers.[11] In similar fashion were created, in a descending order, the feudal lords and the district and village heads.[12] At each of these levels, the function of the superior was to unify the ideas of his subordinates in terms of his own and, in turn, to model his ideas on those of his superior. "Upon hearing good or evil one shall report it to a superior. What the superior thinks to be all right all think to be right; what the superior thinks to be wrong all shall think to be wrong."[13] Rewards are to be awarded to those who conform to the scheme and punishments imposed on those who go contrary to it.[14] It is important to emphasize here that the chain of command does not stop simply at its terrestrial head, the emperor, but only with Heaven itself[15]—which constitutes a living and conscious entity. The above structure has many points worthy of a more detailed analysis, the doctrine of centralization, the concept of the delegation of authority, the role of rewards and punishments, the nature of hierarchy and the belief in a moral Heaven, but for the present we shall limit ourselves to a descriptive survey of Mo Ti's thought and reserve a critique till later.

Another related and crucial aspect of Mo Ti's search for order lies in his doctrine of universal love which holds that all particular affections and sentiments are the source of evil and conflict. In this concept there are shades of Taoist ideas as it points out that all specific relationships are, by their very nature, exclusive. It aims therefore at the abolition of the polarities inevitably consequent upon such affiliations. Mo Ti analyzes disorder by defining it as "just the lack of filial piety on the part of the minister and the son towards the emperor and father."[16] Since the son loves himself more than the father, he benefits himself to the detriment of the latter, and the same is true of the thief because he too loves his own family more than that of others and therefore robs the latter for the benefit of his own.[17] Thus the interminable internecine and inter-state warfare of his time could be similarly seen to be rooted in an unthinking and excessive devotion to one's cause and interests at the necessary expense of those of others. On the other hand,

> "If everyone in the world will love universally; states not attacking one another; houses not disturbing one another; thieves and robbers becoming extinct; emperor and ministers, fathers and sons, all being affectionate and filial—if all this comes to pass the world will be orderly. Therefore, how can the wise man who has charge of governing the empire fail to restrain hate and encourage love?"[18]

Two things are to be noted in this connection; Mo Ti is not opposed to the values implicit in filiality but simply asks that they be expanded beyond the limits imposed by a strictly familial interpretation of the term. In other words he demands that these values be universalized and made universally applicable and he proposes three requirements which would functionally define filiality: (a) that it enrich the poor, (b) increase the few, (c) provide stability and order.[19] The second point follows from just such a universalization and echoes the same point made earlier in connection with the Taoists. In so far as he argues against differentiated relationships he is destroying all the lateral links in the state which can diffuse and blunt the vertical pressures of autocratic and centralized rule. It is true that this is not the rationale for Mo Ti's espousal of universal love, but the doctrine can easily be utilized by those whose main interest is in the maximization of political control.

The three doctrines enunciated above, the emphasis on utilitarianism, the necessity of Agreement with the Superior and the desirability of universal love can be said to constitute the bed-rock of Mo Ti's system, but each of these possesses themes which deserve to be further explored, and to these we now turn. Needless to say, the tenets adumbrated above are all part of an integrated system, and a point made in one context will necessarily have implications in the others. To commence, we have seen that the natural condition of men is divisive and fratricidal and to curtail this certain standards are necessary. In this context, the principle of Agreement with the Superior is a methodological tool of use only when it is a question of implementing a standard—in itself it offers none. How then are these basic codes of conduct to be determined? Mo Ti is convinced that but a few people are good in this world and therefore general guidelines prescribing obedience to parents, teachers and rulers are of limited use in that the number of these who are worthy of emulation are in the minority.[20] The only stable entity is Heaven, and its characteristics are to serve as a paradigm for earthly virtues. "Heaven is all-inclusive and impartial in its activities, abundant and unceasing in its blessings, and lasting and untiring in its guidance."[21] He goes on to deduce from this that Heaven approves of love and abhors that which militates against it. The cardinal proof of its impartiality and universality lies in the fact that it accepts sacrificial offerings from all.[22] This is what establishes the basis for Mo Ti's stringent egalitarian bias. For him, virtue is the sole distinguishing feature amongst men and the only criterion which the ruler should employ in his selection of officers. "If capable, even a farmer or an artisan would be employed—commissioned with high rank, remunerated with liberal emoluments, trusted with important charges, and empowered to issue final orders."[23] But virtue is not just a general moral condition but implies the capacity, the technical ability, to convert ideas into deeds. Consistent with his utilitarian perspective, Mo Ti has little time for doctrines incapable of implementation—they are but ways of wearing out one's mouth.[24] Virtue becomes a means for standardizing ranks, determining functions and granting rewards; "Therefore ranks should be standardized according to virtue, tasks assigned according to office, and rewards given according to labour spent."[25] It is precisely this equation between function, performance and remuneration that was to be one of the guiding principles of the Legalists, and its importance for bureaucratic practice is obvious. In the same context Mo Ti makes it clear that his espousal of virtue and righteousness is not for their intrinsic value but because they are functionally effective and pay rich dividends in terms of strong and orderly government. Rewards and high ranks are not given for the sake of honouring virtue *per se* but because they are necessary for the performance of governmental duties.

> "For, if his rank were not high, people would not respect him; if his emoluments were not liberal, people would not have confidence in him; if his orders were not final, people would not stand in awe before him. To place these three (honours) upon the virtuous is not so much to reward virtue as to bring about the success of the enterprise (of government.)"[26]

Having thus institutionalized the dictates and standards of Heaven and incorporated them into a system whereby, through Agreement with the Superior and the equilibrium established between performance and rewards, they can subserve concrete administrative ends, Mo Ti naturally comes out firmly against the concept of rule by generalists as opposed to trained technicians. Government for him is as detailed and technical an enterprise as any craft and he equates it with one in terms of the necessity of specialization: "As the gentleman of the world cannot be butchers of dogs and pigs, they would refuse when asked to be such. Yet, although they are not capable of being ministers in a state, they would accept it when asked to be such. Is this not perverse?"[27] Here again he is at one with the Legalists and opposed to the Confucians in supporting specialists against generalists. But the acceptance of the meritocratic principle does not imply the destruction of hierarchy—indeed it is of particular importance in Mo Ti's system of Agreement with the Superior. He makes it quite clear that the standards are not of democratic origin but that the people get them from the scholars, they from the lords, the lords from the emperor, and the emperor himself from Heaven.[28] The egalitarianism of Mo Ti is thus, despite his vaunted utilitarianism, of an almost metaphysical character. It does not mean that all men are equal—for we have seen their virtue to vary, nor does it mean that they are free either to establish their own norms or to obey their own social dicates since both of these are to be determined by the Superior. The sole basis for this dogma consists in the belief that since Heaven is impartial in receiving gifts whether they be from prince or peasant, men must all be equal. It is a simple derivative of the non-differentiating nature of Heaven.

But whatever its origins, the principle attains its true significance in the context of administration. The advantage of equality here is simply that it does away with a rigid ranking system which may stand in the way of the most efficient bureaucratic organization. One of the reasons which Mo Ti asserts for establishing virtue as the only condition of employment is precisely mobility—the prevention of fixed positions: "When emoluments are distributed in proportion to achievements, officials cannot be in constant honour and people in eternal humility."[29] But the point is not that it is just for those of common birth to have a chance to attain to high station but that keeping the door open to ability wherever it may be found is pragmatically desirable for the sake of efficiency. The operative factor is really expediency rather than social justice.

The centralization principle expressed in the Agreement with the Superior is seen to be fostered rather than weakened by the delegation of responsibility. Mo Ti is astute enough to see that the total concentration of power in the ruler's hands is not advisable—for the pragmatic reason that he may well be unable to sustain the burden of such responsibility.

> "Having been crowned, the emperor, realizing the impossibility of unifying the world just by his own senses of hearing and sight, choses the understanding, virtuous, sagacious and wise of the world and installed them as the three ministers, sharing with them the duty of unifying the standards in the empire."[30]

But Mo Ti also sees that it is precisely such delegation of authority which enables a greater degree of central control: "The emperor is like a spirit in his hearing and sight."[31] And this because he seeks resort to the powers of others in order to magnify his own. Mo Ti's firm commitment to the ideas of government by specialists, his emphasis on centralization and the need for implicit obedience to the superior all point to a kind of technocratic totalitarianism aided by the pressures of rewards and punishments and the desire for wealth, honour and safety.[32] And this would certainly be so if Mo Ti's primary loyalty was to the ruler. But the omnipotent entity in his scheme is not the ruler but Heaven, which constitutes the ultimate source of his most important dogmas. Thus it is through Heaven's intervention that a virtuous man is elevated to the rank of an emperor in order to end the suffering and chaos engendered by the plurality of standards.[33] Further, it alone offers that standard which is commonly acceptable, and its canons of universality, impartiality, abundance and incessant endeavour are those which government should seek to make its own.[34] The doctrine of universal love, again, can be seen to be a corollary of one of Heaven's attributes—its impartiality and love. The idea of reciprocity is fundamental to the dogma of universal love and it has an exact parallel in the context of one's relationship to Heaven. "When I do what Heaven desires, Heaven will also do what I desire."[35] This belief in a cognizant and functioning Heaven which awards what it likes and punishes what it dislikes through natural calamities[36] is a vital part of Mo Ti's system, and its role in militating against mere wilful tyranny is made manifest through the king's subordination to it. It was mentioned above that the hierarchy envisaged by Mo Ti does not terminate with the ruler but only with Heaven:

> "But to carry the process of identification with the superior up to the Son of Heaven and not further up to Heaven itself—then the jungle from Heaven is yet unremoved. Thereupon Heaven would send down cold and heat without moderation, and snow, frost, rain and dew untimely."[37]

Again, as in the case of his egalitarianism, the test he employs to determine the primacy of Heaven is that of sacrifice. Thus, *apropos* of the impermissibility of the emperor establishing his own standards at will, he says—"But I have not yet heard of Heaven invoking the emperor for blessing. So I know Heaven gives the standard to the emperor."[38] In the political realm, therefore, Heaven, by constituting a system of values independent of the emperor, makes it impossible for the ruler to formulate his own specific political values. In other words, although centralization is possible, indeed vital, the values so centralized are not brought into being under the aegis of the ruler's own authority. It is fitting, while on the topic of Heaven, to stress that although Mo Ti sees Heaven as a conscious and moral entity, he does not regard it as a deterministic one. He categorically rejects the idea of a fate in whose hands man is a helpless pawn and argues that the acceptance of fate is the overthrow of righteousness and the consequent decline of order.[39] A belief in fate is particularly deleterious in that it weakens the faith in the potency of individual actions on which the scheme of Agreement with the Superior—and its implied system of rewards and punishments—depends. Thus the fatalists can say—"Whoever is rewarded by the superior is destined to be rewarded. It is not because of his virtue that he is rewarded."[40] Here Mo Ti shows considerably greater sophistication than the Legalists in realizing that, even for the efficacy of rewards and punishments, one has to acknowledge a basic degree of human freedom—a man's performance simply cannot be seen as the pure result of an automatic interaction between pleasure and pain. A totally deterministic belief will not lead to the attempt to escape pain or procure pleasure. In addition to Heaven and the Superior, Mo Ti adduces yet another source of order, that of the spirits of the middle realm—as distinguished from Heaven above and man below. They too, like Heaven, are omniscient, and therefore a powerful agent for ensuring rectitude. "One may not act disrespectfully even in woods, valleys or solitary caves where there is no man. Spirits and ghosts are watching everywhere."[41]

There is admittedly a seeming discrepancy between the secular, pragmatic tone of Mo Ti and his profound belief in Heaven and spirits. But this apparent dichotomy vanishes once we regard his utilitarianism not as a philosophical stance but as a way of attaining the order exemplified by Heaven.[42] Popularly defined, utilitarianism is a concern for tangible benefits as opposed to supposedly non-productive enterprises. Despite the fact that Mo Ti does not expressly ackowledge the point that the dividing line between the useful and the useless is a very difficult one to draw and that the apparently useless can, in fact, turn out to be very useful, this is a point which does emerge in his discussion of elaborate funeral ceremonies. The methodological framework which Mo Ti adopts to determine the necessity for funeral ceremonies is admittedly utilitarian in the general sense; the questions he poses are thus whether such institutions are capable of enriching the poor, increasing the few, removing danger and regulating disorder.[43] Since they are seen to be incapable of these, they are condemned.[44] This is quite consistent with the basic postulates from which he commenced, but later on he tacitly admits that mourning does have a value although it may not meet his rigidly functional criteria. He thus says—"Even regarding clothing and food, which are the necessities of life, there are rules. How then can there be none regarding funerals and burials which are the necessities of death?"[45] In general, Mo Ti values the utilitarian ethic, not for itself, but because it conduces to the general good. The aim of his cautious frugality is not so much utility as order. A society and a government which are wasteful and extravagant are bad not because luxuries are bad *per se*, but because they are not in a position "to contribute to the benefits of the people at present."[46] In brief, Mo Ti's consistent concern, whether it be in the fields of architecture, clothing or food, is to establish the importance of the economic element in the establishment of order, and the principle of utility derived from this concern is of final importance because ". . . the people bacome more unruly as the state becomes poorer."[47] The fact that Mo Ti tends towards utilitarianism as a policy rather than as an ideology is somewhat strikingly revealed in a conversation he has with a potter-farmer of the name of Wu Lu.[48] The latter is truly utilitarian because he completely equates the performance of a concrete, basic activity with righteousness. Mo Ti's argument against him—who might be expected to be his ideal—is revealing. His logic is that insofar as no one man can cultivate enough food or weave sufficient clothing to feed and clothe all the people in the world, it is futile to become a farmer or a weaver. The only way in which to attain success in such an infinite enterprise would be to teach the principles of the ancient sages (i.e., his own doctrines) to all in the sure confidence that "when the rulers adopt my principles their states will be orderly.[49] . . . And for this reason . . . I have greater merit than those who plough and feed, and weave and clothe."[50] Whatever the merits of the reasoning, this defence of the pedagogic profession concedes that the intangible—although seemingly not productive—can in fact be more worthwhile than specific and concrete jobs, and a dimension is introduced which makes it impossible to distinguish between the useful and the not-useful by bringing into question the very definition of practicality. It is therefore necessary to exercise some caution in categorizing Mo Ti's thought as utilitarian, although that term has been used here as the most convenient available. The fact that, for Mo Ti, utilitarianism is but a means of realizing Heaven's scheme on earth, or even conversely that Heaven is but a rationalization for the justification of certain pre-conceived values that he wants to reify, means that he is in a position to escape the dilemma confronting all purely utilitarian thought, a dilemma brilliantly expressed by Lessing in his question, "What is the use of use?"[51] Mo Ti tacitly concedes that "use" cannot be elevated into a goal by itself, that it has to serve an end greater than itself which, in the last analysis, has an intrinsic worth of its own and is not just a means to yet another provisional end. The goals of Mo Ti's system possessed of an absolute worth are the values of Heaven. And, as we have seen above, Mo Ti is not strictly utilitarian even in the more popular sense which seeks to separate practical activity from supposedly non-productive ideation.

Before concluding, it may be useful to add a few words on Mo Ti's stand regarding rewards and punishments. We have already seen that they are an important element both in the context of Agreement with the Superior and in that of elevating the virtuous to office where it acts to reinforce the desired correlation between rank and performance. Nevertheless Mo Ti does not regard punishment purely in its physical aspect. He concedes that punishments as such are unimportant, what matters is the form in which they are implemented—and it is in this, rather than in the physical nature of the punishments themselves, that antiquity differed from the present day. When punishments are applied employing instruction and admonition, they are properly so-called, when not so accompanied, they are merely "a code of five tortures"[52] and ineffectual. This aversion to brute force as a motive power is also evident in his statements regarding the necessity of the superior loving his subordinates. This is not just a derivative of the idea of universal love but a conclusion springing from an astute perception regarding the nature of obedience: "Whoever orders his people to identify themselves with their superiors must love them dearly. For the people will not obey orders except when they are ordered with love and held in confidence."[53] He sees clearly that the entire idea of subordination will be effective only if the people know it is for their welfare—if this certitude is lacking no degree of rewards and punishments would succeed in ordering the state.[54] Thus, even though Mo Ti's system, despite its egalitarianism, does not countenance democratic forces in theory, public sentiment does play a substantial role in determining the success of his hierarchic scheme, for he realizes that government has to accord in some degree with the public in order to be stable. "When the administration of the ruler answers to the desires of the people there will be order; otherwise there will be confusion."[55]

It will become apparent, when dealing with the Legalists, that there is much in common between them and the doctrines of Mo Ti. These affinities are most marked in the fields already noted—those of an emphasis on the material aspects of government, the breakdown of particular affiliations in favour of uniform and universal relationships and the overriding importance of implicit obedience to the Superior. These similarities, however, should not blind one to equally significant differences. Mo Ti does not place a blind faith in the purely mechanical efficacy of rewards and punishments as a method of rule; the doctrine of a just and far-seeing Heaven mitigates unbridled authoritarianism and, not least significant, is the fact that although he too stresses the importance of centralization,[56] he does not see this as an end which is to be attained through aggressive war. It is true that Mo Ti's arguments against offensive warfare are mostly couched in expedient terms, those of the loss of lives and property and the needless interruption of production, but war is also bad in that it violates the basic tenets of Heaven's order: "For universal love the standard is righteousness. For partiality it is force."[57] This is a tenet which, at the methodological level at any rate, the Legalists would find hard to accept.

CHAPTER VIII

The Logic of Power

CHAPTER VIII

Section 1. The Political Context of Legalism

This section is concerned with providing a survey of the political and social forces which constitute the setting of the political philosophies of our concern. The purpose here is not to undertake an exhaustive and detailed study of these historical events but to indicate that the common concern underlying the various doctrines of this period—the concern with order—is firmly rooted in the decline of Chou feudalism and in the desperate attempts to create a new system capable of replacing it. The present section will briefly describe the salient features of this process through the Spring and Autumn (*Ch'un Ch'iu*, 722-464 B.C.) and Warring States (*Chan Kuo*, 463-221 B.C.) periods and its culmination in the unification of China under Shih Huang-ti and Li Ssu.

The dramatic centralization which is the most significant feature of this period can perhaps be best illustrated by the observation that of the 1,773 states held to have been brought into being under the aegis of the Chou shortly after they overthrew Shang in ca. 1112 B.C., only about 170 survived in 772 B.C. and by the end of the *Ch'un Ch'iu* in 481 B.C. these had been further reduced to 13.[1] At the end of the ensuring period of the *Chan Kuo* these too had been subsumed into the house of Ch'in—the founder of the first united Chinese empire in 221 B.C. This drastic simplification of the political scene was the outcome of the interaction of a complex of forces operative both within each state and between the states. Shortly after the overthrow of the Shang, the new Chou rulers instituted a system of government somewhat akin to European feudalism.[2] Lands were apportioned to relatives and allies, and even some of the old Shang nobility were allowed to retain their old territories under the suzerainty of the Chou.[3] Such delegation of power and diffusion of authority were probably necessitated by the impossibility of directly ruling vastly increased territories; nevertheless, an attempt was made *via* the fictive device of the Son of Heaven concept and the emphasis placed on ritual and familial ties to bind the feudal lords to the Chou ruler and thus maintain a degree of centralization. During the early stages, the fact that not only the minor lords in the royal demesne but also the lords of the various states belonged to the royal family must have enabled the system to work reasonably well.[4] The feudal lords were hierarchically structured into five gradations, those of Duke (*kung*), Marquis (*hou*), Earl (*po*), Viscount (*tzu*) and Baron (*nan*),[5] while the knights (*shih*) constituted the lowest level of the nobility. Theoretically, they all owed their positions to the king, and their fiefs were revocable, while they owed tribute and military aid to the Chou court.[6] Within their lands, however, they were supreme, and could establish their own tax system, labour force, army and capital city.[7] Below these privileged strata were the merchants, artisans, peasants and slaves of whose lot little is known. There seems little doubt, however, that the peasants were initially bound to the land with no rights of purchase or sale thereof with their role consisting primarily of serving the lord with corvée, grain and cloth taxes.[8]

Even before the end of the Western Chou in 770 B.C., there is some evidence that this ordered, stratified society was beginning to crumble. For instance, the growing separation of the peasant from the land is testified to by the *k'o-ting* tripod of this period which records the Chou king as making seven grants of land in only one of which there is mention of serfs being part of the property.[9] Similarly, the evidence of the expulsion of King Li (832 B C.), the tenth monarch of Chou, as the result of a popular uprising is an indication of the growing strength of public sentiment.[10] These incidents only lightly mark the tendencies which were to develop into maturity in the succeeding *Ch'un Ch'iu* period, but the fact that they were already manifest, however marginally, in the Western Chou indicates that even prior to 770 B.C. social forces antagonistic to feudalism were beginning to bourgeon in the body-politic. This being so, the shift of the Chou capital from Hao near modern Sian to Lo-i occasioned by the invasion of the nomadic Jung in 770 B.C. can be seen primarily as a catalyst furthering social and political change. While in the period of the Western Chou the evidence of change is very slight, in the later *Chan Kuo* period one witnesses an already mature process moving inexorably towards its culmination—for this reason we shall concentrate mostly on the *Ch'un Ch'iu* period in which, falling as it does between these two periods, we are in a position to witness the growing definition of the forces propelling socio-political change.

It has already been noted that by the 8th century B.C. only about 170 states remained and of these a few were already beginning to become prominent, such as Lu, Cheng, Wei, Sung, Chi, Ch'en, Ts'ao, Ts'ai, Ch'i and Chou itself, states which were to survive through most of the *Ch'un Ch'iu* period.[11] These states constituted what are sometimes known as the Chou or central states for they are seen as belonging to the central core as opposed to the 'barbaric' or semi-civilized states on the periphery such as Ch'in and Chin to the west and northwest, Ch'u in the Yangtze valley, and Wu and Yueh to the southeast.[12] As we shall see, the distinction tends to become an increasingly tenuous one as these states begin to play a widening role in the politics of the central states and eventually one of them, Ch'in, imposed its dominance on the whole country. Walker points out that the process of consolidation, that is, the process of the aggrandizement of states at the expense of others, was manifest as early as 707 B.C. and that too at the expense of the supposedly revered Chou monarch in the course of a battle between Chou and Cheng.[13] Even more indicative of the decline of the Chou house is the fact that by 652 B.C. the succession in Chou was being determined by a group of the more powerful states.[14] In the period under discussion, the greatest expansion was on the part of Chin—an expansion so rapid and uncontrolled that it split up into the three states of Han, Wei and Chao in 403 B.C. But although the example of

Chin is the most prominent, it was by no means alone in its pursuit of territory. Even Lu, the conservative state of Confucius, made at least eighteen additions to its territories[15] while Ch'i did even better. The importance of Ch'i resides not only in the fact of its military prowess and steady expansion but also because it was the first state to fully realize that the exigencies of the time demanded a drastic reorganization of the military and administrative structure, and it was this governmental rationalization, undertaken by Kuan Chung, the minister of Duke Huan of Ch'i, that enabled the latter to become the first *Pa* or Lord Protector of the states in 679 B.C.[16] The essential principle underlying Kuan Chung's administrative and economic reforms was that of centralization. The entire population was divided into twenty-one divisions (*hsiang*) of which six were professional and functional and the remaining fifteen regional. The fifteen regional divisions were further divided into three groups of five each, and each of these groups contributed an army on the basis of one soldier per family.[17] Thus a common system sufficed for both the civilian and military structures. Within the *hsiang* itself, the lines of authority were clearly delineated and the leaders of the *hsiang* were required to report to the ruler once a year on the affairs under their control. The criterion of advancement was to be merit rather than privilege and in fact the whole organization bears considerable resemblance to that which we have seen adumbrated by Mo Ti. It is perhaps not insignificant in the context of Kuan Chung's espousal of meritocracy that he himself did not owe his position to birth—he was not a member of the ruling house[18]—but to his own ability. This system obviously does away with the diffuse pattern of authority so characteristic of feudalism and replaces it with a cohesive organization in which both responsibility and decision are more precisely demarcated. Feudal loyalty is now replaced by the obedience springing from functional subordination, and organizational efficiency is maximized by excluding factors which are extraneous to merit. His reforms on the economic front similarly conduce to the increase of state power through rationalization. The *Shih Chi* credits him with the controlling of prices and the rectification of weights and measures.[19] In order to add to the fiscal resources of the state he instituted a salt and iron monopoly and this obviously constitutes a method of social control as well.[20] The degree of emulation that these reforms fostered is ample proof of the fact that they were regarded as the obvious solutions to the problems of the day. The organization developed by Duke Wen of Chin (635-628 B.C.) closely approximated that of Kuan Chung and the same is probably true of the reforms of Ch'u, Cheng and Lu.[21]

The new organizational patterns developed by Kuan Chung were also timely in terms of the international situation, for it was about this time that the southern state of Ch'u became a serious rival to the hitherto supreme Chou states and as Walker puts it "The Ch'i ruler, because of the internal strength of his own state was able to assemble the princes of the others to oppose Ch'u's armies which were invading Cheng."[22] The acknowledgment of Duke Huan of Ch'i as the first Lord Protector in 679 B.C. has a twofold significance. Insofar as this dignity was conferred upon the Duke with full royal assent, it symbolized a further retreat of the Chou monarch into a purely ritualistic status and, in strictly political terms, the League of Chou states which the institution of the Lord Protector presupposed was now to ensure that battles would not simply be between individual armies but between opposing confederations. This is not to deny the existence of alliances prior to 679 B.C. but to point out that the concept of collective security necessarily implies an expansion of the scale of war.[23] The League however by no means involved the abrogation of the autonomy of individual states—on the contrary, amongst the Chou states at any rate, it was the one way of ensuring their independence because the Hegemon or Lord Protector was always keen on winning their allegiance in any prospective campaign against one of the major non-Chou states. The League headed by Ch'u functioned on more authoritarian lines. There will be more to say on the general issue of the techniques developed to deal with newly conquered territory below,[24] but for the present suffice it to say that Ch'u was particularly known for the elimination of the states which it conquered and their total assimilation into its own territory. An example of this is furnished by its absorption of the state of

Ch'en in 534 B.C.[25] Its blatant determination to seize every possibility of gain—although in this it probably differed from other states only in degree—is expressed by the statement of one of its generals, Tzu-fan, in 576 B.C., "When we can gain the advantage over our enemies, we must advance without consideration of covenants."[26] This candid Realpolitik ethic seems to have made some of its allies somewhat uneasy and we find the states of Huang and Chiang switching their allegiance to Duke Huan of Ch'i in 648 B.C.[27] In general, the smaller states had to play a very delicate balancing game in order to preserve their sovereignty in the face of pressure from the larger states. Thus the *Ch'un Ch'iu* and *Tso Chuan* chronicle the attempts of the state of Lu to follow its own policies and yet keep in harmony with Ch'i between 681 and 643 B.C. and later with Chin from 640 to 510 B.C.[28] Very often a small state was in a position to determine the balance of power in a critical fashion and thus drew upon itself the unwelcome attentions of more powerful states. Walker cites Cheng as an almost archetypal case of a small—though by no means helpless—state constantly vacillating between the Northern and Southern Leagues in an attempt at staving off attacks from the stronger side, and simultaneously endeavouring to improve its own situation—thus in 642 B.C., on the death of Duke Huan of Ch'i, Cheng shifted its allegiance to the Ch'u camp.[29] Walker characterizes the role of Cheng as that of the "passive balancer" since its function of maintaining an equilibrium was essentially a negative one, and contrasts it with that of Ch'in—which he regards as an "active balancer."[30] Thus in 600 B.C. Ch'in attacked Chin when she feared the latter was getting too strong vis-a-vis Ch'u,[31] and in 615 B.C., fifteen years earlier, Ch'in had joined Chin in attacking Ch'u fearing that Ch'u had finally won the allegiance of the axial state of Cheng.[32] Ch'in again balanced the odds in 589 B.C. by assisting Chin in its attempts at pressuring Ch'u to desist from an invasion of Wei.[33] It was this kind of constant equalization—either on the part of states like Cheng struggling to preserve their freedom of manoeuvre or on that of stronger states like Ch'in strong enough to act decisively on their own behalf—which constituted the uneasy balance of power in the *Ch'un Ch'iu* period. The emergence of the state of Wu in the southeast to a position of political significance in 568 B.C. introduced a new dimension into the situation.[34] Chin, whose power had been declining in possible consequence of its inability to develop an administrative structure capable of coping with its incessant territorial expansion, immediately looked to Wu as a counter-balance to its archrival Ch'u.[35] After 562 B.C. however, Ch'in exerted itself on behalf of Ch'u motivated by the concern that the latter would succumb to the Chin-Wu axis and thus upset the power equation.[36] With the continuing decline of Chin, the tension and balance was maintained by the rivalry between Ch'u and Wu, both states of the south. This new development completely obviated the initial intent of the League system which was to preserve a semblance of order among the Chou states and thus protect them from the barbaric outsiders. Now the stability of the Chou states themselves depended on the balance between two barbarians—the central states were no longer politically pertinent.

The political configuration alters again with the fragmentation of Chin into the states of Han, Wei and Chao in 403 B.C. —the date which marks the beginning of the *Chan Kuo* period, a period during which the above-mentioned states along with Ch'u, Ch'i, Yen and Ch'in constituted the major political entities.[37] Ch'in no longer played the role of the "active balancer" but became one of the major participants in the struggle. As distinct from the earlier North-South Leagues, the pattern of alliances were now East-West and North-South, those of Ch'in and its enemies respectively.[38] By the earlier part of the 4th century B.C. Ch'in was already proving its military superiority and in 318 B.C. it inflicted a crushing defeat on the states of Han, Chao, Wei, Yen and Ch'i, and six years later Ch'u suffered a similar fate.[39] Having seriously debilitated its rivals, the next step was the annihilation of the once sacrosanct house of Chou—and this was done in 256 B.C.[40] It was, nevertheless, only thirty-five years later, in 221 B.C., that Shih Huang-ti finally overcame the surviving opposition and became the first ruler of a unified China. This brief account of the spectacular account of Ch'in has left out one of the cardinal reasons for its political prowess. Much as the power of Ch'i in the 7th century B.C. is explicable in terms of the reforms of Kuan Chung, so the emergence of Ch'in into the central arena of Chinese politics is linked with the changes introduced by Lord Shang Yang during this holding of high office in Ch'in between 359 and 338 B.C.[41] According to the *Shih Chi*, his main reforms were as follows: dividing the entire country into forty-one *hsien*[42] (prefectures) under the control of prefects (*ling*) and assistants (*ch'eng*);[43] attempting to break up the patriarchal family by ordaining that people who had two males or more in the family of an undivided household had to pay double taxes[44] and further forbidding fathers and sons, elder and younger brother from living together in the same house;[45] establishing a system of mutual control by dividing the population into groups of fives and tens who were responsible for supervising each other's behaviour and were commonly culpable and subject to punishment in the event of a crime;[46] the creation of a hierarchy quite independent of birth and based exclusively on military merit, divided into eighteen degrees, which was to be the sole criterion by which status and rank were to be determined;[47] finally, the standardization of weights, scales and measures.[48] It will be apparent that the primary features of these changes were the dissolution of hereditary positions and privileges, as also—*via* the system of division into *hsiens*—the destruction of local centres of authority which could pose a threat to central power. The attempt at centralization did not just stop at the abolition of feudal obstacles to such a policy but aimed further at the destruction of the family—apparently seeing clearly that the atomized individual without social and familial support would prove politically most tractable. Another reform which is attributed to Shang Yang is one which opened the land to private purchase. The problem is a controvesial one as the *Shih Chi* limits itself to the bare observation that "he opened up the longitudinal and horizontal paths and the border country . . . ."[49] The logic of such an action is clear if the aim was to reduce the power of hereditary feudal groups because the creation of an independent peasantry with land-holding rights would necessarily render their position insecure, but, if indeed Shang Yang was responsible for such a measure, it seems to have merely shut the door on one problem to open it to another. The purchaseability of land, far from emancipating the peasant, merely resulted in the accumulation of land in the hands of the wealthy and the peasant simply substituted the rigours of serfdom for the bondage of impossible rents.[50]

Clearly the constant and unremitting pressures of interstate conflict would necessitate, on the grounds of sheer survival, a thorough-going revamping of internal structures in order to withstand them. It may now be useful to turn to a related aspect of the same issue and see the development of changes within the states—changes no doubt reinforced and accentuated by the exigencies of interstate conflict. Here too we shall note the same tendencies towards simplification, centralization and conflict.

Hsu Cho-yun in this work on social mobility in ancient China between 722 and 222 B.C.[51] has pointed out that the familial nature of early *Ch'un Ch'iu* society and government soon made way for a new functional type. Thus, for example, in all the states with the exception of Ch'u, no ruler's son served as Chancellor after 513 B.C. nor were new noble families of political influence founded by the scions of rulers who ruled after this period.[52] He goes on to say "The end of the intimate conjunction of the state and family may be said to have occurred when brothers and sons of rulers no longer automatically, by reason of birth alone, shared in the power to rule. At the end of the *Ch'un Ch'iu* period no brother or son of a ruler held the Cnancellorship of any state but Ch'u."[53] These lacunae were increasingly filled by ministers who were members of families which had originated as cadet branches of the royal house but had grown increasingly separate in the course of time. Examples of such families are those of Chi, Meng-sun and Shu-sun in the state of Lu, and Han, Wei and Chao in that of Chin.[54] But the internecine fighting between these powerful houses drastically reduced their number and weakened the ministerial class as a whole, and here again the state of Chin can serve as an example. It had more than ten great families in the earlier part of the *Ch'un Ch'iu* and these dwindled to the three whose partition of the country was to bring the period to an end.[55] Hsu Cho-yun holds that the ministerial class derived from the members of great families begins to shrink at about the same time that the emergence of the lowest class of the nobility—the *shih*—can be noted, that is roughly in the *Chan Kuo* period, although the paucity of information makes a detailed account of the transition impossible.[56] Nevertheless, his analysis of the differences between the Chancellors of the *Ch'un Ch'iu* and *Chan Kuo* periods does indicate the rise of a new type. Unlike their predecessors of the earlier periods, the *Chan Kuo* Chancellors did not hold the office for any definite period but were entirely subject to the royal will. They were men of no one background and sprang from diverse origins, while their loyalties were commanded by the monarch whom they happened to be serving at any given moment.[57] They were, in other words, administrative mercenaries serving anyone who could afford their services. An important point which Hsu Cho-yun makes regarding these Chancellors is that, again with the exception of Ch'u, they were either close relatives of the ruling house or outsiders like Shang Yang. The great families which had hitherto been their recruiting ground seem to have vanished. This is of obvious significance as it points out the greater authority accruing to the ruler—freed from feudal restraints, he is now aided by men totally dependent upon him. And this dependence is illustrated materially by the fact that in the *Chan Kuo*, unlike the *Ch'un Ch'iu* officials begin to receive salaries;[58] they have become, in the fullest sense of the term, the king's men. The *shih* class, without hereditary positions but nevertheless possessed of education, thus came to constitute the bulwark of the ruler. The scholar-statesman so common in our period and of whom Confucius constitutes perhaps the best known example, mostly belonged to this class. Relentless competition both within and between states necessitated a system of government which enabled the ruler's control to be as untrammeled as possible, and even by the end of the *Ch'un Ch'iu* the common practice was to appoint magistrates to govern the districts of a state rather than to partition them between the feudal lords—the ministers of Chin for example "divided the territory of defeated rulers into ten districts, each governed by a magistrate who was not an enfeoffed vassal."[59] Ability, under the sheer pressure of functional necessity, became the deciding factor, and the

Marquis Wen of Wei, 446-397 B.C., was willing to consider his own brother and an obscure outsider on equal terms for the office of Chancellor.[60] The fragmentation of states, as in the case of Chin, occasioned by the emergence into statehood of what had hitherto been families, offered an opportunity for the *shih* who had been household dependents to become ministers in the new state.[61] The rise of the *shih*—dependent upon ability and needing to master the intricacies of the increasingly complicated system of statecraft—is no doubt closely linked with the development of bureaucratic organization, and Hsu Cho-yun is surely right in seeing the role of the great pedagogic schools —Confucian, Mohist or Legalist—as being at least partly that of instructing its pupils in what was rapidly becoming the specialized skill of governing.[62]

These changes in the political and social fields were paralleled by those in the commercial and technological realm As early as 545 B.C. the story of Ch'ing Feng of Ch'i in the *Tso Chuan* who was apparently in a position to transfer his assets first to Lu and then to Wu indicates the existence of transferable wealth,[63] and the evidence for metallic currency in the *Chan Kuo* years is well attested.[64] Commercial activity was also aided by the political institution of the League which, from its first meeting under the aegis of the Duke Huan of Ch'i in 681 B.C., averaged two meetings every two years till the end of the *Ch'un Ch'iu*. Merchants frequently accompanied the diplomatic missions and, as Walker points out, the city in which the meetings were held must have profited substantially from the lengthly visit of the large delegations.[65] The fact that commerce was a very paying proposition is also very clearly attested to by Shang Yang's pressing concern that people be not tempted away from agriculture—the mainstay of the state—by the conspicuous blandishment of effortless profit which commerce was thought to hold. And part of his aversion for mercantile endeavour certainly springs from this fear.[66] Quoting Chang Kwanchih, Hsu Cho-yun points out that cities in the later *Ch'un Ch'iu* and *Chan Kuo* periods underwent considerable expansion changing from fortified strongholds to commercial centres,[67] and the fact that a new class of artisans and skilled workers was beginning to emerge is attested to by the establishment of a special administrative cadre, the *kung-cheng*, to supervise them in the states of Ch'i and Ch'u.[68] It is a possibility that one of the reasons for this growing prosperity was the introduction of iron sometime during the *Chan Kuo*, but it would perhaps be unwise to lay too much stress on a technological innovation which was yet to achieve its full measure of efficacy.[69] All the tendencies cursorily surveyed above—interstate conflict, internal consolidation within states, the gestation and birth of a bureaucratic class totally dependent on the ruler's acknowledgment and reward of their ability and the new avenues of wealth opened by commerce—all point to the breakdown of the feudal order, an order whose gradual senescence made such developments possible and whose depleted resources proved incapable of keeping the tensions engendered in check within the old framework. The theoretical works on Legalism which we shall now study have to be seen in this setting—that is, a considerable magnification in the scope and resources of power because internecine conflict, while reducing the total number of rulers, made those who remained more powerful than ever, not only in terms of territory controlled but also, as we have seen, internally. The fluidity of social classes dissolved the old hierarchical stratifications but produced no new definition in their stead. The collapse of the feudal system was as much one of values as of political control, and it was increasingly clear that on this, no less than on the socio-political front, the task of demarcating the lines of a new system devolved upon the ruler.

The most revealing symptom of the decline of feudal order is perhaps the oft-noted replacement of *li* (ritual, etiquette) by *fa* (law or model). In place of the implicitly understood social codes of conduct of the feudal age came the generalized, undifferentiated, explicit and public formulations of objective law. The famous statesman Tzu-ch'an of Cheng who, like Kuan Chung and Shang Yang was a firm believer in centralization and not bound by the traditions of the past, had tripods cast in 536 B.C. inscribed with legal codes and the same publication of legal edicts took place in Chin in 513 B.C.[70] But, as we shall see, it would be a very one-sided judgment if one were to literally equate the Legalists with law exclusively. Their concerns span the whole range of problems surveyed above, the magnification and preservation of state power, the methods open to the ruler in terms of bureaucratic techniques and personnel and the overriding question of finding a new principle in terms of which the state could be rendered cohesive again. It was less *fa* as legal institutions *per se* which interested them than *fa* as a model, a creation of objective standards applicable in diverse fields. A description of Legalist concerns in this sense is the object of the succeeding section.

CHAPTER VIII

Section 2—Legalist Theory

This survey of the theory of Legalism will centre around the two acknowledged classics of the School, the *Book of Lord Shang* (*Shang-chün Shu*) and the *Han Fei Tzu*. Duyvendak in his analysis of the former has concluded that it is a composite work of which some of the sections are of considerable antiquity whereas the others date from the third century B.C.—an evaluation which is in general accord with the researches of Chinese scholars.[71] Further, he points out on the basis of grammatical analysis and particle usage that the work most resembles the text of the *Han Fei Tzu* and ascribes a probable date of the third century B.C. to that work as well.[72] The question whether these works are, in fact, the creations of their putative authors is a debatable one, but for the moment be it simply noted that they reveal a high degree of thematic unity despite occasional contradictions of relatively minor import and thus possess a conceptual cohesiveness despite their probable composite authorship.

Moreover, falling as they do in the period of the third century B.C., they can be regarded as representative of a particular view towards political power current in our period. The *Kuan Tzu*, a work ascribed to the famous Ch'i statesman Kuan Chung, is also often acknowledged as a Legalist classic. It is' however, a work as composite in character as it is in authorship[73] and Confucian, Taoist and Legalist ideas are all crowded together with no attempt made at reconciling contradictions. For this reason, the *Kuan Tzu* is not analyzed in the present work but wherever conceptual parallels exist between it and the two works mentioned above they have been pointed out in the notes.

The relationship between the *Shang-chün Shu* and Shang Yang is a very difficult one to determine, but it will suffice for present purposes to see if there is a satisfactory concordance between the facts of Shang Yang's life as we know them from the *Shih Chi* and the tenets adumbrated in the work itself. The *Shih Chi*[74] makes mention of the various reforms noted in the last section—the division of the people into fives and tens bound by a system of mutual responsibility,[75] an attack on the family,[76] the establishment of a hierarchy of military merit,[77] the division of the country into thirty-one *hsien* or districts[78] and the possible opening up of land to private ownership.[79] Few of these reforms find exact equivalents in the Book itself; the scheme for the division into groups of fives[80] appears as also the idea of establishing a hierarchy founded exclusively on military merit, but this latter only in a paragraph which Duyvendak holds to be of a later date, possibly later than the third century B.C.[81] There is no mention of opening up the land to private ownership, nor of the division of the country into thirty-one *hsien* nor categorically of the measures designed to destroy the family. But the lack of a one-to-one relationship should not blind one to the essential similarity of perspective between what Ssu-ma Ch'ien tells us of Shang Yang and the *Shang-chün Shu*. The primary features of the biography, the importance attached to the reliability and clarity of the law, its utility in guiding people to the desired goals, the emphasis on war and agriculture as the two basic prerequisites for any viable state, the importance of awarding office on the basis of merit and the general desirability of breaking down particular and divisive loyalties as inimical to the interests of the state are all to be found in the Book. It is therefore possible to agree with Duyvendak when he concludes that although "It is impossible to say in how far these ideas in the oldest parts of *Shang Tzu* have any direct connection with Shang Yang. . . . there is therefore nothing improbable in the tradition, which calls him the initiator of this policy."[82] In other words despite differences or omissions of detail, there is no great reason to doubt a generic similarity between the ideas of the Book and those attributed to Shang Yang by the *Shih Chi.* The same may be said to be true of the relationship between Han Fei Tzu and the text which bears his name. Judging again by the compatibility of the content of the work and his biography in the *Shih Chi,*[83] it is hard to discern any marked discrepancy between the perspectives of the two. Needless to say, this is not to claim that the text as we know it is the exclusive work of the eronymous author but to stress the fact that the work does deal precisely with those issues of improving laws and institutions, balancing proficiency and office and strengthening the position of the ruler which Ssu-ma Ch'ien credits him with an interest in.[84]

To turn now to the content of these works, the fundamental concern of both is the strengthening of the state in the widest political sense. This, of course, was also the concern of the various philosophers dealt with above, but part of the importance of the Legalists is that they are the first to try and analyze the problem of order from first principles guided neither by tradition, hallowed truths or transcendental beliefs, but directly on the grounds of practical reason. The first victim of this iconoclastic approach was the sanctity of antiquity, the archetypal modes of rule attributed to the legendary emperors Yao and Shun. The *Shang-chün Shu* asserts, "Therefore a sage, if he is able to strengthen the state thereby, does not model himself on antiquity, and if he is able to benefit the people thereby, does not adhere to the established rites."[85] He goes on to point out that the preceding dynasties had all attained supremacy by different rites—in other words that the patterns of antiquity in themselves were not uniform and therefore could not be said to constitute a stable model for all time.[86] The *Han Fei Tzu* argues along identical lines and states that those in the present age who praise the ways of yore would be figures of ridicule.[87] Its main point is that human nature has not altered but the appearance of change is induced by the fact that circumstances have become increasingly constrictive. The amity of earlier days was due to the paucity of people and the relative abundance of goods whereas the discontent and strife of the present are due to the opposite. Thus, in good environmentalist fashion, it concludes, "circumstances change with the age and measures change according to circumstances."[88] The *Shang-chün Shu* similarly sees disorder as the result of increasing numbers and the propensity of people to favour their own and discriminate against others.[89] Given the impotence of the past as a model for the present, the clue for order was seen to lie in human nature, and this is described by the *Shang-Chün Shu* in the following terms: "The people are only interested in obtaining profit and it depends on what their superiors encourage, what they will do."[90] The *Han Fei Tzu* echoes this sentiment: "Profit is the means whereby the people's hearts are won."[91] From this it is but a step to the calculus of pleasure and pain which constitutes the main mechanism of political control advocated by the Legalists. If rewards were based on what the people desired and punishments on what they feared, an automatic equilibrium could easily be established on the stable basis of the immutable principles underlying human nature. "Generally speaking, the order of All-under-Heaven must accord with human feelings. Human feelings have likes and dislikes, wherefore rewards and punishments can be applied."[92] The *Shang-chün Shu* holds an identical view, though in general it may be said to stress the punitive aspect of the doctrine leading to the association of Shang Yang's name with *fa*—here defined as punitive law: "The fact that penalties are heavy makes rank the more honourable, and the fact that rewards are light makes punishments the more awe-inspiring."[93] It is precisely by the manipulation of this principle that people can be made to undertake perilous and arduous occupations like agriculture and war, for "the people, when alive scheme for profit, and when in danger of death, are anxious for fame."[94] Thus, if agriculture is the only road to profit and war the only road to fame, the people will be industrious and martial. The essential pre-condition for the smooth functioning of rewards and punishments is that they be definite and that the law on which they are based be clear and firm, and this is repeatedly stressed both in the *Shang-chün Shu* and in the *Han Fei Tzu*.[95]

This dependence on the pleasure-pain principle is noticeable at every level of the Legalist system. It would be altogether wrong, as has been pointed out frequently, to regard the idea in a purely judicial light, susceptible as it is to managerial and bureaucratic organization.[96] Thus the doctrine of *shu* — translated as 'tact' or 'methods'[97] — which is associated with the name of Shen Pu-hai[98] and known to us primarily through the *Han Fei Tzu*, is reducible to the same basic principle. The *Han Fei Tzu* defines it as follows: "Tact is the means whereby to create posts according to responsibilities, hold actual services accountable according to official titles, exercise the power over life and death, and examine the officials' abilities."[99] Here rewards and punishments are utilized to establish a system of administrative mensuration: "Whenever any task is accomplished, he (i.e., the ruler) holds to its result. And out of coincidence and discrepancy between the consequences of tasks accomplished and the covenants of words uttered reward and punishment are born."[100] It constitutes the means whereby official merit may be accurately judged and office bestowed in accordance with that merit. Creel is thus quite justified when he sees in this "at least the seeds of civil service examination and merit rating, and of imperial government through a systematically controlled bureaucracy."[101] The belief in a meritocratic officialdom is also to be found in the *Shang-chün Shu* as is also the described method of determining ability: "Thus the way in which intelligent princes utilized their ministers was that their employment was made dependent on the work which they had done and rewards were bestowed on the merits which they had acquired."[102] *Shu*—'method' or 'tact'—as just defined is identical with the doctrine of *hsing-ming*, also associated with Shen Pu-hai, which "is to demand actual performance on the basis of the title held, thus honouring the ruler and humbling the minister, exalting superiors and curbing inferiors."[103] Both Fung Yu-lan and Creel[104] have pointed out the similarity between this and the Confucian *Cheng-ming* or Rectification of Names mentioned earlier, but whereas Confucius had in mind the categories of the family and the feudal hierarchy, the Legalists were concerned with its use as a bureaucratic instrument.

Another concept of some significance in Legalist thought

arises from the attention paid to the nature of political power. Even Mencius had noted, "Great is the influence of position,"[105] and this can be said to be the gist of the celebrated utterance attributed to Shen Tao in the *Han Fei Tzu*:

> "The flying dragon rides on the clouds and the rising serpent strolls through the mists; but as soon as the clouds disperse and the mists clear up, the dragon and the serpent become the same as the earthworm and the large-winged black ant, because they have lost what they rested on. If worthies are subjected by unworthy men, it is because their power is weak and their status is low; whereas if the unworthy man can be subjected by the worthies, it is because the power of the latter is strong and their status is high."[106]

The *Han Fei Tzu*, in adducing a critique of this doctrine, admits of the potency of the mystique of position but declines to accept that such potency is sufficient in and of itself and without talent, to ensure good rule.[107] It would appear to be likely, however, that what may have been meant was that without the utilization of *shih*—that is, without the power accruing to sheer 'position' described above—it would be impossible to use the methods and thus ensure good rule. The three cardinal tenets which have been briefly enunciated, the ideas of *fa* (law), *shu* (methods) and *shih* (position), and which have been seen to be associated with Shang Yang, Shen Pu-hai and Shen Tao respectively, all form part of the same integrated system. The attempt made by Creel to establish a dichotomy between the *fa* of Shang Yang and the *shu* of Shen Pu-hai would not seem to be either justified or useful. He posits a stringent opposition between *fa*, which he sees as being devoted to harsh penal law, and *shu*, which he regards as being fundamentally indifferent to such law and more concerned with the methods used by the ruler in dealing with his officials.[108] While it is certainly true that the *Shang-chün Shu* is very insistent on the idea of law in its punitive aspect, holding that heavy penalties are an index of the ruler's love for his people,[109] it is to be noted that the *Han Fei Tzu*—which Creel holds is far more devoted to *shu*—is by no means without similar sentiments.[110] On the other hand, the *Shang-chün Shu* is not without frequent references to the 'methods' to be utilized in supervising officials, an instance of which we have already given above.[111] What is more significant, however, is the similarity in spirit between *fa* and *shu*. Both systems rely on basically identical factors: the need to establish an objective standard by which men can be ruled, the formation of a measure by which their acts may be evaluated and the creation of a mechanism by which men will strive to attain the goals deemed desirable by the ruler and avoid the opposite. On the other hand, as Creel asserts,[112] the *Han Fei Tzu* itself distinguishes between the two and castigates Shang Yang for lacking *shu* and Shen Pu-hai for being without *fa*, both courses being fatal.[113] But this point, far from substantiating the disjunction made by Creel, merely emphasizes the necessary complementarity and non-exclusiveness of the two doctrines. As mentioned above, it would perhaps be most accurate to view the difference between *shu* and *fa* as the same principle operating at different levels. *Fa* is the means by which the people are given a standard and thus controlled, while *shu* performs the same function at the level of officialdom. They are both ultimately contingent upon the rewards and punishment principle—a fact made manifest by the overriding importance placed on self-interest, the motive force in family affections no less than in the state at large.[114]

It would nevertheless be simplistic to see in Legalism nothing more than the cynical manipulation of pleasure and pain, central though these may be to its system. As Ch'en Chi-t'ien has pointed out, the law of the Legalists comprises the meanings of administrative systems, policies and rewards and punishments all fused into an indissoluble whole.[115] Moreover, as has been mentioned, the term *fa* combines the meanings of both 'law' and 'model' and it is imperative that both these connotations be kept in mind.[116] Further, any estimate of Legalism would have to take into account its aspirations to render government independent of the vagaries of fortune and ability which plague individual rulers. In other words, it would need to be seen as an attempt to render government impersonal. It is this depersonalization of the governmental function, as distinct from the use of force alone, which fundamentally opposes it to Confucianism in which the role of the ruler as moral exemplar is vital. It is also this endeavour which gives Legalist theory its marked Taoist flavor. If Legalism were seen purely in terms of the manipulative techniques of pleasure and pain as employed in administrative techniques and harsh punitive laws, it would appear to be nothing more than a methodology aiming at the maximization of the power of the ruler. That this has a large element of truth is undeniable, but there is another dimension to the doctrine which should not be ignored—its idealism.

In talking of the ideal ruler, the *Han Fei Tzu* says:

> "Therefore, when governing the state he rectifies laws clearly and establishes penalties severely in order to rescue all living beings from chaos, rid All-under-Heaven of misfortune, prohibit the strong from oppressing the few, enable the old and the infirm to die in peace and the young and the orphan to grow freely, and see to it that the frontiers be not invaded, that ruler and minister be intimate with each other, that father and son support each other, and that there be no worry about being killed in war or taken prisoner. Such is one of the greatest achievements, yet the stupid men do not understand it and condemn it as misgovernment."[117]

This could be a Confucian utopia except for the punitive clauses, but these have to be seen in the context of the incorrigible self-seeking characteristic of men. Given this quality, every indulgence of it simply makes men more intractable and their plight more desperate with the result that a punitive act is really one of clemency for it curbs, albeit coercively, self-interest and the evils consequent upon it. It is for this reason that the *Han Fei Tzu*, quoting Lao-tzu, mourns—"Misery, Alas! is what happiness rests upon."[118] Severe penalties and heavy convictions are hated by the people, but it is precisely by those that their safety is secured.[119] The *Shang-chün Shu* shares the same view; it sees that "Punishment produces force, force produces strength, strength produces awe, awe produces kindness. Kindness has its origin in force."[120] Again, "Indeed, in making the people correct, one always attains what they like by means of what they dislike, and one brings about what they dislike by means of what they like."[121] In other words, the policy is aimed at the "abolishing of penalties by means of penalties."[122] Further, the law which ensures stability and the equilibrium of the state and which is dependent on punishments and strictures for its efficacy is not a mere creature of the ruler's whim to be altered and disregarded at his fancy, but something which should hold the ruler, too, in check. The *Shang-chün Shu* says, "Only an intelligent ruler loves right standards and values good faith and will not, for the sake of self-interest, harm the law."[123] The *Han Fei Tzu* in a similar vein asserts that the "Tao of the intelligent sovereign is true to the law, and his law is true to the mind."[124]

It is also the *Han Fei Tzu* which lays particular stress on the impersonality of the ruler—which is tantamount to stressing the paramountcy of the law—and this for reasons which are strongly colored by expediency. It argues that the ruler must hide his desires, views and opinions so that the ministers will not be able to shape their own to conform to his.[125] It is only, so to say, against the blankness of the ruler that the true nature of the ministers stands revealed. Thus, "leave the ruler's wisdom, then you will find the minister's intelligence; leave the ruler's worthiness, then you will find the minister's merits; and leave the ruler's courage, then you will find the minister's strength."[126] The secrecy which we saw Lao-tzu enjoin upon the ruler here finds a utilitarian basis. A constant tension exists between the king and those who surround him based on the fact that their relations are founded exclusively on self-interest, which is, as noted, the dominant if not the exclusive force in all human relations. "Every minister, in his heart of hearts, does not necessarily love the ruler. If he does, it is for the sake of his own great advantage."[127] The easiest way by which the ruler can control his ministers without revealing his own likes and dislikes is by using the twin handles of commendation and chastisement which it is vital that he firmly secure in his own hands all the time and never delegate to his subordinates. This principle, in turn, feeds into the doctrine of *shu* already outlined above;

"Whenever a minister utters a word, the ruler should in accordance with his word assign him a task to accomplish, and in accordance with the task call the work to account. If the work corresponds with the task, and the task corresponds with the world, he should be rewarded. On the contrary, if the work is not equivalent to the task, and the task not equivalent to the word, he should be punished. Accordingly, any minister whose word is big but whose work is small should be punished. Not that the work is small, but that the work is not equivalent to the name. Again, any minister whose word is small but whose work is big should also be punished. Not that big work is not desirable but that the discrepancy between the work and the name is worse than accomplishment of the big work."[128]

The last portion is particularly significant: it emphasizes that what is important is the operation of the mechanical balance which weighs every performance in terms of the stated intent and not in terms of the personal approval or disapproval that the work itself elicits from the ruler. The crucial factor is the precise equivalence, and in utilizing this criterion the ruler is saved from the follies and deceptions attendant upon subjective evaluation; an objective standard has been wrought.

It is this objectification of the means of ministerial and political control which enables the ruler's role to be discussed in Taoists terms:

"The sceptre should never be shown. For its inner nature is non-assertion. The state affairs may be scattered in the four directions but the key to their administration is in the centre. The sage holding this key in hand, people from the four directions come to render their meritorious services, and they will exert their services by themselves."[129]

The power in the state should never be divided, and the methods by which that power is sustained never divulged, for the good reason that the ruler can never rely completely upon his ministers. The importance of unitary control is further stressed: "Tao is never a pair. Hence it is called one.

Therefore the intelligent ruler esteems singleness, the characteristic feature of Tao."[130] But it is important to remember that the non-divisibility of the ruler's potency and power does not imply that he assumes the impossible task of personally undertaking all specialized functions and specific administrative tasks. This is the road to disaster, and the wise ruler, manipulating the reins of pleasure and pain, limits himself to a supervisory capacity:

> "Likewise the state is the carriage of the ruler; the august position is his horse. If the ruler does not know how to drive the carriage, then even though he exhausts himself, he cannot avoid chaos. If he knows how to drive, he will remain in the place of ease and joy and accomplish the achievement of the emperor and the king."[131]

What the *Han Fei Tzu* advocates is a centralization of values but a delegation and decentralization of administrative responsibilities.

Just as in the case of the paradox which we encountered in the context of deterrent punishment—whereby punishments abolish punishments—so in the administrative field we have a similar attempt to make self-interest the axel on which the whole system rotates and which prevents the deleterious consequences of individual self-interests. It is the desire for personal profit which drives a wedge between the minister and the ruler and leads to the necessity of the latter firmly securing the instruments of power—*shu*—in his own hands. But the Legalists' attempt to transform this defect into their greatest asset by discerning that it is precisely because men are motivated by self-interest that they can be manipulated and hence human weakness becomes the king-pin of their system. The degree to which the success of their system is seen to depend on cupidity and cowardice is revealed in the following quotation: "Not encouraged after being rewarded and honoured and not afraid after being punished and disgraced—in other words, not transformed after the four methods are applied—then such ministers will be removed."[132] It is in a statement like this that the revolutionary opposition to Confucius really becomes glaringly manifest. The sturdy and unshakeable integrity of personal conscience is what—precisely because of its resistance to manipulation—the Legalists most abhor. The reversal of values is complete. For the Legalists, however, the eradication of selfishness is possible only through the employment of selfishness:

> "Order and strength are due to the law; weakness and disorder, to its crookedness. If the ruler understands this principle, he must rectify rewards and punishments but never assume humanity towards his inferiors. Rank and emolument are due to meritorious services; censure and punishment to criminal offences. If the minister understands this, he must exert his strength even at the risk of his life but never assume loyalty to the ruler. Thus, with the ruler well versed in the practice of inhumanity and the minister in that of disloyalty, it is possible to rule All-under-Heaven."[133]

In another instance it is made clear that the intrusion of love between subject and ruler would upset the entire mechanism of government because such love constitutes an unstable and incalculable element: "As to why the people work for me, it is because of my position. Suppose I discard my position and attempt to win the hearts of the people with love. Then, as soon as I happen to slacken my love, they will no longer work for me. Therefore I extirpate the policy of love."[134] Here the idea of impersonality is directly linked with the notion of *shih*, the position which will be violated by personal emotion as they are seen to be incompatible. The logic of the impersonality of rule is, therefore, a multifaceted one; although interconnected they can be divided into a number of aspects. Depersonalized government ensures that those closest to the throne are unsure as to the precise locus of authority and are therefore powerless to affect or corrupt it—"So quiet it rests without footing; so vacant, it cannot be located."[135] Independent as it is of the ruler's personal desires, it constitutes an external and objective standard which precisely demarcates the officials responsibilities. Lest it should be felt that there is a contradiction between these two points, it may be pointed out that the amorphousness of the ruler does not dull the precision of the standard—on the contrary, by separating one from the other, it establishes the standard as existing, as it were, transcendentally, in a realm of cosmic validity. To continue, unitary control of power is combined with administrative delegation again by the device of separating the essence of government from the specific performance of bureaucratic tasks. But the final endeavor of impersonalism is to create a system which can afford to be indifferent to the quality of the ruler who heads it—one which can, in short, be autonomous. The attempt of all systems-makers is to create one which is better than the men who compose it and on whose talents it does not have to depend, and the Legalists were no exception. Thus it is frequently asserted that the great blessing of standards is that they enable good rule without presuming upon any exceptional qualities in the ruler: "Suppose an average sovereign abode by law and tact and an unskillful carpenter used compasses, squares and rulers, certainly there would be no mistake in a myriad cases."[136] Again,

> "If they uphold the law and make use of their august position, order obtains; if they discard the law and desert their august position, chaos prevails. Now suppose you discard the position and act contrary to the law and wait for Yao and Shun to appear and suppose order obtains after the arrival of Yao and Shun, then order will obtain in one out of one thousand generations of continuous chaos."[137]

The Legalists are therefore not legislating for those of exceptional abilities and virtues because they are dealing with those from whom not too much can be expected: "What can be practised only by wise men should not be made a law, because the people are not all wise."[138] For this reason it is imperative that laws be clear and punishments definitive. Now it is because the heterodox and diverse doctrines of the *literati* blur the distinction of standards that they are to be condemned.

"Similarly, if a minister always praises the early kings for

> the greatness of their virtues and longs after them, he is a defamer of his ruler . . . . Therefore, the minister who neither extols the worthiness of Yao and Shun, nor admires the achievement of T'ang and Wu, nor speaks well of the nobleness of the ancient heroes but applies all his strength to observing the law and devotes his mind to serving the sovereign, is a loyal minister indeed."[139]

They also stand condemned by the criterion of utility which aims at the pure strengthening of the state through agrarian and military might. The *Han Fei Tzu* asks, "Erudite, learned, eloquent and wise as Confucius and Mo-tzu were, if Confucius and Mo-tzu would never till and weed farming land, what could they contribute to the state?"[140] And it concludes that "clarifying laws and statutes by forbidding literary learning and concentrating on meritorious services by suppressing private advantages are public benefits."[141] The need to keep the people ideologically unperturbed and docile finds particularly emphatic expression in the *Shang-chün Shu* where it is also seen to be connected with the utilitarianism which so strongly marks Legalism. While the *Han Fei Tzu* concentrates on the Taoist imperturbability of the ruler, the *Shang-chün Shu* looks at the means by which the people can be made to attain that tractable quiescence so vital to the efficient functioning of the law. It regards agriculture and warfare as the basis of the Legalist state, but not solely from the point of view—important as it is—of economic viability and military prowess, but also from that of the efficacy of these occupations in keeping the people drained and docile. It holds that, for example, if people are kept stupid by the application of the the right standards they will turn to agriculture and thus render the country peaceful and free from peril.[142] An entire section of the work is devoted to the problem of keeping people weak.[143] The clue to the paradox is given in the opening lines—"A weak people means a strong state and a strong state means a weak people."[144] The two avenues of advancement are the onerous ones of war and agriculture and both subserve the aim of keeping the state strong and the people weak.[145] Any activity which enriches the individual, such as trade, and thus strengthens him, *ipso facto* weakens his fear of the law and thus prepares the way for the downfall of the state.[146] There is thus a congruence between the demands of utility and the need for keeping the people in a state of unheeding simplicity. Similarly, while the mechanism of rewards and punishments is required to good people into agriculture and war, these activities, in turn, help to keep them weak and subservient to the state.[147] It may be noted, by way of parenthesis, that here too the play on weakness and strength and the emergence of one from the other reveal the logic of paradox evidenced above in the use of punishments to abolish punishment and the manipulation of self-interest to create an impartial law.

It would perhaps be appropriate to terminate this survey of Legalist thought by reviewing the reforms of the most Legalist politician of our period—Li Ssu, the minister of Shih Huang-ti, the Ch'in emperor who finally unified China in 221 B.C. Such a review does not reveal any new conceptual dimensions for the reforms constitute an institutional culmination of patterns and trends which had been in progress for some time. The failure, however, of the Legalist endeavour to create a system independent of the vagaries and deficiencies of the ruler is manifest in the fact of the singular brevity of the Ch'in dynasty which survived barely three years after the founder's death in 210 B.C. Even in purely theoretical terms it is obvious that far from creating a system utilizable by the average person, the techniques of *shu* required considerable sophistication for its successful application. Fundamentally, the issue raised by the Legalists is whether it is sufficient for legislation to be concerned exclusively with observable mensurable behavior and nothing else. From their point of view this limitation of attention to the surface is justified by their conviction that benevolence and rectitude are matters of birth and fate and thus not inculculable pedagogically.[148] Since human nature is thus not alterable, it has to be dealt with in terms of its one abiding characteristic, selfishness. The dependency on self-interest, and the reliance on the mechanics of pleasure and pain which this implies, reduce people to puppets galvanized into appropriate action by the ruler. But by thus devalorizing people politically—that is in terms of value which transcend profit—the Legalists merely ensure that the entire cohesiveness of the body-politic depends upon the ruler. Self-interest being, by its very nature, a centrifugal and divisive force, its espousal as the principal factor in rule means that the people as a whole lack a centre of gravity and this results in the unwanted paradox that the sole unifying factor in the state is the ruler—and that in a system which aims at the abolition of government by government.[149] In this sense, therefore, far from creating an autonomous system—an acephalous organization—it instead develops one in which the ruler is of paramount significance. On the other hand, as Chén Chi-t'ien and others point out,[150] the doctrine of *shu* is of manifest importance in bureaucratic practice. The above critique is not aimed at denying this, but at pointing out that bureaucracy alone is incapable of maintaining a viable governmental system. The Han compromise which used bureaucratic techniques for governmental organization but which also allowed for a span of human interests and affections going beyond profit and pain was to prove far more successful and stable.

The reforms of Li Ssu devoted as they are to issues of rationalization and centralization do not vary a great deal from those attributed to Shang Yang. That Li Ssu was well acquainted with Legalist theory and was working on the basis of its tenets can be deduced not only from the fact that he was a fellow student of Han Fei Tzu when they were both studying under the famous Confucian positivist Hsün-tzu, but also from many of his pronouncements. Thus in a memorial to Shih Huang-ti's successor, Erh-Shih, he outlines the doctrine of *shu*, the idea of using heavy punishments as a deterrent, the undesirability of the ruler partaking in the specific details of administration and the notion of *shih* or position.[151] In this context he mentions the names of Han Fei Tzu and Shen Pu-hai—with whom we have seen the concept of *shu* to be associated.

To proceed now to the concrete reforms, the most important is perhaps the division of the entire country into thirty-six *chün* (commanderies) further subdivided into *hsien* (districts) each in the joint command of a civilian and military officer.[152] This measure, along with the forced removal of 120,000 noble families from their land to the capital at Hsien-yang in 221 B.C. abolished the last vestiges of feudal property.[153] The reform was only the termination of a long policy of centralization initiated by Shang Yang when, as we have seen, in 350 B.C. he divided the whole of Ch'in into 31 *hsien.* The origin of these administrative units is debatable; the *hsien* is said to have originated in Ch'in around 688 B.C. as a way of controlling newly conquered lands directly from the centre as opposed to the method of feudal delegation. The *chün,* in a somewhat similar manner, is said to have been developed by Wei as a militarized buffer zone in about 400 B.C.—again under central control—against the barbarian tribes on the borders of the Chinese states.[154] These devices were not inevitably anti-feudal as we do hear of families possessing or being given *hsien,*[155] but it would be fair to agree with Bodde that in theory "the *hsien* system tended to weaken feudalism,"[156] and its appropriateness for such a function is amply demonstrated in Li Ssu's use of it as a centralizing measure. Another act aiming in the same direction was the melting down of all the feudal armory and the destruction of feudal fortifications to make insurrections difficult.[157]

Li Ssu's other measures are also concerned with the enforcement of unitary control and internal rationalization. Thus they include the unification of the Chinese script[158] and currency[159] and the construction of a network of roads for military purposes.[160] Again like Shang Yang, and doubtless for similar reasons, he favoured agriculture at the expense of commerce. In one of his proclamations Shi Huang-ti announces that "he has elevated agriculture and proscribed what is secondary (i.e., commerce)."[161] And Li Ssu in 213 B.C. happily affirms that "now the clans and the heads of families apply themselves to agriculture and artisan labour."[162] Perhaps the Legalist measure for which Li Ssu is most notorious is his memorial of 213 B.C. which led to the famous Burning of the Books. The arguments he adduced for such a measure are exactly those we find in the *Han Fei Tzu* directed against the fissiparous and divisive activities of the scholars. He is quoted in the *Shi Chi* as saying

> "When they (i.e., the scholars) hear orders promulgated, they criticize them in the light of their own teachings. Within (the court) they mentally discredit them, and out-

> side they criticize them upon the streets. To cast disrepute on the ruler they regard as a thing worthy of fame; to accept different views they regard as high (conduct); and they lead the people to create slander. If such conditions are not prohibited, the imperial power will decline above, and partisanship will form below."[163]

Thereupon he requested permission to destroy the works of poetry and history (what were later to become the Classics of the *Shih Ching* and the *Shu Ching*) along with the various philosophical works. Works of utilitarian or supposedly utilitarian import were preserved, such as those on medicine, pharmacy, divination by the tortoise and milfoil and on agriculture and arboriculture.[164] As Bodde points out, the damage done by this measure was limited, and considerably less than that occasioned by the sacking of the capital Hsien-yang by the rebels in 206 B.C.[165] The primary victims were probably the state histories apart from that of Ch'in and the philosophical writings which, lacking widespread dissemination among the people, could not be reconstructed with the same facility as the Confucian works.[166] Here again Li Ssu was not breaking fresh ground, for Mencius mentions that the feudal lords of his time frequently destroyed historical records to prevent the past from holding witness against them.[167] In all his reforms therefore, Li Ssu was no innovator either in concept or in implementation but his contribution lay in extending measures which had received piecemeal implementation throughout the entire land on a uniform basis.

Before concluding this discussion, one last point may be made. In dealing with the *Han Fei Tzu* and the *Shang-Chün Shu* we have noted that the enormous power vested in the ruler is not to be confused with a justification of arbitrary tyranny, and the ruler is expected to maintain a distinction between the public and the private interest. This indeed is vital to the smooth functioning of the 'methods.' Now Li Ssu too holds to this distinction on which the entire existence of impersonal rule is contingent and counsels restraint, but at the same time there is a tendency to undermine the distinction between the two realms in the interest of placating the ruler.

Thus, "When an able man possesses the empire, he does nothing else but use the empire exclusively so that it will accord with his own (desires). This is the value of possessing the empire."[168] Further in the same memorial he says, "Therefore he is able for himself alone to follow a mind of complete unrestraint, and no one dares to oppose him."[169] Although it is possible that he is simply describing in terms of Taoist exaggeration the complete ease and absence of concern that marks the ideal ruler, one is left with the impression that the fatal transition is being made from the ruler as unmoving mover, mysterious and unformulatable in his desires, to one for whom the empire is simply a source for self-indulgence. *Shu* becomes less an objective mechanism than a tool for relentless exploitation. It was by tensions engendered by this form of misuse—implicit perhaps in Legalism—that the empire of Ch'in was supplanted a brief fourteen years after its founding; a point which lends substance to the observation of the *Han Fei Tzu* that *shih* or position alone is not sufficient to guarantee the security of the state.

In summation, the genealogy of Legalism is reasonably clear. Confucius is the first to sound the warning that the accepted values of the family and feudalism were collapsing and needed to be refurbished. He himself hoped for a restoration of these old forms, but the point is that his teachings established the question of the formation of political and social value systems as the most valid and pressing one of the times—and this of course merely underlined the same issues which were being posed even more forcefully by the course of contemporary socio-political events. Mo Ti's theory regarding the Agreement with the Superior—stressing as it does vertical definition as opposed to lateral affiliation—clouds the distinction between state and society and makes the Superior all-important, a tendency which becomes even more marked when augmented by Hsün-tzu's deep-seated pessimism regarding human nature. The problem facing the Legalists was how to establish a state given the baseness of men. The two vital requirements were coercion, the application of external force to prevent unwanted acts—necessary because moral education was powerless to alter men—and impersonality—because the all-too-evident foibles of human nature had to be circumvented. The first of these is evidenced, particularly though not exclusively, in the emphasis on *fa* both as punitive and as commendatory in the *Shang-chün Shu* while the latter finds its expression in the importance attached to *shu* by the *Han Fei Tzu*. Both these ideas, though particularly that of impersonality, are strongly coloured by Taoist thinking. The *Lao-tzu* is firm on the issue of keeping the people in a simple and unperturbed state, and this condition is greatly facilitated by the use of law, as also by the system of rewards and punishments implicit in it, in propelling people into the 'weakening' professions of war and agriculture. Equally, the equation of the ruler with the fish who never leaves the deep and therefore remains an unpredictable and unknown force to his ministers, thus preventing their exploitation of him, is the essence of the notion of impartiality. It has been said earlier that the distortions and excesses of Legalist thought may to some extent be the result of attempting to institutionalize the uninstitutionalizationable teachings of Taoism. Like Confucianism, although from a very different angle, Taoism is particularly concerned with ontology, its endeavour is to alter the being of men, and it is singularly aware that the attempt to define this being in any definitive sense, be it social, political or otherwise, is to deform and falsify it. External forms therefore are of no importance to it, and yet Legalism, which uses a similar terminology, is concerned with nothing but externalities, the observable behaviour of men. Its impersonality is therefore not that of unformulatable being but a form of bureaucratic discretion. This externality of Legalism opposes it to both Confucianism and Taoism. However, it is precisely the fact that the "inner-directed' man plays no role in their scheme that makes it so seductive a governmental philosophy, for it leads, as we have seen with Li Ssu, not only to administrative centralization, but to the abrogation of a pluralistic value system and its replacement by state dogma.

CHAPTER IX

Conclusion

CHAPTER IX

The very nature of the source materials utilized in this study will serve to highlight the essential and irreducible differences between the Chinese and Indian perspectives. With the possible exception of Arthaśāstra literature—and we have attempted to indicate that the gulf between it and the Dharmasūtras is not as great as is often assumed in terms of fundamental attitudes towards political authority—it is clear that the Indian thinkers do not see the problem of order as a political issue but as a sacro-social one. Further, the problem is seen to be solved if the categories of the *varṇāśramadharma* can be faithfully sustained, and these categories—as distinct from the agencies required for their protection—are sacrally ordained and transcendentally sanctified. Or perhaps it would be more accurate to say that the policing agencies partake of a sacred character only in so far as they are faithful to their protective role. With the Chinese, on the other hand, the problem of order is preeminently a political one, and the issue is quite self-consciously analyzed by the authors whom we have studied—a fact that stands in marked contrast to the almost incidental role accorded to temporal authority as such in the Indian works. Moreover, despite the emphasis in Confucius on what we have termed the five basic values and that in Mo Ti on Heaven, it is generally true that the Chinese works have a more secular view of society and the state.

It is tempting, at first sight, to attempt an equation between the hierarchy of castes and that of Confucius and to see them both as immutable social forms which stand in the way of monolithic centralization. This view certainly has a substantial measure of truth in terms of the discrete nature of castes in India and the stringent attempts made by the Legalists to break down the values of the Confucians which they saw as standing in the path of the imposition of state-determined dogma in China. But this valid similarity also tends to blur distinctions of some importance between the two systems. The caste system is not a political form although the Regnum does find a place within it. The values intrinsic to it are not political—if by that we understand that it does not aim at an increase of temporal authority—and in fact throughout the preceding survey we have noted the tension and barely latent opposition between the sacred social order and the executive agent, a tension which is summed up in the oppositional complementarity of the syzygy scheme of the Regnum and the Sacerdotium. We have also seen, in the section on the *Kauṭilīya Arthaśāstra,* that the pluralism of values implicit in the caste system automatically assures that no one value scheme, such as for example that which aims at the magnification of state power, can ever become paramount without destroying the system. The Confucian system, like the Brahmanical scheme, accepts certain social values and the external forms which overtly express them as being of the greatest importance, and they are, in this respect, alike in being wedded to concrete social schemes. But, unlike the Śāstric order, there is no dichotomy between the social and the political, what conduces to political personal virtue also conduces to success. It may here be parenthetically noted that what distinguishes Confucius from the Legalists is not the fact that the latter are more 'political' than he is but that they assert that temporal imperium is not only independent of personal worth but often opposed to it. Hence the significance of Shang Yang's 'weakening the people' and his dictum that a strong state requires a weak people. This fusion of the personal and the political, indeed the social and the political, does not mean, as we have seen, that Confucius regards social forms as relative, for it can be argued that it is only in the content of certain specific social forms that government can be successful, but it does mean that the whole scheme is far more politicized than the Śāstric structure.

The Śāstras do not claim that the *varṇāśramadharma* and the values which it embodies can be justified in political or utilitarian terms, and certainly it is explicable only in sacral and not in empirical ones. But in the case of the Confucians, because of the essentially political nature of their scheme, a justification is always sought on empirical grounds. The question which underlies the Confucian debate with the Mohists and the Legalists is whether a man can be really worthy of rule if he be not loyal, sincere, filial and practice forms exemplifying these virtues—in other words, whether or not the Confucian means are efficacious, a term which has no place in a discussion of the Brahmanical order. Thus the Confucian hierarchy is really a unitary construct in terms of values—a common yardstick sufficces for both the good official and the dutiful son since, theoretically, one has to be the latter before becoming capable of the former. The *varṇāśramadharma*, on the other hand, as was discussed in the section on the *Arthāśastra* of Kauṭilya, has a value system with a dual aspect and this was seen to be responsible for the strange contrast between Kauṭilya's drastic methods and the surprising modesty of his ends. This duality, which makes a value absolute in a given caste category but relative to the whole, stems from the essential pluralism of the caste system, a pluralism which would be shattered by allowing any one value to be absolute in terms of the whole. Thus, despite the similarities between the Confucian and Śāstric structures, they are, in fact, unitary and pluralistic value-systems respectively. It is this fact which enabled the Confucians, in the tims of the Han, to establish a compromise with Legalist principles, since despite the extent of their other differences, they both countenanced a unitary value structure. Conversely, the gulf between the polyvalent Śāstric scheme and the unified scheme pre-supposed by the Buddhist perspective regarding political authority was far too wide to permit a similar type of accommodation.

Another angle of comparison which suggests itself is the similarity between what may be termed the heterodox foes of the traditional systems in India and China, namely Buddhism and Legalism. An affinity between these two is certainly shocking and unjustified if seen in the overall context of their philosophies, but it is justified if viewed in terms of what their attitudes imply for political power. It is clearly no accident that both Buddhism and Legalism do not regard any given social institution as being sacrosanct—and the lack of any counter-balance stemming from a pre-existing social order ensures that the political agent will be seen as the origin of any such order and be accorded a commensurate prestige and power. We have seen that the Buddhists derive kingship from pure necessity—kings are necessary to curb the chaos engendered by the conflict of selfish interests. The fact that society in itself lacks any degree of cohesive power is also illustrated by the devalorization of the caste system. The king thus becomes paramount; he not only prevents internecine conflicts but imposes a degree of integration upon a discrete heap of individuals. The king is not only the state, but the motive power behind the creation of society. This is precisely the case with the Legalists as well. We have attempted to show that the endeavour to create a system of automatic rule based on the mechanism of self-interest leads to a similar elevation of the ruler who becomes the sole means of holding the state together. Seen in this light, and however anamalous it may seem, Aśoka and the Ch'in policy exemplified by Shih Huang-ti have much in common. Here again the ultimate aims and purposes of the two rulers obviously differ to the point of being polar opposites. but the significant point is that they both regard society as a synthetic creation engendered by political will. To be sure the policies operated at somewhat different levels: Shih Huang-ti's primary concerns—as those of his predecessors—were with the abolition of feudalism and the creation of a monolithic state, both materially and—via the Burning of the Books—ideologically, while Aśoka's, despite certain similar concerns (such as his determination to keep order among the hill peoples for example) were with the formation of a universal and unifying social ethic—that of Dhamma. But this difference, along with that which is constituted by the opposition between Shih Huang-ti's emphasis on force and that of Aśoka on pacifism, must not blind one to the fact that in both cases the dynamic was an executive one. With Aśoka, unlike in the Śāstric scheme, the Regnum creates the Sacerdotium instead of merely protecting it—and by create we mean, as clarified above, not that he regarded the ethic *per se* as his own creation, but that the modalities of its expression were regarded as his responsibility. And Shih Huang-ti, in definitively substituting *fa* (law) for *li* (rites and rituals) similarly subordinates social forms to the will of the executive power.

The strange congruence between the formidable monarch who first unified China and the great pacifist emperor matches the parallelism in the general historical configurations of India and China in our period. In both places it is a time of fierce inter-state conflict marked by expanding monarchial ambitions. The common trend is away from discrete political units to large monolithic states, a trend that culminates in the achievements of Ch'in in China and the Mauryas in India. And in both instances the states which summed up and exemplified the forces and tendencies of the time were outsiders to the main hallowed cultural centres. In both cases what occurred was not the fulfillment and development of traditional forms but their abolition. The political values of Buddhism are not mature extensions of the Brahmanical ones but are diametrically opposed to them. And in much the same way, although perhaps not to the same extent, the Legalist values contravene those of the preceding Confucian school despite their both being unitary systems. The fact that the old order was being dissolved through war, expansion, and the weakening of traditional institutions with nothing immediately at hand to replace them provides some basis for the perception of Shih Huang-ti and Aśoka of the state and society as a virtual *tabula rasa* on which new forms, devised by them, were to be inscribed. The freedom from traditional restraints which both enabled and necessitated the growth of monarchical power to provide a substitute for the ancient scheme is what is particularly striking about both monarchs. But this freedom is precisely a result of the breakdown of the old traditional forms, and the similarity based on this freedom illustrates not a cultural affinity between China and India but simply that, in our period, both India and China had become, as it were, "deculturized." That is to say, they had lost or abandoned organic forms of society and government and were compelled to the conscious utilization of political power in the endeavour to synthetically create new ones and it is this which gives the policies of Aśoka and Shih Huang-ti a modern ring.

This period of hiatus which was sought to be filled with executive action was a temporary phenomenon, and with its passing the ephemeral similarities which we have noted between India and China also came to an end. In India the emergence, or recrudescence, of Brahmanical forms in Magadha shortly after the collapse of the Mauryas rendered the problem of fabricating a social consciousness out of whole cloth invalid, while in China the Legalist Confucianism of the Han tempered the harsh principles of Legalism with consideration for forms of relationships other than that between the subject and the state—thus reducing its sterile artificiality and total dependence on positivistic means. Whether or not Indian political thinking and practice would have become bureaucratized, like that of the Chinese, given continued state support for Buddhism—or any similar doctrine which denied society an intrinsic regulatory power—must remain a matter for speculation, but it was impossible so long as the *varṇāśramadharma* held undisputed sway.

The central issue regarding the *varṇāśramadharma* and its relation to administrative unity and centralization has been a topic of considerable discussion, and in the work of Bouglé we have what may be considered a fairly representative viewpoint. He views the *varṇāśramadharma* as a purely divisive force—"the most active principle of disintegration that the world has ever known"[1]—and he goes on to remark that "they [i.e., the Hindus] enact a paradox in that they can only be united in the cult which divides them."[2] Dumont, in his analysis of the caste system, clearly sees what Bouglé had failed to perceive—that the caste system is a unity and has to be viewed as a holistic entity based on the interdependence of its separate parts. He notes, in other words, that the oppositions within the caste system are also modes of complementarity, and here again we meet the ever-present syzygy principle. This, however, does not dispose of Bouglé's point that politically the caste system is a disruptive force as it militates against the formation of a central authority, but it does have an intimate bearing on the subject. If we accept that the caste system, viewed internally, is an integrated unity, then we have to accept it as a principle of order in itself. Bouglé's cardinal error is in persistently viewing order as a political problem in need of an executive agent to ensure uniformity. The idea of a sacro-socially induced order with pluralistic and dissimilar values is inconceivable to him. He is right if he means that the caste system is antipathetic to the formation of a homogenized and monolithic state but not in equating this fact with atomization and chaos. Dumont, as we have noted, does not make this error, but he too fails to note the full implications of the concept of social order. He does recognize that although the king is needed as the caretaker of the *varṇāś-ramadharma*, in the ultimate analysis the king exists for the *varṇāśramadharma* and not vice—versa, but does not go on to stress that the *varṇāśramadharma* thus creates an insuperable obstacle to the growth of absolute and despotic temporal power. The very fact that the *varṇāśramadharma* is not conducive to patterns of centralization and administrative unity is what guarantees the prevention of totalitarian forms—that is, forms devised and imposed by executive diktat.

Seen in this light, the bureaucratization and centralization of China would seem to be intimately linked with the absence of this kind of hallowed social form. Two cyclical points of general validity may be noted in this context: insofar as the problem of order was seen as a political one, a political solution had to be formulated for it—and this was the creation of a bureaucracy; secondly, the active existence of a bureaucracy prevents—or at least hinders—the development of autonomous social forms. Viewed from a slightly different angle, the absence of a self-regulatory social order demands the compensation of bureaucratic control, and this bureaucratic control, in turn, widens the gap between the ruler and the ruled—an extreme example of which is constituted by Shih Huang-ti. It is frequently assumed that hierarchy is opposed to egalitarianism, and that, since egalitarianism is equated with liberty, hierarchy and liberty are incompatible. The egalitarian totalitarianism of the Ch'in exposes the fallacy of such a perspective and reveals the fact that hierarchy, whether that of caste or of the patriarchal family, was the force which intervened between the individual and the relentless reality of state power. Never was it more true that freedom lies in having many masters.

NOTES

Chapter I

[1]Ananda K. Coomaraswamy, *Spiritual Authority and Temporal Power in the Indian Theory of Government* (New Haven, Conn. : American Oriental Society, 1942), reprinted by Krause Reprint Corporation, New York, 1967. I am substantially indebted to this brilliant work for the discussion that follows as also for the references to the original works quoted.

[2]*Ibid.*, p. 50.

[3]Of the vedas, Coomaraswamy concentrates on the *Artharvaveda* and the *Ṛgveda*.

[4]Coomaraswamy, *Spiritual Authority* . . ., pp. 42-43.

[5]*Ibid.*, p. 43.

[6]*Ibid.*, p. 8.

[7]*Ibid.*, pp. 10-11, note 13.

[8]*Ibid.*, p. 3.

[9]*Ibid.*, pp. 51-63.

[10]*Ibid.*, p. 65.

[11]*Ibid.*

[12]*Ibid.*, p. 50.

[13]*Ibid.*

[14]*Ibid.*

[15]*Ibid.*

[16]*Ibid.*, p. 24.

[17]*Ibid.*, p. 68.

[18]Arthur A. Macdonell, *A History of Sanskrit Literature* (Delhi : Motilal Banarsidass, 1971), pp. 207-221.

[19]P. V. Kane, *Hisory of Dharmaśāstra* (5 vols. in 7 : Poona : Bhandarkar Oriental Research Institute, 1930-68), Vol. I, pp. 10-13. See also, *The Sacred Laws of The Aryas, Part I, Āpastamba and Gautama*, trans. by Georg Bühler in *The Sacred Books of the East*, ed. by Max Mueller (Delhi : Reprint by Motilal Banarasidass, 1965), Vol. II, pp. x, xi (hereinafter referred to as *Āpastamba* or *Gautama*).

[20]*Gautama*, XI.1.

[21]*Ibid.*, XI.14.
[22]*Ibid.*, XI.9.
[23]*Ibid.*, XI.10.
[24]*Ibid.*, XI.19.
[25]*Ibid.*, XI.20-21.
[26]J. Duncan M. Derrett, "The Role of Dharmaśāstra in Modern Comparative Legal History," in *Madras Law Journal* (June, 1966), pp. 43-56.
[27]*Ibid.*, p. 53.
[28]*Āpastamba*, 1.3.11.34.
[29]*Ibid.*, 1.5.15.4.
[30]*Ibid.*, 2.5.10.8.
[31]*Ibid.*, 1.7.20.10.
[32]*Ibid.*, 1.7.20.13.
[33]*Ibid.*, 1.9.27.15 and 1.10.29.1.
[34]*Ibid.*, 1.9.27.18.
[35]*Ibid.*, 2.5.10.12,13,14,15.16.
[36]*Ibid.*, 1.9.25.4.
[37]*Ibid.*, 1.9.25.5.
[38]*Gautama*, XXIII.14.
[39]*Āpastamba*, 2.11.28.1.
[40]*Gautama*, XII.26.
[41]*Ibid.*, 40.
[42]*Ibid.* 29.
[43]*Ibid.*, 30.
[44]*Ibid.*, 32-33.
[45]*Ibid.*
[46]*Āpastamba*, 1.9.27.10.
[47]*Gautama*, XI.19.
[48]J. Duncan M. Derrett, *Religion, Law and the State in India* (London : Faber and Faber, 1968), pp. 167-169.

Chapter II

[1]Macdonnel, *Sanskrit Literature*, p. 181.
[2]*Ibid.*
[3]Hemachandra Raychaudhuri, *Political History of Ancient India* (Calcutta: University of Calcutta, 1963), p. 167. (Hereinafter referred to as *PHAI*.)
[4]*Ibid.*
[5]*Ibid.*, p. 164.
[6]*Ibid.*, p. 58.
[7]J. C. Heesterman, "Brahmin, Ritual and Renouncer," *Wiener Zeitschrift für die Kunde Sud und Ostasiens*, Band VIII, 1964, p. 14.
[8]*Ibid.*
[9]*Ibid.*

[10]*PHAI*, p. 168.

[11]*Ibid.*, p. 58.

[12]*Ibid.*, p. 69.

[13]G. P. Malalasekera, *Dictionary of Pāli Proper Names*, Vols. I-II, Pali Text Society (London: Luzac and Co., 1960), Vol. II, p. 813. (Hereinafter referred to as *DPPN*.)

[14]*PHAI*, p. 95.

[15]*Ibid.*, p. 112.

[16]T. W. and C. A. F. Rhys Davids, trans., *Sacred Books of the Buddhists*, Vol. II, Part I, 111.1., Humphrey Milford (London: Oxford University Press, 1923), p. 145. (Hereinafter referred to as *SBB*.)

[17]A. L. Basham, *Studies in Indian History and Culture*, (Calcutta: Sambodhi Publications Private Ltd., 1964), p. 77.

[18]*PHAI*, p. 199.

[19]*Ibid.*, p. 204.

[20]Thomas R. Trautmann, "Consanguineous Marriages in Pāli Literature" (paper presented at the 181st meeting of the American Oriental Society. Cambridge, Mass., April 6-8, 1971), p. 4.

[21]Vishudhanand Pathak, *History of Kosala* (Benares: Motilal Banarsidass, 1963), p. 235.

[22]Basham, *Indian History and Culture*, p. 78.

[23]*PHAI*, p. 220.

[24]*DPPN*, Vol. I, p. 194.

[25]*PHAI*, p. 233.

[26]*Ibid.*, p. 235.

[27]E. J. Rapson, ed., *The Cambridge History of India*, Vol. I, *Ancient India* (Delhi: S. Chand, 1968), p. 281. (Hereinafter referred to as *CHI*.)

[28]*PHAI*, p. 261.

[29]J. W. McCrindle, trans., *The Invasion of India by Alexander the Great as described by Arrian, Q. Curtius, Diodorus, Plutarch and Justin*, (Archibald Constable and Co., 1896), p. 177.

[30]Thomas R. Trautmann, *Kauṭilya and the Arthaśāstra* (Leiden: E. J. Brill, 1971), pp. 59, 66.

[31]*PHAI*, p. 270.

[32]*Ibid.*, p. 273.

[33]K. A. N. Sastri, *A History of South India* (Madras and New York: Oxford University Press, 1955), p. 79.

[34]*Ibid.*, pp. 85-86.

[35]*PHAI*, p. 296.

[36]Romila Thapar, *Aśoka and the Decline of the Mauryas* (Oxford: Oxford University Press, 1961).

[37]*Gautama*, IX. 20.

[38]*CHI*, p. 158.

[39]*Ibid.*, p. 160.

[40]*SBB*, Vol. II, 91. 13-14, p. 113.

[41]*PHAI*, p. 174.

[42]*Ibid.*, p. 207.

[43]*Ibid.*, p. 277. see also Trautmann, *Kauṭilya and the Arthaśāstra*, pp. 183, 185.

[44]McCrindle, *Ancient India as described by Megasthenes and Arrian*, reprinted (with additions) from the *Indian Antiquary*, 1876-77 (revised 2nd edition: Calcutta: R. C. Majumdar, 1960), p. 15.

[45]*Ibid.*, p. 41.

[46]*Ibid.*, pp. 87-88.

[47]*Ibid.*, p. 86.

[48]*Ibid.*, p. 41.

[49]*The Kauṭiliya Arthaśāstra*, trans. by R. P. Kangle, Parts I, II, III (Bombay: University of Bombay, 1963), Part II, 1.12.6. (Hereinafter referred to as *ARTH.*)

[50]McCrindle, *Ancient India as. . .*, p. 41.

[51]*ARTH*, 2. 36.1-4.

[52]*Ibid.*

[53]*Ibid.*, 2.6.2.

[54]*Ibid.*, 2.22.1-7.

[55]*Ibid.*, 2.16.2.

[56]*Ibid.*, 2.16.6.

[57]*Ibid.*, 2.12.23.

[58]*Ibid.*, 2.23.1.

[59]*Ibid.*, 2.12.23.

[60]*Ibid.*, 2.30.4, 2.31.1.

[61]*Ibid.*, 2.33.6.

[62]*Ibid.*, 2.33.7.

[63]*Ibid.*, 2.18.1.

[64]McCrindle, *Ancient India as. . .*, p. 85.

[65]*ARTH*, 5.3.38.

[66]*Ibid.*, 5.3.41.

[67]*Ibid.*, 2.1.4.

[68]*Ibid.*, 2.35.2.

[69]*Ibid.*, 2.35.1., 2.35.6.

[70]*Ibid.*

[71]*Ibid.*, 2.35.8.

[72]*Ibid.*, 1.13.16.

[73]*Ibid.*, 5.2.2.

[74]*Ibid.*, 2.1.17.

[75]*Ibid.*, 2.1.13-14.

[76]*Ibid.*, 4.13.17.

[77]*Ibid.*, 2.24.11.

[78]*Ibid.*, 2.1.20.

[79]*Ibid.*, 2.1.21.

[80]*Ibid.*, 3.9.33.

[81]*Ibid.*, 3.18.7, 3.19.4.

[82]*Ibid.*, 3.1.39.

[83]*Ibid.*, 3.1.45.

[84]*Ibid.*, 2.35.2.

[85]*Ibid.*, 3.9.15.

[86] *Ibid.*, 4.1. 2-3.
[87] *Ibid.*, 3.14.2-12.
[88] *Ibid.*, 11.1.1.
[89] *Ibid.*, 10.3.43.
[90] *Ibid.*, 9.1.18.
[91] *Ibid.*, 1.5.17.
[92] *Ibid.*, 6.2.13-22.
[93] *Ibid.*, 7.1.2-5.
[94] *Ibid.*, 7.1.32.
[95] *Ibid.*, 7.1.13.
[96] *Ibid.*, 7.16.3.
[97] *Ibid.*, 7.2.1.
[98] *Ibid.*, 7.8.8.
[99] *Ibid.*, 12.1.10-25.
[100] *Ibid.*, 7.16.17-23.
[101] *Ibid.*, 7.16.26.
[102] *Ibid.*, 7.16.28.
[103] *Ibid.*, 7.16.23.
[104] *Ibid.*, 7.16.30.
[105] *Ibid.*, 7.16.33.
[106] *Ibid.*, 13.4.52, 10.3.26.
[107] *Ibid.*, 1.4.3.
[108] *Ibid.*, 7.16.26.
[109] *Ibid. PHAI*, 207.
[110] Basham, *Indian History and Culture*, p. 77.
[111] *Ibid.*
[112] *Ibid.*
[113] *ARTH*, 1.15.23.
[114] *Ibid.*, 1.1.1.
[115] *Ibid.*, 5.5.11.
[116] Pathak, *History of Kosala*, pp. 232-233 .
[117] *ARTH*, 1.3.5-9.
[118] *Ibid.*, 1.3.16.
[119] *Ibid.*, 4.13.43.
[120] *Ibid.*, 1.4.13-15.
[121] *Ibid.*, 1.4.12.
[122] *Ibid.*, 3.19.8.
[123] *Ibid.*, 5.3.1-24.
[124] *Ibid.*, 3.1.39.
[125] *Ibid*, 13.5.14, 13.5.10.
[126] *Gautama*, XI 19, 20.
[127] Louis Dumont, *Homo Hierarchicus*, trans. by Mark Sainsbury (London: Weidenfeld and Nicolson, 1970).
[128] *Ibid.*
[129] *Ibid.*
[130] *Ibid.*, p. 152.
[131] *ARTH*, 13.5.9-10.
[132] *Ibid.*, 13.4.62.

[133] *Ibid.*, 13.5.14.

[134] Dumont, *Homo Hierarchicus*, pp. 97-106.

[135] *Ibid.*, p. 66.

[136] *ARTH*, 1.3.14-15. See also 1.3.16.

Chapter III

[1] M. Winternitz, *History of Indian Literature*, trans. by S. Ketkar, Vols. I-II (Calcutta: University of Calcutta), Vol. II, Buddhist Literature and Jain Literature, pp. 15, 247.

[2] T. W. and C. A. F. Rhys, Davids trans. *Sacred Books of the Buddhists*, Vol. IV, Part III, Diii 84-85, Humphrey Milford (London: Oxford University Press, 1923), p. 81.

[3] Mahāvastu, Vol. I, trans. J. J. Jones, *Sacred Books of the Buddhists*, Vol. XVI (London: Luzac and Co., 1949), pp. 285-286.

[4] *Ibid.*, p. 291.

[5] *Ibid.*, p. 292.

[6] *Ibid.*, p. 293.

[7] Davids, *Sacred Books of the Buddhists*, Vol. IV, Part III, Diii 93-96, pp. 88-91.

[8] *Ibid.*, Diii 82, p. 78.

[9] *Ibid.*, Diii 96-97, p. 92.

[10] *Ibid.*, Diii 97, p. 93.

[11] *Ibid.*, Diii 98, p. 94.

[12] *Ibid.*

[13] A. K. Warder, *Indian Buddhism* (Delhi: Motilal Banarsidass, 1970) p. 165.

[14] *Ibid.*, p. 171.

[15] Macdonell, *History of Sanskrit Literature*, p. 189.

[16] Heesterman, "Brahmin, Ritual and Renouncer."

[17] *Ibid.*, p. 2.

[18] *Ibid.*, p. 10.

[19] *Ibid.*

[20] *Ibid.*, p. 7.

[21] *Ibid.*, p. 12

[22] *Ibid.*, p. 14.

[23] *Ibid.*, p. 23.

[24] *Ibid.*

[25] Bhagavad-Gita, 2.19.

[26] *Les Inscriptions d'Aśoka*, trans. by Jules Bloch Societé d'edition "Les Belles Lettres" (Paris, 1950, 13th MRE), p. 128.

[27] *Ibid.*, p. 129.

[28] *The Sacred Laws of the Aryas, Part II, Vasiṣṭha and Baudhāyana*, trans. by Georg Bülher in *The Sacred Books of the East*, ed. by Max Mueller (Delhi: Reprint by Motilal Banarsidass, 1965) Vol. II, xix, i (hereinafter referred to as *Vasiṣṭha* or *Baudhāyana*).

[29]*Ibid.*, XIX.2.
[30]*ARTH*, 1.4.3.
[31]*Ibid.*, 1.4.16.
[32]*Ibid.*, 1.4.7-10.
[33]Bloch, 13 MRE.
[34]*Ibid.*
[35]*The Laws of Manu*, trans. by Georg Būlher, *Sacred Books of the East*, Vol. XXV, (New York: reprint by Dover Publications, 1969), VII. 103. (Hereinafter referred to as *Manu*.)
[36]Bloch, 7th. PE.
[37]Thapar, *Aśoka*, p. 198.
[38]*Ibid.*, p. 198; *PHAI*, pp. 354-355.
[39]Bloch, p. 96.
[40]*Ibid.*, 11th, RE, p. 120.
[41]*Ibid.*, 12th, RE, p. 124.
[42]*Ibid.*, p. 122.
[43]*Ibid.*
[44]A. L. Basnam, *History and Doctrines of the Ājīvikar* (London: Luzac and Co., 1951), pp. 134-141.
[45]*Ibid.*, p. 135.
[46]*Ibid.*, p. 138.
[47]Bloch, 1st. RE, p. 91.
[48]*Ibid.*, p. 92.
[49]*Ibid.*, 4th, RE, p. 98.
[50]*Manu*, II. 17.
[51]Robert Lingat, *The Classical Law of India*, trans. by J. Duncan M. Derrett (Berkeley: University of California Press, 1973), p 200.
[52]I. e., the Bhābra, Rummindei and Nigalisāgar inscriptions and the Schism Edict.
[53]Bloch, 3rd, MRE, p. 96.
[54]*Ibid.*, 5 MRE.
[55]*Ibid.*
[56]*Ibid.*, 6th MRE, p. 107.
[57]*Ibid.*, pp. 108-109.
[58]*Ibid.*
[59]*Ibid.*, p. 121.
[60]*Ibid.*, p. 124.
[61]*Ibid.* 1st. Separate Edict of Kaliṅga.
[62]*Ibid.*, MRE 6, p. 109.
[63]*Ibid.* Mysore and Central Regions, p. 150.
[64]Thapar, *Aśoka*, pp. 173-174.
[65]Bloch, PE 1.
[66]*Ibid.*, PE 2.
[67]*Ibid.*, PE 4.
[68]*Ibid.*, PE 7.
[69]*Ibid.* I have chosen to retain 'meditation' in the sense in which Bloch uses it when he says "superiorité de la meditation individuel e

sur les interdictions externes" on p. 37. The term 'persuasion' would not lend itself to this meaning. See also p. 39.

[70]Louis Dumont, *Religion, Politics and History in India* (Paris/The Hague: Mouton Publishers, 1970), p. 74.

[71]*Ibid.*, p. 75.

[72]Bloch, MRE 6.

[73]*Ibid.*, Mysore and Central Regions, Minor Rock Inscription, p. 146.

Chapter IV

[1]Bühler's Introduction to *Manu*, p. xcii.

[2]*Ibid.*, xcix.

[3]*Manu*, XI.75.

[4]*Ibid.*, VII.35.

[5]*Ibid.*, VIII.3.

[6]*Ibid.*, VII.4.

[7]*Ibid.*, VII.5.

[8]*Ibid.*, VII.8.

[9]*Ibid.*, VII.17.

[10]*Ibid.*, VII.24.

[11]*Ibid.*, VII.20.

[12]Bühler's Introduction to *Manu*, xlvi.

[13]*Manu*, VIII.3.

[14]*Ibid.*, VIII.8.29.

[15]*Ibid.*, VIII.138.

[16]*Gautama*, XII.43.

[17]*Manu*, VIII.319-331,

[18]*ARTH*, 2.1.4.

[19]*Manu*, VII.115-117.

[20]*Ibid.*, VIII.401-402 *ARTH*, 2.16.2-8.

[21]*Manu*, VII.128. *ARTH*, 2.21.1.

[22]*Manu*, VIII.403. *ARTH*, 2.6.2.

[23]*Manu*, VIII.399.

[24]*ARTH*, 1.4.3.

[25]*Manu*, VII.101.

[26]*Ibid.*, VII.102.

[27]*Ibid.*, IX.251.

[28]*Ibid.*, IX.261.

[29]*Ibid.*, VII 158.

[30]*Ibid.*, VII.107.

[31]*Ibid.*, VII.120.

[32]*Ibid.*, VII.138.

[33]*Ibid.*, VII.130.

[34]Bülher's Introduction to *Manu*, liv-lv.

[35]Trautmann, *Kauṭilya*, p. 186, Table 7.4.

[36]Dumont, *Homo Hierarchicus*, p. 153.
[37]Bloch, 13th. RE, p. 130.
[38]*Manu*, 1.85.
[39]Lingat, *Classical Law*, p. 184ff.
[40]*Ibid.*, p. 182.
[41]*Manu*, XI.159.
[42]*Ibid.*, IV.250.
[43]*Ibid.*, III.15-19.
[44]*Ibid.*, IX.53.
[45]*Ibid.*, IX.66.
[46]*Ibid.*, V.157, IX.76.
[47]Lingat, *Classical Law*, p. 187.
[48]*Ibid* , p. 169ff.
[49]*Ibid.*, p. 169.
[50]*Manu*, VIII.3.
[51]Lingat, *Classical Law*, pp. 200-202.
[52]*Ibid.*
[53]*Ibid.*, p. 200.
[54]*Manu*, VII.28.
[55]Coomaraswamy, *Spiritual Authority and Temporal Power. . .*, p. 24.
[56]*Ibid.*, p. 8.

Chapter V

[1]*The Chinese Classics, Vol. I.—Confucian Analects*, *The Great Learning*, *The Doctrine of the Mean*, trans. by James Legge (Hong Kong : 1960), *Analects*, II.21.1. (Hereinafter referred to as *Confucian Analects*, *The Great Learning*, or *The Doctrine of the Mean*.) See also Liang Ch'i-ch'ao, *History of Chinese Political Thought During the Early Tsin Period*, trans. by L.T. Chen (New York : AMS Press, 1969), pp. 45, 51.

[2]*Analects*, II.1.

[3]*Ibid.*, VIII. 18.

[4]*The Great Learning*, 4.

[5]*Ibid.*, 6-7.

[6]*Li-chi*, *Book of Rites*, trans. by James Legge. Edited with Introduction and study guide by Ch'u Chai and Winberg Chai, Vols. I and II (New York : University Books, 1967), Li Yun 2.15. (Hereinafter referred to as *Li-Chi*.) In the Introduction to the work, the compilation of the text as it has come down to us is traced to the first century B.C.—pp. lvff. This being so, the references to and the quotations from the *Li-chi* are not to be taken as being directly attributable to Confucius but only as illustratively amplifying ideas present in his system. With reference to the emulative nature of good government, see also Liang Ch'i-chao, *History of Chinese Political Thought During the Early Tsin Period* (New York : AMS Press, 1969), pp. 45, 51.

[7]*Analects*, XII.18.

[8] *Ibid.*, XIII.3.2, 6.

[9] *Ibid.*, XII.11.1. See Also Liang, *History of Chinese Political Thought . . .*, pp. 47-48.

[10] *Doctrine of the Mean*, 2.9.

[11] See the Speach of the Duke of Chou, *Shu Ching, The Book of Documents*, ed. and trans. by Bernhard Karlgren, reprinted from Museum of Far Eastern Antiquities Bulletin 22 (Stockholm, 1950), Book IX.16, wherein he refers to filiality and fraternal affection as "the laws of our nature given by Heaven to our people."

[12] *The Doctrine of the Mean*, 2.3.

[13] *Li-chi*, Li Yun, 4.9-10.

[14] *Ibid* , 1.4

[15] *Ibid.*, IV.5.

[16] *Ibid.*, 1.10.

[17] *Analects*, XVII.11.

[18] *Li-chi*, Tseng Tzu Wen 2.7.

[19] *Analects*, VIII.2.

[20] *Li-chi*, Li Yun, 4.5.

[21] *Ibid.*, Wen Wang Shih Tzu, 1.16.

[22] *Ibid.*, Yueh Chi, 1.3.

[23] *Analects*, III.3.

[24] *The Great Learning*, Comm., X.2.

[25] *Li-chi*, Kung-tzu Hsien Chu, 1-3.

[26] *Ibid.*

[27] *Ibid.*, Li Yun, 2.13. For a somewhat different discussion of the same theme, see H. G. Creel. *Confucius, The Man and The Myth* (New York : John Day, 1949), p. 135 ff, where he tends to see Confucius in a more purely empiricist light as one who functioned on the basis of experience.

[28] *Analects*, XVII.3.

[29] *Ibid.*, XVII.2.

[30] *Li-chi*, 2.15.

[31] *Analects*, II.3.1-2.

[32] *Ibid.*, XII.19.

[33] *Ibid.*, XV.4.

[34] *Li-Chi*, 2.15.

[35] *Analects*, XIII.1.1.

[36] *Ibid.*, IV.14.

[37] *Ibid.*, IV.16.

[38] *The Great Learning*, Comm. X.23.

[39] Analects, XI.16.1.

[40] *Ibid.*, IX.6.1 and XIII.4.3.

[41] *Ibid.*, XIII.5.

[42] *Ibid.*, XII.7.1.

[43] *Li-chi*. Fang Chi, 1-2.

[44] *Ibid.*, 4.

[45] Analects, IX.25.

[46]1.1.1.1-6, *The Works of Mencius, The Chinese Classics* Vol. II, trans. by James Legge (Hong Kong : Hong Kong University Press, 1960). (Hereinafter referred to as *Mencius*).

[47]*Ibid.*

[48]Ibid., 1.1.7.3.

[49]*Ibid.*, 2.1.5.2-5.

[50]*Ibid.*, 1.1.7.20. See also Liang, *History af Chinese Political Thought*, p. 59.

[51]*Ibid.*, 1.1.7.22.

[52]*Ibid.*, 1.2.4.1.

[53]*Ibid.*, 1.2.3.6-7 ; also 1.2.5.4.

[54]*Ibid.*, 1.2.12.1-2.

[55]*Ibid.*, 3.1.2.1.

[56]*Ibid.*, 2.1.6.1.

[57]*Ibid.*, 6.1.1.1.

[58]*Ibid.*, 6.1.1.2.

[59]*Ibid.*, 6.1.6.5.

[60]*Ibid.*, 6.1.6.7.

[61]*Ibid.*, 6.1.7.3 ; also 6.1.7.1.

[62]*Ibid.*, 7.1.15.2.

[63]*Ibid.*, 7.2.4.2-6.

[64]*Ibid.*, 1.1.7.12.

[65]*Ibid.*, 2.1.3.1.

[66]*Ibid.*

[67]*Ibid.*, 2.1.3.2. See also Fung Yu-lan, *A History of Chinese Philosophy*, Vol. 1, trans. by Derk Bodde (Princeton : Princeton University Press, 1952), p. 112.

[68]*Ibid.*, 1.1.7.17.

[69]*Ibid.*, 1.1.7.16.

[70]*Ibid.*, 1.2.8.2-3. See also Fung, *Chinese Philosophy*, Vol. I, p. 113.

[71]*Ibid.*, 5.1.5.1-2.

[72]*Ibid.*, 5.1.5.4.

[73]*Ibid.*, 5.1.6.3.

[74]*Ibid.*, 5.2.9.1-4.

[75]*Ibid.*, 1.2.7.3.

[76]*Ibid.*, 5.1.6.2.

[77]*Ibid.*, 7.2.14.1.

[78]*Ibid.*, 1.2.7.4.

[79]*Ibid.*, 1.1.7.12.

[80]*Ibid.*, 4.1.1.3.

[81]*Ibid.*, 3.1.5.3.

[82]*Ibid.*, 3.1.5.4.

[83]*Ibid.*, 3.2.9.9. Fung. *Chinese Philosophy*, Vol. I. pp. 113-114, sees the justification for hierarchy in Mencius to be a purely rational one—that of the division of labor. This is based on Mencius' dictum that "Some labour with their minds, and some labour with their strength. Those who labour with their minds govern others; those who labour with their strength are governed by others. Those who are

governed by others support them; those who govern others are supported by them." Mencius, 3.1.4.6. But it will be obvious in the context of his strictures against Mo Ti that the importance he places on distinctions far transcends purely utilitarian considerations and that they possess an intrinsic significance.

[84]*Ibid.*, 6.1.6.7.

[85]*Analects*, XVII.2.

[86]4. 23. p. 65, *The Works of Hsüntze*, trans. by Homer H. Dubs (Taipei : Ch'eng Wen Publishing Co., 1966). Reprint of original edition published by Arthur Probsthain London, 1928. Hereinafter referred to as *Hsuntze*.

[87]*Ibid.*, 4. 23. p. 66.

[88]*Ibid.*, 9.3. p.124.

[89]*Ibid*, 9.12. p.124.

[90]*Ibid*. For other similar discussions on the nature of hierarchy in Hsün-tzu, see Ch'ü T'ung-tsu, *Law and Society in Traditional China* (Paris : Mouton, 1965), p. 227, 229-230. Also Fung, *Chinese Philosophy*, p. 305, for the relationship between Hsün-tzu's Rectification of Names—in this respect similar to that of Confucius—and hierarchy: "Names (*ming*) were made in order to denote actualities (*shih*), on the one hand so as to make evident the noble and the base, and on the other to distinguish similarities and differences." Also Donald J. Munro, *The Concept of Man in Early China* (Stanford : Stanford University Press, 1969), p. 26, for a treatment of the same theme and pp. 89-90 for a discussion involving the related topic of the role of *li* and *yi* in controlling man's infinity of desires.

[91]*Hsüntze*, 9.12. p. 124.

[92]*Ibid.*, 10.1. p. 151.

[93]*Ibid.* It is worth remarking here that it is knowledge rather than morality which leads to the establishment of social institutions. In other words, the formation of societies is a tribute, not to human goodness, but to human intelligence. See Fung, *Chinese Philosophy*, p. 296, for the role of the mind (*hsin*) in knowing the social norms. See also Munro, *The Concept of Man*, p. 79.

[94]*Hsüntze*, 23.4, p. 306.

[95]*Ibid.*, 23.7-8, p. 313.

[96]*Ibid.*, 8.6, p. 96.

[97]*Ibid.*, 19.14, p. 235.

[98]*Ibid.*, 21.5. p. 264.

[99]*Ibid.*, 8.21, p. 115. See also 9.11, p. 135.

[100]*Ibid.*, 17.2. p. 174. Apropos the issue of the impersonality of Heaven, Y. P. Mei in "Hsün-tzu's Theory of Education," "*Tsing Hua Journal of Chinese Studies*, New Series 11, No. 2 (June, 1961), 362, points out the apposition and complementarity between the concept of an impersonal Heaven and that of the evil of man. See also Fung, *Chinese Philosophy*, p. 286.

[101]*Hsüntze*, 9.11, p. 135.

[102]*Ibid.*, 19.3. p. 220.

[103]*Ibid.*, 23.2. p. 303.

[104]*Ibid.*, 23.1. p. 302. For a different view of the role of the doctrine of evil in Hsün-tzu, see Munro, *The Concept of Man*, pp. 77-81, where he holds that this aspect of Hsün-tzu has been wrongly emphasized at the expense of the truly principal theme of his work—the problem of the allocation of scant resources and the role of the mind (*hsin*) in controlling man's social behavior in this context. It would still appear, however, that any discussion of man's social behaviour would necessarily imply some attitude towards the issue of human nature, and thus the doctrine of evil retains its importance.

[105]*Hsüntze*. 23.1-2, p 302.

[106]*Ibid.*, 23.2, p. 304.

[107]*Ibid.*, 23.3. p. 304. See also Homer H. Dubs, *Hsüntze, Moulder of Ancient Confucianism* (London : Arthur Probsthain & Co., 1927), pp. 80ff.

[108]*Hsüntze*, p. 305.

[109]*Ibid.*, 19.14. p. 234. Dubs, *Hsüntze*, p. 81, also touches on this issue when he says in passing, "Hsüntze never raised the question as to whether this training presupposed the capacity to receive it; he merely saw that the training was received."

[110]*Hsüntze*, 2.22. p. 52.

[111]*Ibid.*, 23.8. p. 313.

[112]*Ibid.*, 17.14-14. p. 177.

[113]*Ibid.*, 23.8. p. 314.

[114]*Ibid.*, 23.4. p. 306.

[115]*Ibid.*, 9.3. p. 123.

[116]*Ibid.*, 8.17-19. p. 182.

[117]*Ibid.*, 8.24. p. 83-4.

[118]*Ibid.*, 7.25. p. 84.

[119]*Ibid.*, 15.11-12. p. 169-70.

[120]*Ibid.*, 18.2. p. 190.

[121]*Ibid.*, 7.23. p. 82.

[132]*Ibid.* Dubs is of the opinion that it may be an expansion of *Analects*, XV.30. See footnote 3, p. 32.

[123]*Hsüntze*, 1. 3. p. 32. Regarding the externality of Hsün-tzu, Mei, in his perceptive article on "Hsün-tzu's Theory of Education," p. 365, show that for Hsün-tzu, unlike Mencius, education is not an organic growth but "a quantitative accumulation (*chi*)," but yet he assumes that such accumulation can naturally arrive at spiritual enlightenment. In Mei's words, "Accumulation here seemed to be capable of following a quantitative procedure but producing qualitative results." This contradiction constitutes a parallel in the educational field to the one already noted in his treatment of Heaven and man's nature. As Mei goes to note, the externality evidence in his view of education as "accumulation" is symptomatic of his emphasis on control from the outside; similarly rituals and ceremonials are seen as forms to be observed, that is to say, as objective standards rather than as objective correlatives.

[124]See *Analects*, XVII.2, where he inveighs against the mere external form of ritual.

[125]*Mencius*, 7.1.36 1-2.

[126]*Hsüntze*, 18.6. p. 194.

[127]*Ibid.*, 18.6. p. 195.

Chapter VI

[1]Lao Tzu, *Tao Te Ching*, trans. by D. C. Lau (London : Penguin Books, 1963), p. 174. He sees the date of the work as belonging to the third century B. C., and Burton Watson in his translation of the *Complete Works of Chuang-tzu* (New York : Columbia University Press, 1968), sees both the works being known in their present form in the second century B. C. See p. 8. This writer is aware of the complexity of the issue regarding the dating of the Tao-Te Ching and is inclined to follow the argument of the two scholars whose translations have been used in this study. For other studies see Hu Shih, "A Criticism of Some Recent Methods Used in Dating Lao-tzu" *Harvard Journal of Asiatic Studies*, No. 2 (1937), 373-397, and Fung, *Chinese Philosophy*, pp. 170-172. (Hereinafter referred to as *Lao Tzu* and *Chuang Tzu*.)

[2]Lau, *Lao Tzu*, p. 32.

[3]*Ibid.*, 1.XXV.57.

[4]*Ibid.*, 1.XXVII.62.

[5]*Ibid.*, 11.XXXVIII.63.

[6]*Ibid.*, 1.VIII.21.

[7]*Ibid.*, 2.LIII.121.

[8]*Ibid.*, 2.LXXII.175.

[9]*Ibid.*, 1.XXX.69a.

[10]*Ibid.*, 1.XXIX.66.

[11]*Ibid.*, 1.XVIII.42.

[12]*Ibid.*

[13]*Ibid.*

[14]*Ibid.* 2.XXXVIII.83.

[15]*Ibid.*, 1.XXV.58.

[16]*Ibid.*, 1.II.4.

[17]*Ibid.*, 1.II.7.

[18]*Ibid.*, 1.II.5.

[19]Fung, *Chinese Philosophy*, p. 174, feels that the blurring of opposites is more a feature of Chuang-tzu's thought than that of Lao-tzu's, but he goes on to give examples from Lao-tzu, pp. 178, 183, 185, where precisely this ambiguity is revealed in discussions on Being and Non-being, oneness and duality, etc. It would be wiser to assert that this attitude is perhaps more stressed in Chuang-tzu, but it is by no means absent in Lao-tzu. Chang Ch'i-chun, *Lao-tzu Yen-Chiu* (Hong Kong, L658), pp. 63, 91, is more inclined to accept the relativist nature of lao-tzu's thought.

[20]Lau, *Lao Tzu*, 1.II.7.
[21]*Ibid.*, 1.III.10.
[22]*Ibid.*, 1.XVI.38.
[23]*Ibid.*, 1.XXX.69a.
[24]*Ibid.*, 1.XXX.69b.
[25]*Ibid.*, 1.XXXV.77.
[26]*Ibid.*, 1.XI.27.
[27]*Ibid.*, 1.X.24.
[28]*Ibid.*, 1.XVII.39.
[29]*Ibid.*, 1.XXVIII.64. See also his note on p. 86 equating "vessels" with specialists. Also introduction, p. 37.
[30]Lau, *Lao Tzu*, See Introduction, p. 45, and 2.LV.125.
[31]*Ibid.*, 1.XIX.43.
[32]*Ibid.*, 1.III.9.
[33]*Ibid.*, 1.XXXVII.81.
[34]*Ibid.*
[35]*Ibid.*, 2.LXI.141-142a.
[36]*Ibid.*, 2.LXVI.160.
[37]*Ibid.*, 162.
[38]*Ibid.*, 2.LVII. 132.
[39]*Ibid.*, 1. XXXVI. 80.
[40]*Ibid.*, Introduction, pp. 38-39.
[41]*Ibid.*, 1.V.14.
[42]Burton Watson, trans., *The Complete Works of Chuang Tzu* (New York and London : Columbia University Press, 1968), 2.39.
[43]*Ibid.* 2.40.
[44]*Ibid.*
[45]*Ibid* , 5.75.
[46]*Ibid.*, 6.81.
[47]*Ibid.*, 1.33 7.93.
[48]*Ibid.*, 1.35.
[49]*Ibid.*, 5.74.
[50]*Ibid.*, 6.78.
[51]*Ibid.*, 7.93.

Chapter VII

[1]Mei, Yi-Pao, trans. *The Ethical and Political Works of Motse* (Westport Conn.: Hyperion Press, Inc., 1973). Original Arthur Probsthain Publication, 1929, 1.V.18. (Hereinafter referred to as *Motse.*)
[2]*Ibid.* I.V.20.
[3]*Ibid.*
[4]*Ibid.*, I.V.21.
[5]*Ibid.*, I.V.20.
[6]*Ibid.*

[7]*Ibid.*, III.XI.55. In the note on the same page, Mei explains his translation of Yi as idea.

[8]*Motse*, III.XI.55.

[9]*Ibid.*

[10]*Ibid.* 56.

[11]*Ibid.*

[12]*Ibid.*, III.XII.60-61.

[13]*Ibid.*

[14]*Ibid.*

[15]*Ibid.*, 58.

[16]*Ibid.*, IV.XIV.78.

[17]*Ibid.*, 78-79.

[18]*Ibid.* 80.

[19]*Ibid.*, VI.XXV.123-4. For the difference between this attitude and that of the Confucians, see Liang, *History of Chinese Political Thought*, p. 94.

[20]*Motse*, I.IV.13-14.

[21]*Ibid.*

[22]*Ibid.* 15.

[23]*Ibid.*, II.VIII.32.

[24]*Ibid.*, XL.XLVI.217.

[25]*Ibid.*, II.VIII.33.

[26]*Ibid.*

[27]*Ibid.*, XII.XLVII.225. For a treatment of the topic of specialization in Mo Ti, see Y. P. Mei, *Motse, The Neglected Rival of Confucius* (London : Arthur Probsthain, 1934), pp. 116-117.

[28]*Ibid*,, VII.XXVI.136. Mei, *Motse* . . . , p. 119, also deals wlth the meritocratic nature of the Mohist hierarchy.

[29]*Ibid* , II.VII.33.

[30]*Ibid.*, III.XII.60.

[31]*Ibid.*, 67.

[32]For a different interpretation of the monopolization of power implicit in the principle of Agreement with the Superior—the political heart of the Mohist system—see Hsiao Kung-ch'üan, *Chung-kuo Cheng-chih Szu-hsiang Shih*. Vol. I (Chungking, 1945), pp. 101-104—where he argues that, insofar as the Superior only unifies pre-existing opinions, the system is essentially democratic and dependent upon catering to the public interest and sentiment for its efficacy. Even if we accept the somewhat dubious postulate that centralization policies require the support of the people, it is still beyond argument that centralization, in itself, limits a plurality of views and Hsiao himself acknowledges this when he refers to the principle of Agreement with the Superior as a politically restraining force. And, it may be remarked, a restraining force which demands a very high degree of uniformity—something which is necessitated by the Babellike confusion which Mo Ti sees as prevailing among men who are without a Superior. Mei, *Motse*, pp. 115-116, tends to see a parity between the ruler and the people as they are both subordinate to Heaven. Although this is indisputable, it ignores the

functional differences between the Superior and the inferiors. Liang, *History of Chinese Political Thought*, pp. 105ff, acknowledges the conflict between Mo Ti's egalitarian bias and the authoritarianism of his political structure as does T'ao Hsi-sheng. *Chung-kuo Cheng-chih Ssu-hsiang Shih*, Vol. I, Taipeh, p. 97. Both accept the fact that Mo Ti's system tends to autocracy but, as Liang implies, an autocracy limited by the moral probity of Heaven.

[33]*Motse*, III.XI.56.

[34]*Ibid.*, I.IV.14.

[35]*Ibid.*, VII.XXVI.136.

[36]*Ibid.*, VI.XXV.128.

[37]*Ibid.*, III.XII.63.

[38]*Ibid.*, VII.XXVI.137.

[39]*Ibid.*, IX.XXXV.184.

[40]*Ibid.*, 186.

[41]*Ibid.*, VIII.XXXI.165.

[42]Hsiao *Chung-kuo Cheng-chih Ssu-hsiang*, Vol. I, p. 104, states that Mo Ti's belief in a conscious Heaven is really a matter of reinforcing the political restraints of the Agreement with the Superior with a religious one. In this sense, although his belief in a living Heaven may not in itself be rational, the function it tends to sub-serve is certainly pragmatic and utilitarian. This should not be taken to mean that religious sanctions are cynically used to bolster political power but rather that the principles of order which the ruler is supposed to exemplify are principles of a celestial validity.

[43]*Motse*, VI.XXV.124.

[44]*Ibid.*

[45]*Ibid.*, 134.

[46]*Ibid.*, VIII.XXXII.175.

[47]*Ibid.*, I.VI.23.

[48]*Ibid.*, XIII.XLIX.248.

[49]*Ibid.*, 249.

[50]*Ibid.*

[51]Hannah Arendt, *The Human Condition* (New York : Doubleday Anchor, 1959), p. 135.

[52]*Motse*, III.XII.64.

[53]*Ibid.*, III.XIII.77.

[54]*Ibid.*, III.XII.66.

[55]*Ibid.*, III.XIII.70

[56]*Ibid.*, V.XVIII.106.

[57]*Ibid.*, VII.XXVIII.155.

Chapter VIII

[1]Richard Louis Walker, *The Multi-State System of Ancient China* (Hamden, Conn. : The Shoe String Press, 1953), p. 20. (Hereinafter referred to as *MSAC*.) Derk Bodde, basing himself on the *Li-chi*, gives

the number of states existing in the early years of the Chou as 1,763. See Derk Bodde, *China's First Unifier* (Hong Kong : Hong Kong University Press, 1967). Walker's figure is based on that of Ma Tuan-lin in *Wen Hsien T'ung-k'ao* (Shanghai : Commercial Press, 1936), pp. 2059b. For the social changes which accompanied and accentuated this process of political simplification, see Hsu, Cho-yun, *Ancient China in Transition* (Stanford : Stanford University Press, 1968), pp. 24ff.

[2]Ch'i Ssu-ho, "The Investiture Ceremony of Chou," in *Chinese Social History*, trans. and ed. by E-Tu Zen Sun and John De Francis (New York : Octagon Books, 1966), p. 38. (Hereinafter referred to as *CSH*.)

[3]Chang, Yin-lin, *Feudal Society of the Chou Dynasty*, in *CSH*, p. 21. See also *MSAC*, p. 6, as also H. G. Creel, *The Origins of Statecraft in China* (Chicago and London : University of Chicago Press, 1970), Vol. I, pp. 70-71. In General, however, Creel believes that the Chou, despite their policy of delegation, were more centralized than is commonly believed. See also, Derk Bodde, *Feudalism in China in Feudalism in History*, ed. by Rushton Coulborn (Princeton : Princeton University Press, 1956), p. 53.

[4]*CSH*.

[5]*Mencius*, 5.2.3.

[6]"The Investiture Ceremony of Chou," in *CSH*, p. 38.

[7]"Feudal Society of the Chou Dynasty," in *CSH*, p. 21.

[8]*Ibid.*, p. 23.

[9]*Ibid.*

[10]*Ibid.*, p. 25.

[11]*MSAC*, p. 20.

[12]*Ibid.*, p. 22.

[13]*Ibid.*, p. 26.

[14]*Ibid.*, p. 27.

[15]*Ibid.*, p. 28.

[16]*Ibid.*, p. 34.

[17]*Ibid.*, p. 32ff.

[18]"Feudal Society of the Chou Dynasty," in *CSA*, p. 22.

[19]See translation of the *Shih Chi* biography of Kuan-tzu in Evan Morgan, *A Guide to Wenli Styles and Chinese Ideals* (London : Arthur Probsthain and Co., 1931), p. 120. The Biography also credits him with encouraging trade—a policy diametrically opposed to that followed by other Legalist administrators like Shang Yang and Li Ssu.

[20]*MSAC*. p. 33.

[21]*Ibid.*, p. 34.

[22]*Ibid.*

[23]Walker states that the scope of warfare was magnified after the battle of Ch'eng-pu between the Chou and southern leagues in 632 B.C. *MSAC*, p. 124, n. 60.

[24]See the discussion regarding the *chün* and *hsien*, pp. 181-182 in text.

[25]*CSH*, pp. 38-39.

[26]*Ibid.*, p. 54.
[27]*Ibid.*, p. 38.
[28]*Ibid.*, p. 49.
[29]*MSAC.*, p. 50.
[30]*Ibid.*, p. 52.
[31]*Ibid*
[32]*Ibid.*
[33]*Ibid.*
[34]*Ibid.*
[35]*Ibid.*, p. 53.
[36]*Ibid.*
[37]Bodde, *China's First Unifier*, p. 2.

[38]*Ibid.*, p. 4. The members of the so-called 'perpendicular alliance' against Ch'in were Chao, Yen, Wei, Ch'u, Ch'i and Han. See W.K. Liao, trans. *The Complete Works of Han Fei Tzu* (London : Arthur Probsthain and Co., 1959), Vol. 1, 1.1.1-2. Hereinafter referred to as *Han Fei Tzu.*

[39]*Ibid.*
[40]*Ibid.*, p. 5.

[41]J. J. L. Duyvendak, trans. *The Book of Lord Shang* (London : Arthur Probsthain and Co., 1963), p. VIII. (Hereinafter referred to as *The Book of Lord Shang.*)

[42]*Ibid.*, p. 18, n. 2. Duyvendak claims the figure to be erroneous and states it to be 31 *hsein.*

[43]*Ibid.*
[44]*Ibid.*, p. 15.
[45]*Ibid.*, p. 18.

[46]*Ibid.*, p. 14. It may be noted that the division into fives, probably inspired by Kuan Chung, is also to be found in the reforms of Tzu-ch'an. See *MSAC*, p. 67. See also W. Allyn Rickett, trans. *Kuan-Tzu* (Hong Kong : Hong Kong University Press, 1965), XVIII, 57.82. All future references to the *Kuan-tzu* will be based on this work. (Hereinafter referred to as *Kuan-tzu.*) The translation of the *Kuan-tzu* by Wen Kung-wen and T'an Po-fu entitled *Economic Dialogues in Ancient China* (Carbondale, III : Lewis Maverick, 1954) has also been consulted, as has the *Kuan-tzu*, Vols. 1-5, collated by Tai Wang (Taipeh, 1965).

[47]*Kuan-Tzu*, Tai Wang Cheng-chiao, p. 15.
[48]*Ibid.*, p. 19.
[49]*Ibid.*, p. 18.
[50]*Ibid.*, pp. 53-54.

[51]Hsu, Cho-yun, *Ancient China in Transition* (Stanford : Stanford University Press, 1968). (Hereinafter referred to as *ACIT.*)

[52]*Ibid.*, p. 31. Ch'u appears to have been an exception in that it early developed a centralized system of administration with the officials—although frequently related to the dynasty—being appointed on the basis of merit and subject to removal. Hereditary office and feudal independence were minimal or non-existent. See H. G. Creel, "The Beginnings

of Bureaucracy in China : The Origin of the Hsien," in *What Is Taoism?* (Chicago : University of Chicago Press, 1970), pp. 149-152.

[53]*Ibid.*

[54]*Ibid.*, p. 34. Barry Burden Blakely, "Regional Aspects of Chinese Socio-political Development in the Spring and Autumn Period (722-464 B.C.) : Clan Power in a Segmentary State" (unpublished Ph.D. dissertation, The University of Michigan, 1970), pp. 320-327, notes considerable regional variation between states in terms of the relationship between kinship structure and political influence, but he accepts (pp. 333-334) that in all states there was a rise of collateral lineages, thus testifying to the weakening of the central lines.

[55]*Ibid.* See starred note.

[56]*Ibid.*, p. 37.

[57]*Ibid.*, p. 51.

[58]*Ibid.*, p. 154.

[59]*Ibid.*, pp. 93-95.

[60]*Ibid.*, p. 93.

[61]*Ibid.*, p. 68.

[62]*Ibid.*, p. 100ff.

[63]*MSAC*, p. 16.

[64]*ACIT*, p. 64.

[65]*MSAC*, p. 91.

[66]*The Book of Lord Shang*, 2.179-183.

[67]*ACIT*, p. 137. For an archaeological description of some Ch'un Ch'iu and Chan Kuo cities, see Paul Wheatley, *The Pivot of the Four Quarters* (Chicago : Aldine Publishing Co., 1971), pp. 136-150.

[68]*MSAC*, p. 18.

[69]*ACIT*, p. 137. Bodde, China's First Unifier, p. 170, takes a somewhat opposed view.

[70]Ch'en, Ch'i-t'ien, in *Fa-chia Shu-yao*, p. 843. See also, Fung yulan, *A History of Chinese Philosophy*, Vol. I, trans. by Derk Bodde (Princeton : Princeton University Press, 1969), p. 313 and *MSAC*, p. 67.

[71]*The Book of Lord Shang*, p. 159. See also Chang Hsin-cheng, *Wei-shu T'ung-k'ao* (Shanghai, 1939, reprint 1954). pp. 769-771.

[72]*The Book of Lord Shang*, p. 158. See also Chang, *Wei-shu T'ung-k'ao*, pp. 774-783.

[73]*Kuan-tzu*, p. 11.

[74]*The Book of Lord Shang*, p. 8ff.

[75]*Ibid.*, p. 14.

[76]*Ibid.*, pp. 15, 18.

[77]*Ibid.*, p. 15. *Kuan-tzu*, VI, 16.94, also supports a hierarchy based on service.

[78]*Ibid.*, p. 18.

[79]*Ibid.*

[80]*Ibid.*, 18.287. A scheme which also appears in the *Kuan-tzu*, XVIII, 57.82.

[81]*Ibid.*, 17.275, see p. 139 for dating.

[82]*Ibid.*, p. 92. For a similar opinion see Ch'en, Lieh, *Fa-chia Cheng-chih Che-hsueh* (Shanghai, 1929), pp. 11-12.

[83]*Han Fei Tzu*, Vol. I, p. XXVII.

[84]*Ibid.*

[85]*The Book of Lord Shang*, 169. See also *Kuan-tzu*, 1, 2 and XX, 64.144.

[86]*Ibid.*, 1.171-3. See also *A History of Chinese Philosophy*, p. 317.

[87]*Han Fei Tzu*, Vol. II, 19.49.276.

[88]*Ibid.*, 19.49.278.

[89]*The Book of Lord Shang*, 1.169.

[90]*Ibid.*, 23.316.

[91]*Han Fei Tzu*, Vol. II, 17.45.229.

[92]*Ibid.*, 18.48.258.

[93]*The Book of Lord Shang*, 5.208.

[94]*Ibid.*, 6.219.

[95]*Ibid.*, 4.260-1, *Han Fei Tzu*, Vol. I.2.6.44-5, *Kuan-tzu*, VI, 16.90.

[96]Ch'en Chi'-ti'en, *Fa-chia Shu-yao*, 853-854. See also H.G. Creel, "Fa-chia : 'Legalists' or 'Administrators'?" in *What is Taoism* ?, pp. 92-120.

[97]W.K. Liao translates the term as 'tact.'

[98]For a detailed discussion of Shcn Pu-hai, see H.G. Creel, "The Meaning of Hsing-ming," "The Fa-chia : 'Legalist' or 'Administrators'?" in *What is Taoism* ?, pp. 79-121. (Hereinafter referred to as "Fa-chia.")

[99]*Han Fei Tzu*, Vol. II, 17.43.212. See also *A History of Chinese Philosophy*, p. 319.

[100]*Han Fei-tzu*, Vol. I, 1.5.34.

[101]"The Fa-chia : 'Legalist' or 'Administrators' ?," *What is Taoism*?, p. 95.

[102]*The Book of Lord Shang*, 9.240.

[103]"The Fa-chia: 'Legalists' or 'Administrators' ?," p. 86.

[104]*History of Chinese Philosophy*, p. 325; also "The Fa-chia," p. 86, n. 45.

[105]*Mencius*, 7.1.XXXVI.1.

[106]*Han Fei Tzu*, Vol. II, 17.40.119. See also *Kuan-tzu*, 1, 2 and XX, 64.

[107]*Han Fei Tzu*, Vol. II, 17.40.200.

[108]"The Fa-Chia," pp. 93, 102, 103.

[109]*The Book of Lord Shang*, 4.200. Also *Kuan-tzu*, VI, 16.97.

[110]See *Han Fei Tzu*, Vol. I, 9.30.292.

[111]*The Book of Lord Shang*, 6.225 and 13.254.

[112]"The Fa-chia," p. 114.

[113]*Han Fei Tzu*, Vol. II, 17.43.213-4.

[114]*Ibid.*, Vol. I, 5.17.146.

[115]*Fa-chia Shu-yao*, p. 853.

[116]*The Book of Lord Shang*, p. 102.

[117]*Han Fei Tzu*, Vol. I, 4.14.124.

[118]*Ibid.*, Vol. I, 6.20.175-6.

[119] *Ibid.*, 4.14.124. The importance of punishing minor crimes severely for their deterrent effect is also found in the *Kuan-tzu*, VI, 16.91.

[120] *The Book of Lord Shang*, 4.204.

[121] *Ibid.*, 7.229-30.

[122] *Ibid.*, 13.259.

[123] *Ibid.*, 14.261.

[124] *Han Fei Tzu*, Vol. I. 8.25.265. Also *Kuan-tzu*, VI, 16.90.

[125] *Ibid.*, 1.5.31.

[126] *Ibid.*

[127] *Ibid*,, 2.7.51.

[128] *Ibid.*, 2.7.48-9.

[129] *Ibid.*, 2.8.52. See also 1.5.31 and *Kuan-tzu*, I, 2 and XX, 64-127. For a good example of the link between Taoism and stringent punitive Legalism, see *Kuan-tzu*, XVI, 49 and XII, 36-37.175.

[130] *Ibid.*, 55. See also *Kuan-tzu*, VI, 16-100, which says, "Therefore it is said : Your political power is not something to be granted to others."

[131] *Ibid.*, Vol. II. 14.35.134.

[132] *Ibid.*, 13.34.88.

[133] *Ibid.*, 14.35.117; see also *The Book of Lord Shang*, 4.199-200.

[134] *Ibid.*, 14.35.126.

[135] *Ibid.*, Vol. I. 1.5.32.

[136] *Ibid.*, 8.27.270. *Kuan-tzu*, VI, 16.95.

[137] *Ibid.*, Vol. II. 17.40.204-5.

[138] *Ibid.*, 18.47.250.

[139] *Ibid.*, 20.51.316.

[140] *Ibid.*, 18.47.251.

[141] *Ibid.*, *The Book of Lord Shang* is even more explicit, see 4.197.

[142] *The Book of Lord Shang*, 2.177. See also Chen Lieh, *Fa-Chia Cheng-chih Che-hsueh*, pp. 16-17.

[143] *Ibid.*, paragraph 20, "Weakening the People."

[144] *Ibid.*, p. 303.

[145] *Ibid.*, p. 83. It may be mentioned that while the *Kuan-tzu* emphasizes agriculture, it is anti-war in general, VII, 18.55-60.

[146] *Ibid.*, 20.307.

[147] *Ibid.*, 8.234-5.

[148] *Han Fei Tzu*. Vol. II. 19.50.307.8.

[149] *Ibid.*, 20.53.324. What may be meant by these possibly pseudo-Taoists statements is simply that conditions can be created in which punishments and government are not invoked—not ones in which they don't exist. In a similar spirit Li Ssu claims that one rule is no rule—Fa-chia Hsu-yao, p. 852.

[150] *Fa-chia Shu-yao*, p. 853-854.

[151] *China's First Unifier*, pp. 38-41.

[152] *Ibid.*, p. 135.

[153] *Ibid.*, p. 143.

[154]*Ibid.*, pp. 135-143. Creel holds the differing view that *hsien* originated in Ch'u. He argues that Ch'u had a weaker kinship structure than the Chou states and was thus in a better position to develop a device which so violated the old principle of delegation. *What Is Taoism*?, pp. 149-152.

[155]*China's First Unifier*, p. 138.

[156]*Ibid.*, p. 139.

[157]*Ibid.*, p. 178.

[158]*Ibid.*, p. 160.

[159]*Ibid.*, pp. 171-172.

[160]*Ibid.*, p. 175.

[161]*Ibid.*, p. 171.

[162]*Ibid.*

[163]*Ibid.*, p. 23.

[164]*Ibid.*, pp. 23-24.

[165]*Ibid.*, p. 163.

[166]*Ibid.*, pp. 164-165.

[167]*Ibid.*, pp. 162-163.

[168]*Ibid.*, pp. 137-38.

[169]*Ibid.*, p. 42.

Chapter IX

[1]Celestin Bougle, *Essays On the Caste System*, trans. by D.F. Pocock (Cambridge: Cambridge University Press, 1971), p. 142.

[2]*Ibid.*

Bibliography

Chinese

Arendt, Hannah. *The Human Condition.* New York: Doubleday Anchor, 1959.

Blakeley, Barry Burden. "Regional Aspects of Chinese Socio-Political Development in the Spring and Autumn Period (722-464 B.C.): Clan Power in a Segmentary State." Unpublished Ph.D. dissertation, The University of Michigan, 1970.

Bodde, Derk. *China's First Unifier.* Hong Kong: Hong Kong University Press, 1967.

Bodde, Derk and Clarence Morris. *Law in Imperial China.* Cambridge, Mass.: Harvard University Press, 1967.

Chan, Wing-tsit. Translator. *The Way of Lao Tzu.* Indianapolis, Ind.: The Bobbs-Merrill Co., 1963.

Chang, Ch'i-chun. *Lao-tzu Yen-chiu.* Hong Kong, 1958.

Chang, Hsin-ch'eng. *Wei-shu T'ung-k'ao.* Changsha, 1939.

Ch'en, Chi-t'ien. *Fa-chia Shu-yao.* Chung-yang Yen-chiu yuan Li-shih Yu-yen Yen-chiu So, Taipeh, 1970.

Ch'en, Lieh. *Fa-chia Cheng-chih Che-hsueh.* Shanghai, 1929.

Ch'ü, Tung-tsu. *Law and Society in Traditional China.* Paris: Mouton Publishers, 1965.

Coulborn, Rushton. Editor. *Feudalism in History.* Princeton: Princeton University Press, 1956.

Creel, H.G. *Confucius, The Man and the Myth.* New York: John Day, 1949.

Creel, H.G. *What is Taoism*? Chicago: University of Chicago Press, 1970.

Creel, H.G. *The Western Chou Empire*, Vol. I in *The Origins of Statecraft in China*. Chicago: University of Chicago Press, 1970.

Crump, James I. *Studies of the Chan-Kuo T'se*. Ann Arbor, Mich.: The University of Michigan Press, 1964.

Dubs, Homer H. Translator. *The Works of Hsüntze*. Taipeh: Ch'eng-wen Publishing Co., 1966.

———. *Hsüntze, The Moulder of Ancient Confucianism*. London: Arthur Probsthain & Co., 1927.

Duyvendak, J.J.L. *The Book of Lord Shang* [*Shang-chün Shu*] London: Arthur Probsthain & Co., 1963.

Fung, Yu-lan. *A History of Chinese Philosophy*. Vol. I. Translated by Derk Bodde. Princeton: Princeton University Press, 1952.

Granet, Marcel. *La Pensée Chinoise*. Paris: Editions Albin Michel, 1950.

Hsiao, Kung-ch'üan. *Chung-kuo Cheng-chih Ssu-hsiang Shih*, Vol. I. Chungking, 1945.

Karlgren, Bernhard. Editor and translator. *Shu Ching, The Book of Documents*. Reprinted from Museum of Far Eastern Antiquities *Bulletin* 22. Stockholm, 1950.

Lau, D.C. Translator. *Lao Tzu, Tao Te Ching*. London: Penguin Books, 1963.

Legge, James. Translator. *Shu Ching*, Parts I and II, Vol. III in *The Chinese Classics*. London: Trubner and Co., 1865.

———. Translator. *Ch'un ts'ew* with the *Tso chuen*, Vol. V in *The Chinese Classics*. London: Trubner and Co., 1893.

———. Translator. *The Confucian Analects, The Great Learning, The Doctrine of the Mean*, Vol. I in *The Chinese Classics*. Hong Kong: Hong Kong University Press, 1960.

———. Translator. *The Works of Mencius*. Hong Kong: Hong Kong University Press, 1960.

———. Translator. *Li-chi, Book of Rites*, Vols. I-II. New York: University Books, 1967.

Legge, James, Translator. *The Book of Poetry*. New York: Paragon Book Reprint Corp., 1967.

Liang, Ch'i-chao. *History of Chinese Political Thought During the Early Tsin Period*. Translated by L.T. Chen. New York: AMS Press, 1969.

Liao, W.K. *The Complete Works of Han Fei-tzu.* Vols. I-II. London: Arthur Probsthain & Co., 1939.

Mei, Yi-pao. Translator. *The Ethical and Political Works of Motse.* Westport, Conn.: Hyperion Press, Inc., 1973.

———. *Motse, The Neglected Rival of Confucius.* London: Arthur Probsthain & Co., 1934.

———. "Hsün Tzu's Theory of Education, With an English Translation of *Hsün Tzu*, Chap. I, An Exhortation to Learning." *Tsing Hua Journal of Chinese Studies.* New Series II, No. 2, June, 1961.

Morgan, Evan. *A Guide to Wenli Styles and Chinese Ideals.* London: Arthur Probsthain and Co., 1931.

Munro, Donald J. *The Concept of Man in Early China.* Stanford: Stanford University Press, 1969.

Rickett, W. Allyn. Translator. *Kuan-tzu, A Repository of Early Chinese Thought.* Hong Kong: Hong Kong University Press: 1965.

Sun, E-Tu Zen and John De Francis. *Chinese Social History.* New York: Octagon Books, Inc., 1966.

Tai, Wang. Editor. *Kuan-tzu.* Taipeh, 1965.

T'ao, Hsi-sheng. *Chung-kuo Cheng-chih Ssu-hsiang Shih.* Vol. I. Taipeh, 1954.

Walker, Richard Louis. *The Multi-State System of Ancient China.* Hamden, Conn.: The Shoe String Press, 1953.

Watson, Burton. Translator. *The Complete Works of Chuang Tzu.* New York: Columbia University Press, 1968.

Weber, Max. *The Religion of China.* New York: Macmillan Co., 1951.

Wen Kung-wen and T'an Po-fu. Translators. *Economic Dialogues in Ancient China, Selections from the Kuan-tzu.* Carbondale, Ill.: Edited and published by Lewis A. Maverik, 1954.

Wheatley, Paul, *The Pivot of the Four Quarters.* Chicago: Aldine Publishing Co., 1971.

Wilhelm, Richard. Translator. *The I Ching or Book of Changes.* Rendered into English by Cary F. Baynes. Bollingen Series XIX. Princeton: Princeton University Press, 1967.

Indian

Basham, A.L. *History and Doctrines of the Ājīvikas.* London: Luzac and Co., 1951.

———. *Studies in Indian History and Culture.* Calcutta: Sambodhi Publications Private Ltd., 1964.

Bloch, Jules. *Les Inscriptions d'Aśoka.* Paris: "Les Belles Lettres," 1950.

Bouglé Celestin. *La Régime des Castes.* Paris: Librairie Felix Alcan, 1927.

Bühler, Georg. Translator. *The Laws of Manu, Sacred Books of the East.* Edited by Max Mueller. Vol. XXV. New York: Reprint by Dover Publications, 1969.

———. Translator. *The Sacred Laws of the Aryas, Part I, Āpastamba and Gautama.* In *The Sacred Books of the East.* Edited by Max Mueller. Delhi: Reprint by Motilal Banarsidass, 1965. Vol. II.

———. Translator. *The Sacred Laws of the Aryas, Part II. Vasiṣṭha and Baudhāyana.* In *The Sacred Books of the East.* Edited by Max Mueller. Delhi: Reprint by Motilal Banarsidass, 1965. Vol. II.

Coomaraswamy, Ananda. *Spiritual Authority and Temporal Power in the Indian Theory of Government.* American Oriental Series, Vol. 22. New Haven: American Oriental Society, 1942.

Davids, Rhys, C.A.F. and T.W. Translators. *Sacred Books of the Buddhists.* Edited by Max Mueller, Vol. II, Part I. Humphrey Milford. London: Oxford University Press, 1923.

———. Translators. *Sacred Books of the Buddhists.* Vol. IV, Part III. *Dialogues of the Buddha.* Translations from the Dīgha Nikāya. Humphrey Milford. London: Oxford University Press, 1921.

Derrett, J. Duncan M. *Religion, Law and the State in India.* London: Faber and Faber, 1968.

———. "The Role of Dharmaśāstra in Modern Comparative Legal History." Reprint from *Madras Law Journal.* June, 1966, pp. 43-56.

Drekmeier, Charles. *Kingship and Community in Early India.* Stanford: Stanford University Press, 1962.

Dumont, Louis. *Homo Hierarchicus*. Translated by Mark Sainsbury. London: Weidenfeld and Nicolson, 1970.

———. *Religion, Politics and History in India*. Paris/The Hague: Mouton Publishers, 1970.

Ghoshal, U.N. *A History of Indian Public Life*. Vol. II. London: Oxford University Press, 1966.

Heesterman, J.C. "Brahmin, Ritual and Renouncer." *Wiener Zeitschrift für die Kunde Süd und Ostasiens*, B and VIII, 1964, pp. 1-32.

———. *The Ancient Indian Royal Consecration*. Paris: Mouton Publishers, 1966.

Hutton, J.H. *Caste in India*. London: Oxford University Press, 1963.

Jones, J.J. Translator. *Sacred Books of the Buddhists Vol. XVI, The Mahāvastu*; Vol. I. London: Luzac and Co., 1949.

Kane, P.V. *History of Dharmaśāstra*. 5 Vols. in 7. Poona: Bhandarkar Oriental Research Institute, 1930-68.

Kangle, R.P. Translator. *The Kauṭilīya Arthaśāstra Parts I and II*. Bombay: University of Bombay, 1963.

Lamotte, Etienne. *Histoire du Bouddhisme Indien*. Louvain, Publications Universitaire, 1958.

Lingat, Robert. *The Classical Law of India*. Translated by J. Duncan M. Derrett. Berkeley: University of California Press, 1973.

Macdonnel, Arthur A. *A History of Sanskrit Literature*. Delhi: Motilal Banarsidass, 1971.

Macdonnel, Arthur A. and A.B. Keith. *Vedic Index of Names and Subjects*. Vols. I-II. Delhi: Motilal Banarsidass, 1967.

Malalasekera, G.P. *Dictionary of Pāli Proper Names*. Vols. I-II. Pali Text Society. London: Luzac and Co., 1960.

McCrindle, J.W. *Ancient India as Described by Megasthenes and Arrian*. Reprinted (with additions) from the *Indian Antiquary*, 1876-77. Revised second edition. Calcutta: R.C. Majumdar, 1960.

———. Translator. *The Invasion of India by Alexander the Great as Described by Arrian, Q. Curtius, Diodorous, Plutarch and Justin*. Archibald Constable and Co., 1896.

Pathak, Vishuddhanand. *History of Kosala*. Benares: Motilal Banarsidass, 1963.

Rapson, E J. Editor. *The Cambridge History of India*, Vol I. *Ancient India*. Delhi: S. Chand, 1968.

Raychaudhuri, Hemachandra. *Political History of Ancient India*. Calcutta: University of Calcutta, 1963.

Sastri, K.A.N. *A History of South India*. Madras and New York: Oxford University Press, 1955.

Senart, Emile. *Caste in India*. Translated by Sir Denison Ross. London: Methuen and Co., 1930.

Thapar, Romila. *Aśoka and the Decline of the Mauryas*. Oxford: Oxford University Press, 1961.

Trautmann, Thomas R. *Consanguineous Marriages in Pāli Literature*. Paper presented at the 181st meeting of the American Oriental Society, Cambridge, Mass., April 6-8, 1971.

———. *Kauṭilya and the Arthaśāstra*. Leiden: E.J. Brill, 1971.

Warder, A.K. *Indian Buddhism*. Delhi: Motilal Banarsidass, 1970.

Winternitz, M. *History of Indian Literature*. Translated by S. Ketkar. Vols. I-II. Calcutta: University of Calcutta, 1927-33.

Wittfogel, Karl. *Oriental Despotism*. New Haven and London: Yale University Press, 1963.

Index